The Difficult But Indispensable Church

The Difficult But Indispensable Church

Edited by Norma Cook Everist

FORTRESS PRESS
MINNEAPOLIS

THE DIFFICULT BUT INDISPENSABLE CHURCH

Library of Congress Cataloging-in-Publication Data
The difficult but indispensable church / edited by Norma Cook Everist
　　　p. cm.
　　Includes bibliographical references (p.).
　　ISBN 0-8006-3478-0 (alk. paper)
　　　1. Church. I. Everist, Norma Cook

BV600.3 .D54 2002
262'.001'7—dc21   2002021097

Manufactured in the U.S.A.
06　　05　　04　　03　　02　　1　　2　　3　　4　　5　　6　　7　　8　　9　　10

To seminary professors, students, and staff who came before us, shaping worship-centered communities of critical theological reflection, to those who presently work together, faithfully committed to their callings in Christ, and to those who, by God's grace, will come in the future, continuing the tradition of life together wherein learning leads to mission and mission informs learning.

Contents

PART TWO
The Church's Heart:
The Indispensable Power of Christ

PART THREE
The Church of God in Motion:
The Indispensability of Mission

PART FOUR
A CHURCH OF ALL PEOPLE:
THE INDISPENSABLE CHALLENGE

Contributors

The faculty of Wartburg Theological Seminary, Dubuque, Iowa

1. Thomas H. Schattauer is associate professor of liturgics and dean of the chapel. The courses that he teaches use the methods of liturgical history and theology as well as ritual studies to illuminate the patterns and practices of worship in contemporary congregations. His research and writing focus on issues of liturgy, church, and mission in the current cultural context and also on the liturgical work of Wartburg's founder, Wilhelm Loehe. He taught previously at Yale Divinity School and has served as a pastor in congregations in Indiana and Connecticut.

2. Duane H. Larson is president of Wartburg Theological Seminary. He also teaches courses in systematic theology, particularly in constructive theology and the natural sciences. A primary concern of his is leadership development and congregational life and expression of the faith to popular culture. He served as parish pastor in California and as a teaching theologian in Gettysburg, Pennsylvania, before coming to serve at Wartburg Seminary.

3. Ann L. Fritschel is assistant professor of Hebrew Bible. She teaches such courses as Prophets, Psalms, Islam, and the Bible and Film as well as introductory courses in Hebrew Bible. Her research interests include theodicy, suffering, and post-Holocaust theology. Her driving concern is how these relate to parish life. She has served as a pastor in congregations in North Dakota.

4. Daniel L. Olson is professor of pastoral theology and counseling. He teaches courses in pastoral crisis counseling, loss and grief in pastoral perspective, theological anthropology, and introductory courses in pastoral care. He has extensive experience working both as a parish pastor and as a licensed psychologist. His primary research interests at present are in studying human nature at the intersection of biblical theology, evolutionary psychology, and neuroscience.

5. Norma Cook Everist is professor of church and ministry. She teaches courses in educational ministry, leadership, administration, and feminist theology. Her central theological discipline is ecclesiology with an emphasis on theology of methodology, including issues of power and partnership, and the adult learner. As a pastor and a deaconess, she has served suburban and inner-city parish communities in St. Louis, Detroit, and New Haven, Connecticut. She also taught at Yale.

6. James L. Bailey is professor of New Testament. He teaches courses such as Matthew, Mark, 1 Corinthians, and Transforming Bible Study, and team-teaches Jesus and the Gospels, Pauline Letters, and Mission. His research interests include the Sermon on the Mount and Pauline Letters as prototypes for congregational life and practice. He has served as a pastor in Cincinnati, Ohio, and taught at Trinity Lutheran Seminary in Columbus, Ohio, and Concordia College in Moorhead, Minnesota.

7. Duane A. Priebe is Kent S. Knutson Professor of Systematic Theology. Along with basic theology courses, he teaches electives that focus on the person and work of Jesus, creation, and the church. Areas of interest and research include the relationship between theology and biblical theology, hermeneutics, the systematic power of simple structures of thought, Christian faith and religious pluralism, and the question of what God has done in Jesus Christ.

8. Ralph W. Quere is professor of history and theology. He teaches Lutheran Confessions and survey courses in church history. His special focus is history of doctrine and historical theology. He has written about and taught courses in evangelism and has recently focused on outreach to youth. He has served in urban, suburban, rural, and college communities in the East and Midwest.

9. David J. Lull is associate professor of New Testament. He teaches the Pauline Letters, the parables of Jesus, and New Testament. His research interests include the Pauline Letters, parables, hermeneutics, and process theology. He tries to help both trained biblical scholars and nonspecialists to engage the New Testament toward deeper discipleship and mission. He has served as the executive director of the Society of Biblical Literature, as the director of the National Council of Churches Bible translation program, and as a United Methodist pastor in New York.

10. James R. Nieman is associate professor of homiletics. He teaches courses that relate preaching to such subjects as literary genres, the lectionary, and social concerns, as well as introductory courses in preaching. He also teaches workshops and conducts research in local theologies and congregational studies and is interested in emerging issues in ecclesiology. He has served as a pastor in congregations in Iowa and Alaska.

11. Karen L. Bloomquist, an adjunct faculty member (previously associate professor of theological ethics) at Wartburg Theological Seminary, currently is director of the Department of Theology and Studies of the Lutheran World Federation in Geneva, Switzerland. For many years, she directed the Studies Department of the ELCA Division for Church in Society and before that taught at the Lutheran School of Theology at Chicago. She has pastored congregations in California and New York.

12. Craig L. Nessan is associate professor of contextual theology and academic dean. He has served as pastor of Trinity Evangelical Lutheran Church in Philadelphia, Pennsylvania, and St. Mark Lutheran Church in Cape Girardeau, Missouri. He cares that congregations become intentional about Christian discipleship for the sake of mission. He teaches Theology of the Congregation, Church and Ministry, Dietrich Bonhoeffer, and Christian Ethics. His current areas of research are ecclesiology and theological ethics.

13. David A. Ramse is assistant professor of community development and witness and serves as director of the master of arts program "Theology, Development, and Evangelism." He has served for more than twenty years as a missionary on four continents within ecumenical settings. He is a layperson committed to enabling leaders to minister spiritually and physically so that people globally might experience "the abundant life."

14. H. S. Wilson is Wilhelm Loehe Associate Professor of World Mission and director of the Center for Global Theologies. He teaches World Mission, Ecumenism, and Interfaith Dialogues. He is a presbyter of the Church of South India and for several years taught at the United Theological College in Bangalore, India. Prior to coming to Wartburg, he served as executive secretary of the Department of Theology of the World Alliance of Reformed Churches in Geneva, Switzerland.

15. Paul G. Hill is the developer and director of the Center for Youth Ministries of Wartburg Seminary. Paul has thirty-three years of experience in youth and family ministry. He is a certified camp director and adventure facilitator and is the contributing editor to the popular book *Up the Creek with a Paddle: Building an Effective Youth and Family Ministry.* He is currently studying adolescent male development, violence, and faith formation.

16. L. Shannon Jung is professor of rural ministry and director of the Center for Theology and Land of Wartburg Theological Seminary and the University of Dubuque Theological Seminary. He teaches immersion and seminar courses in the practice of rural ministry, leadership, and ecological ethics. His research focuses on strengthening rural congregations and on the theology and ethics of eating. He has been a minister in small Presbyterian churches in Tennessee and Minnesota.

17. Roger W. Fjeld is professor emeritus of church history and president emeritus. He teaches courses in modern church history, American civil religion, and transition from seminary to first call. His research interests are in American Protestant social ethics and American civil religion. He has a special concern for outreach to those who are living their lives outside the faith. He was a home mission developer, assistant to a district bishop, and a unit executive in the national offices of the American Lutheran Church.

18. Winston D. Persaud is professor of systematic theology. He is a native of Guyana, where he served as pastor of his home congregation prior to joining the Wartburg faculty in February 1984. His teaching and research are focused on defining and confessing the gospel of Jesus Christ in a world of religious and nonreligious alternatives. His course offerings include Defining and Confessing the Gospel, the Doctrine of the Trinity, Person and Work of the Holy Spirit, Luther and the Religions, and Liberation Theology.

19. Gwen B. Sayler is associate professor of Hebrew Bible. Prior to coming to Wartburg, she served as pastor at Immanuel Lutheran Church in Watertown, Wisconsin. Her research interests include biblical narratives as a resource for teaching and preaching, the ethics of biblical interpretation, and intertestamental and apocalyptical literature. She is passionate about educational opportunities for the laity and honest biblical conversation about difficult issues.

20. Elizabeth A. Leeper is associate professor of church history. She teaches required courses in early, medieval, and Reformation Christian history and electives such as Wolves in Sheep's Clothing: Heresy in the Early Church and The Virgin and the Harlot: Women in Christianity. Her abiding love is Christianity of the second and third centuries—the wide range of Christian groups, relations with the Roman Empire, and reasons for Christian success. This led to interest in nontraditional Christian groups and cults.

21. Peter L. Kjeseth is professor emeritus of New Testament. After many decades at Wartburg, he has recently retired. For the last several years, he team-taught in the required junior-year courses at Wartburg. He worked intensely with colleague James Bailey on the course Jesus and the Gospels. His special concern is economic justice. He currently teaches at Paulinum, the United Lutheran Theological Seminary, in Windhoek, Namibia.

Foreword

The experience of "difference" describes our public and church life today. Our daily life is vastly different today than it was even a decade ago. Within our own cherished congregational lives, we are surprised not only that things are different from a while ago, but that we in the congregation seem to be so different from one another and have such different opinions about how our lives should lead and be led. Difference has led to recognition that our lives do not fit so well together as we once thought they had or should. We sense that we are overdue for serious talk about our life together.

Except for those who believe that all the questions that so impinge today upon church and culture are answered fully, we know that major, careful conversation about our commonalities and differences of conviction is extremely important for people of Christian faith. We know, too, that such conversation requires immense commitment and energy. It tires us to converse about commonalities and differences of core values. It tires us even more when we together are not able to see well ahead of time the end result. It is difficult to be in serious conversation for which we cannot anticipate the resolutions. We would rather know the destination than engage in the journey. Yet we also know that authentic church life is about such serious talk together.

We pray that this book will help stimulate and guide such faith-full conversation. We live in difficult times. Even life in the church is difficult. But the gospel of Jesus Christ frees believers from fear of difficulty so that we, with the Holy Spirit's inspired guidance, can know abundant life courageously together as Christ's body. Christ's body is indeed his church. And that it is Christ's body means that the church is indispensable.

This book is intended to celebrate the indispensable church, confess its difficulty, and share insight as to how in our congregational life we could know more celebration than challenge.

We write this as members of a particular community of theological reflection who do not do things in lockstep. Rather, we know well the challenges of our own diversity as well as the world's. In our community life together, we have worked, argued, suffered, wept, played, and celebrated. Especially, fed by the Lord's word and the Lord's table, we have celebrated. With no dimming sense of reality of our differences, we have celebrated. And so we would share something of our lives with yours in biblical, theological, and practical terms. We bring to you our own differing perspectives and ultimate common conviction in Christ's reign, in some hope that our perspectives or experiences be not mimicked but, rather, received as gifts for the renewal of the difficult but indispensable church.

Finally, this is not a one-way conversation, nor, we hope, the end of one. The renewal of the church cannot be served by lack of listening, and so we offer our ears as well as our words. Should you find some aid in these reflections or none at all, we invite you to join us in serious talk. We heartily welcome your own words, extended thoughts, and stories. Join us in life together. Work with us for the diversified unity of abundant Christian life together in Christ's indispensable church.

DUANE H. LARSON
President, Wartburg Theological Seminary

Introduction

Life together in a congregation can be difficult. We gather to worship, care for one another in times of crisis, celebrate joyful occasions, and pray for one another. We also worry about the future and disagree about budgets, leadership, ethical stances, and even our identity and image as a congregation. Caught in arguments over difficult decisions, fearful of change, we may resort to denial, blame, and power struggles. Christian people know they are called to love one another, but why in the world is it so difficult to actually be the church?

In a society that reveres individualism, people continue to hunger for community. Many institutions and voluntary associations are available to meet that need. Many currently are floundering. Congregations today face the same dilemma: people want to belong to a community of meaning that draws them close to God, but they face myriad individual responsibilities. And they are busy! They may easily dismiss life in the congregation as one good thing too many. Being "involved" in church becomes dispensable. This book sets forth a clear concept of the radical nature of the Christian community as centered in Christ so that we see it as real and indispensable for life.

Belonging to a congregation and being faithful to one another are difficult. Equally difficult is being the church active in the world. At this point of greatest challenge, we need to recall for ourselves and for one another that it is Christ who brings us together as a gift. We are indispensable to one another's faith and life. Even if the church is often caricatured as irrelevant in today's society, by the grace of God our call to mission is indispensable to the needs of a hurting world. On the Sunday following the terrorist attack of September 11, 2001, on the World Trade Center in New York City, the Pentagon in Washington, and a plane over Pennsylvania, the football stadiums, baseball fields, NASCAR tracks, and Emmy awards auditorium were, as one news commentator put it, "quiet as a church." Houses of faith were overflowing. People of many faiths wanted to gather for prayer and to be empowered to care. They called communities of faith once again to their teaching, preaching, and leadership roles. In community, we receive a historical and global gift of life centered in God's righteousness and God's mercy that goes far beyond the local congregation but which, at the same time, is perhaps most real in its local expression.

The chapters of this book center on the biblical concept of living as the body of Christ in the world. Among the authors, you may notice a range of working theologies of the church. So it is within the local congregation. We hold differing working images and ideas about the church. They may be expressed more implicitly than explicitly through the decisions we make about worship and mission and money.

The Christian church is primarily here to be not admired or criticized but believed. Pastors and lay leaders are frequently embroiled in congregational conflict or disheartened by apathy. They struggle to find enough volunteers. And they are tired. The task may be to believe, for example, that this motley group of people on a street one block off Main Street is indeed the church. Dietrich Bonhoeffer wrote that the Spirit approaches each person in his or her singularity and places that person within the divine community so that the members see one another no longer as claim but as gift.[1] This book seeks to help readers reclaim that gift and believe they really are the community that Christ has redeemed and called them to be.

The authors demonstrate the unity of the church in its diversity. A book by a collection of authors is not unique. Whereas some books by multiple authors take one topic and pursue it and some books stick to one discrete discipline, this book contains a wide range of topics, discussed through diverse disciplines. At times, one might wonder whether the authors are even speaking the same language. You may notice different working definitions of certain terms, such as *pluralism* or *ecclesiology*. So, too, in a congregation people may use the same word, such as *mission*, and mean quite different things. For some, it may mean responsibly caring for the congregation itself; for others, it means reaching out into the neighborhood.

Just as the authors in this book speak in the languages of different academic disciplines, so also in the local congregation members speak various languages from their disciplines of ministry in daily life, such as architecture, agriculture, medicine, education, and finance. The book models in content and process the challenge every Christian community faces to speak different languages; express varying, even conflicting viewpoints; and tell different stories. We do not skirt issues of ecclesiastical authority, especially biblical authority. We broaden the conversation about the church to see it as a complex community comprised of many differing people, with differing interpretations on all sorts of issues. The church congregates in a variety of local assemblies. The challenge is to listen well enough to understand the other and learn to live out our common mission, even while retaining these varied viewpoints and gifts.

The authors of this book belong to a seminary community known for its collaborative style of teaching and its lively life together. We trust one another enough to engage in such a writing process without distracting power struggles. But life in community is not equal to sameness, and writing together can bring out differences we did not know we held. While often we may be expressing similar commitments in different ways, we need to be clear that individual authors may not agree with what another author proposes. We, as a community of authors, made the decision at our first meeting for this project not to write only after we had agreed, nor to synthesize our ideas into a common text. We did exactly the opposite. We sought to push one another outward, to speak carefully in our own particular voices, and to listen even more carefully to one another. How much do we really know what goes on in one another's classroom? How much do parishioners who sit beside one another on a Sunday morning really know about the other's world of telecommunications or social work or real estate?

We dare to welcome such diversity. We continue to reassemble, first of all to listen, to become interested in and even intrigued by the other, not moving too quickly to make the other "just like me" or to define the other person in one's own terms. This, too, is an important task for congregations who engage in moral deliberation on significant issues facing the church today. We invite the readers not only to engage the content of the book but to claim more fully the gift of life in community in their own contexts. Each chapter endeavors to present cutting-edge material. Most important is the comprehensive nature in which the authors together show how these fields relate to community in Christ and the ministry of the church in the world. We believe this exemplifies a holistic understanding of a community of diversity, centered on radical obedience to Christ.

The book is divided into four parts: (1) Personhood in Community: Indispensability in Christ; (2) The Church's Heart: The Indispensable Power of Christ; (3) The Church of God in Motion: The Indispensability of Mission; and (4) A Church of All People: The Indispensable Challenge. Within each part, readers will move back and forth between biblical, theological, historical, and ministerial perspectives. Some linkages between chapters have been noted; others the readers will discover on their own.

Certain themes arise again and again, such as the indispensability of diversity. The church cannot be only a grouping of similar or like-minded people but needs always to be open to the stranger. A church that turns only inward grows sick; mission is an indispensable result of healthy life together. The redemptive core of our difficult life together is simply the grace of God in Jesus Christ.

This book is written for parish pastors, diaconal ministers, associates in ministry, and lay leaders. It is written from a Christian perspective; however, the challenge of living together in a faith community touches, in differing ways, many religions. Although the book is written by faculty members of a Lutheran seminary, not all of the authors are Lutheran. It is written in an inclusive style so that readers from a variety of Christian church bodies will find it relevant and useful. Some chapters refer specifically to historical and contemporary issues in the Evangelical Lutheran Church in America. Most readers will recognize similar issues in other church bodies. The book is academic, but always with a clear focus on the work of parish ministry.

Faith-community leaders can read the book together. Perhaps various members of a staff or a church council will select certain chapters and share them in communal conversation. Readers are invited to bring the specific challenges of their congregation into dialogue with the authors, thus broadening the community. For readers who are theologically trained, the book could serve as a tool for continuing education. Because each chapter is part of the whole but also stands alone, each could serve as a basis for discussion in a cluster or conference or become common reading as part of weekly text study.

We thank Fortress Press, and particularly Harold Rast, for support of this endeavor and for helpful suggestions on how this book could serve its readers. A special word of gratitude to Valerie Way, Connie Rieger, Amy Odgren, and Kevin Anderson for their extraordinary work in compiling the individual manuscripts in their many draft forms, and to student assistant Amy Odgren for her editorial help.

This book was written by professors who were members of the faculty at Wartburg Seminary during the 1999–2000 school year, the turn of the millennium. Already, at the time of publication, one has retired. Others are to come. The community in Christ that is Wartburg Seminary includes all professors and students and staff who served in years past, who are here now, and who will come in future years. So it is with the church, always in motion in God's mission. We are linked inextricably in the body of Christ.

PART ONE

Personhood in Community: Indispensability in Christ

L ife in community poses difficult challenges. If we take seriously the personal needs of individual members, do we neglect the mission of the community? If we focus attention on the call of the community, might we fail to honor the individuality of persons? Whether the faith community be a congregation, a care center, a camp, a campus ministry, a regional judicatory, or an entire church body, just how much diversity can a group tolerate? Theologically centering our life together in Jesus Christ grounds a community to affirm each individual member and the whole body. Not in spite of but *because* of our personhood, we are indispensable to one another. The community accentuates and enfolds the gifts and growing edges, the sufferings and joys, the histories and idiosyncrasies of each person as contributions to the community. Through Christ, we belong to one another.

Beginning with the liturgical center of Christian community, Thomas Schattauer confronts an important issue in many churches today: controversy concerning worship practices labeled "traditional," "contemporary," "blended," or "alternative." The local faith community at worship provides the most profound activity of unity and also the occasion for the deepest division. Schattauer believes the contemporary worship movement does not provide a clear alternative to conventional Christianity. He calls for pursuit of the deepest patterns and practices of liturgical tradition to renew the church as a distinctive community and to activate it for mission in the contemporary world.

Duane Larson asks if a Christian, by definition, is never lonely. Some people painfully report that the loneliest place they have been is a place that promises love and support and then disappoints them. Counter to a primary American goal of personal fulfillment, Larson says the enfleshed community offers something quite different and visionary as a witness in society: the Trinity as the communitarian ground and goal of all life. Justification cannot end with autonomy, with simply any one individual being right with God, but with reconciled relationship. The Trinity is the ground of diversity in unity.

Ann Fritschel provides a biblical perspective on the community's liturgical life by focusing on the psalms, specifically the often-avoided "lament" psalms. This term is rarely used in society, or even in the church. Yet Christian communities long for the opportunity to lament. We need to grieve together as well as to enjoy one another. By looking carefully at Psalm 22, Fritschel goes to the heart of the issue, the idolatrous search for community rather than a search for God. She proposes practical ways a congregation can give people permission to lament while experiencing God's transforming power.

Daniel Olson raises a perplexing difficulty about the relationship of the self to the community. Citing an intriguing body of research, he inquires whether what is good for an individual's mental health, having some control over one's life, might be counterproductive in contributing to healthy communities. People bring their control issues into the congregation, which often results in dependency, blame, or even chaos. Olson uses the biblical concept of steward to help people take charge and relinquish control. He says that this is what God asks of us and what the world needs from us as people living in a community of faith.

Norma Cook Everist concludes the first part of the book by looking at ecclesiological foundations. The church is a human institution that meets human needs, but also much more. It is not just a vehicle for the gospel; it is good news! Three "body of Christ" epistle texts challenge the temptation of individuals and individual congregations to say either "Because I am not like them, I do not belong," or "I have no need of you." She urges the members of the church to "re-member" the body of Christ in claiming and living their communal identity so they can minister in daily life in a pluralistic world.

Seeking Peace in the Assembly

God's Mission, Our Worship, and the World's Hope

THOMAS H. SCHATTAUER

The liturgical assembly expresses both fractured humanity and reconciled community. With the current societal fascination with private, individualized spirituality, what is the place of communal worship? How does the church deal with the consumer mentality of endless personal choice? How can the congregation go beyond worship wars to be a church at worship and a church in mission?

The worship of God in Christ by the power of the Spirit in local gatherings is a source of the profoundest unity among Christians, but the worship of Christian communities is also the occasion of their deepest division. Whether it is what some have called "worship wars" and "trouble at the table,"[1] it is difficult to ignore the divisiveness that characterizes the worship life of many contemporary congregations.

And it has always been so. Precisely at the place where Christians seek to celebrate their unity in Christ, they have manifested a party spirit. The apostle Paul noted the problem already in the Corinthian community. There it seems that the practice of baptism had become entangled in the disputes among factions in the church so that some claimed to belong to Paul, some to Apollos, some to Cephas, some to Christ. "Has Christ been divided?" (1 Cor. 1:13), Paul asks. Divisions were also evident in their practice of the Lord's Supper, where at the common meal some took their fill of food and drink while those less well off went hungry. "When you come together, it is not really to eat the Lord's Supper" (1 Cor. 11:20), Paul warns them. Concerning the songs, teachings, tongues, revelations, and interpretations that individual members brought to their gatherings, Paul instructs them to take care that "all things be done for building up" the community of Christ (1 Cor. 14:26).

The history of Christian worship through the centuries is replete with theological controversy, exclusive claims about the proper form and conduct of worship, and divisive human behavior of every kind. Paul's questions, warnings, and instructions have remained a critical prod for Christians to think and work beyond the divisions that occur within and among their worshiping communities.

One wonders what Paul would have to say to us today when certain labels commonly characterize the gathering for worship—traditional, contemporary, blended, or alternative; when congregations schedule a menu of different services and encourage members to sort themselves out according to their preferences for a certain style of song or leadership; when congregations conduct alternative services at the very same hour in separate spaces; and when congregations are divided by their discussions about these things. Is Christ divided? Is this the Lord's Supper that we celebrate? Are all things being done in a way to build up the community of Christ?

Ferment about Worship

There is an undeniable ferment in contemporary North American congregations about worship, concerning musical style, the style of leadership, and the visual and acoustic environment appropriate to Christian worship. The factors at work in this development are multiple and complex. The effect of our consumer culture upon worshiping communities is certainly one. What we see and hear on televisions and computers about the products we can buy, the experiences we can have, the entertainment we can enjoy, the choices we can make, and the persons we can be profoundly shapes our understanding of the world and ourselves. The electronic message bearers of the consumer marketplace daily rehearse us in the choices that we make as individuals to define ourselves and to construct the world in which we will live.[2] This pervasive cultural message about the self-defining and world-constructing choices available to individuals comes to worship in all of us who lead and participate. It encourages us in patterns and practices of worship that present alternatives from which we can choose what best meets our desires. And it should not surprise us that accompanying the urgent search for alternatives in worship are the popular musical styles of the marketplace; the visual and architectural environment of the mall, the corporate office park, and the auditorium; and the entertaining leadership style of rock bands and television show hosts.

Another significant factor in the contemporary ferment surrounding matters of worship is the quest for something "alternative." But alternative to what? The answer usually given sets the contemporary and the traditional in opposition to each other. What many seem to be seeking is a contemporary alternative to traditional worship, something that relates more immediately to our cultural context and connects more directly to our experience of life today. But is it necessary to set the contemporary search for something alternative in Christian worship over and against the deepest patterns and practices of the liturgical tradition? I would like to suggest that what is being sought is an alternative to conventional worship, not a wholesale opposition to the tradition. The aim is to construct an alternative to *what has passed for tradition in recent memory.* The contemporary worship movement shares this aim with the modern liturgical movement, which has urged the restoration and renewal of tradition as a way beyond conventional understanding and practice.

Conventional Christianity focuses upon the institutional character of the church and the spiritual benefits that individuals receive by their participation. The church exists to perpetuate a certain order in its own life, to support the social and political status quo, and to provide individuals with spiritual nurture. Going to church offers the individual the assurance of forgiveness and the promise of eternal life, and regardless of belief or commitment it grants a measure of social respectability. Conventional worship is clergy dominated, follows an orderly routine, and preserves a "churchly" music, art, and architecture.

The contemporary worship movement carries with it a strong critique of the institutional self-preservation that characterizes conventional Christianity. It seeks to focus the church on the task of connecting more directly with contemporary people and addressing their needs. To do this, it looks to forces at work in the surrounding culture for direction. It adapts the methods of the marketplace together with the style of popular music and entertainment in order to break down the institutional barriers that prevent the church from engaging people today.

The search for an alternative to conventional worship and, by implication, to conventional Christianity also characterizes the work of the liturgical movement.[3] Its goal has not been, as many assume, to preserve tradition and maintain the status quo, but rather through the recovery and updating of earlier Christian practice to renew the church as a distinctive community and to activate it for mission in the contemporary world. Stimulated by the fruits of biblical scholarship and historical liturgical study, the liturgical movement has sought to recover for contemporary practice and understanding the eschatological horizon of the church's worship, and indeed its whole life and mission. The fundamental insight that the liturgical assembly is directed toward the kingdom of God—proclaimed by Jesus Christ and inaugurated by his death and resurrection—

opens the way to a fuller understanding of the significance of worship both for the community of the church and for the life of the world. The communal and cosmic dimensions of the liturgy are understood to encompass the personal within the eschatological purpose of God, in Christ to reconcile the world to Godself (2 Cor. 5:18-19).

This perspective involves a thorough critique of conventional Christianity and substantial proposals for an alternative practice of worship. Like the contemporary worship movement, the liturgical movement represents an alternative to the institutional focus of conventional Christianity. By contrast, however, the communal dimension of the liturgical movement offers an alternative to the individualism of conventional Christianity, and the orientation to the world and its future in God's eschatological purpose provides critical distance from the social and political status quo and the basis for prophetic witness. On these matters, the contemporary worship movement does not provide a clear alternative to conventional Christianity. Devoid of institution and tradition, it intensifies the focus on the spiritual nurture of the individual, and its embrace of the marketplace offers little possibility for prophetic critique.

The Purpose of Liturgical Assembly

How should the church in its liturgical assembly engage people immersed in a consumer culture with all its accompanying values of entertainment and individual choice? Some say embrace it for the sake of reaching out with the gospel message. Others say resist it to preserve the integrity of the gospel and its claims. How do we sort out these competing impulses?

It is not possible even to begin answering that question without first asking about the nature of the church's gathering for worship. What is the purpose of the local liturgical assembly of the church? The Russian Orthodox theologian Alexander Schmemann has provided an answer worth our pondering in this highly compressed statement:

> The proper function of the "leitourgia" has always been to *bring together*, within one symbol, the three levels of the Christian faith and life: the Church, the world, and the Kingdom; . . . the Church herself is thus the sacrament in which the broken, yet still "symbolical" life of "this world" is brought, in Christ and by Christ, into the dimension of the Kingdom of God. . . .[4]

The purpose of the liturgical assembly, according to Schmemann, has to do with how the church enacts a symbol of God's work in Christ to draw the world and its brokenness into the reign of God. In its worship, the local assembly of Christian people shows forth the dynamic relationship of three "communal" realities: the community of the church, the life of the world, and the communion of all things with God that is God's ultimate purpose, what the Scriptures call the "kingdom" or "reign" of God (*basilea tou theou*). The dynamic relationship of these communal realities— church, world, kingdom—is a critical feature of what God has done, continues to do, and will finally accomplish in Christ. This is what the church's liturgical gathering is most deeply about.

Christ the Foundation

The assembly for worship organizes itself around the things of Christ.[5] The Lukan story of the risen Lord's appearance to two disciples on the road to Emmaus already suggests the connections between the presence of Christ and the central elements of the liturgical gathering. The story takes place later on the day of the resurrection, on Sunday. In the midst of their despair over the crucifixion and confusion about reports of an empty tomb, Jesus meets these disciples on the road and "beginning with Moses and all the prophets, he interpreted to them the things about himself in all the scriptures" (Luke 24:27).

Although he remains a stranger to them, at the end of their journey the disciples invite Jesus to stay with them; "when he was at table with them, he took bread, blessed, and broke it, and gave it to them. Then their eyes were opened, and they recognized him" (Luke 24:30-31). The story narratively links certain actions—a meeting on Sunday, the searching of the Scriptures, and the sharing of a meal—to the disciples' encounter with the risen Lord.

These same things characterize the ongoing liturgical assembly of the community of disciples, the church: we meet together on Sunday; the Scriptures are read and interpreted in their witness to Christ; a meal that reveals Christ is taken together.[6] And there is one more connection. Having encountered the risen Lord, the Emmaus disciples go out to join the other disciples in Jerusalem, the place where Israel's hope for a great eschatological gathering of all nations and peoples was focused (for example, Isa. 2:1-4). So, too, the things of Christ around which we organize our liturgical gathering point us to this greater gathering that is God's ultimate purpose with us and for our world. The suggestion in all of these connections is this: the assembly for worship refers us to Christ and through him to a set of interrelated communal realities—church, world, and kingdom. The purpose of worship is to enact a symbol of Christ in the fullness of connection to these communal realities.

Church

The liturgical gathering refers us to the church. The things of Christ at the center of worship are inextricably bound up with the community of Christ. In the words of Dietrich Bonhoeffer, "the church is Christ existing as church-community."[7] The gathering of this community is part of the meaning of Jesus Christ. The word read and proclaimed as a testimony to Christ is heard and received in community. The eucharistic meal is an act of communion among those who share it, as well as with Christ present as its host and its food. Despite the individualistic piety nurtured by much religious practice and understanding, and reinforced by the individualism of contemporary society, the local assembly of Christians around the things of Christ is "the irreducible unit of Christianity," not the individual.[8] Furthermore, this local assembly does not itself exist in isolation but rather in the communion of local assemblies that gather around the things of Christ. The purpose of worship is to enact a symbol of the church.

World

The liturgical gathering refers us to the world. The communion of persons that gathers as the church represents the wider community of people throughout the world in its life before God. In a similar way, the physical stuff of worship, the material elements of the sacraments—bread, wine, and water—as well as the materials of the environment for worship—light, stone, wood, living plants—represents the wider created order.[9] These things are in themselves broken signs of God. The world as a whole, created and sustained by the power of God's word, and persons, created in the image of God, bear a connection to God, but it is a connection that because of sin remains opaque to God's clear and full disclosure to us. This world of all persons and all things, the world of God's creation, is the horizon of all that the particular community of the church does in its gatherings for worship. The liturgical assembly gathers not merely for itself but for this world, into which Christ was born and for which he gave his life. It gathers the world in its brokenness and pain, in its longing and hope for redemption.[10] The purpose of worship is to enact a symbol of the world.

Kingdom

The liturgical assembly refers us to the coming reign of God. The community of the church that gathers in the life of the risen Christ points to and already anticipates the consummation of God's ultimate purpose: the full and encompassing communion of all people and all things in the

reign of God. God's mission in Christ by the power of the Spirit is to draw
the world into a reconciled communion with God, in such a way that the
world is released from brokenness and pain and its longing and hope are
filled by God. The liturgical assembly is about this holy communion,
which is the culmination of God's mission toward the world. The particular work of God for the community of the church and among its people
serves this larger purpose. It exemplifies the judgment of God to which
the whole world is subject and the mercy of God toward which the whole
world lives in hope. The purpose of worship is to enact a symbol of the
kingdom of God.

With this perspective on liturgical assembly as centered on the things of
Christ in relation to the communal realities of church, world, and kingdom, the purpose of worship emerges with greater clarity and in contrast
to what is commonly found in both conventional and contemporary
Christian worship. There worship functions to de-
liver something to the in-
dividual. At worship, the
individual receives some-
thing, understood in
terms of forgiveness of
sins and eternal life or in

"God's mission in Christ by the power of the Spirit is to draw the world into a reconciled communion with God."

terms of spiritual relationship, blessing, power, and gift. In the perspective
being developed here, this purpose of worship to benefit the individual is
set within a larger framework provided by the communal realities of
church, world, and kingdom. Through the gathering for worship, the community of Christ gathers to enact God's mission to the world, to show
forth God's judgment and mercy for all, to witness to and participate in
the reality of God's reign.[11] Worship functions to enact, in the ritual symbol of the assembly gathered around the things of Christ, the world's hope
and its future.

Sharing the Sign of Peace

The sharing of a sign of peace is one moment in the ritual symbol enacted
by the liturgical assembly. It exemplifies in a concrete way how the liturgy
functions to gather the assembly around the things of Christ in connection to the communal realities of church, world, and kingdom. In the
Lutheran Book of Worship (1978), the peace takes place after the prayers of
intercession and before the presentation of the gifts. It consists of two related actions:

1. The presiding minister offers a greeting of peace to the entire assembly, to which the assembly responds:
       p: The peace of the Lord be with you always.
       c: And also with you.
2. The ministers and members of the assembly greet one another,
   saying "Peace be with you" and sharing signs of peace.

The peace that is shared within the assembly is specified as the peace of the
Lord, that is, the peace of the risen Lord Jesus Christ. In John's Gospel,
Jesus offers peace to his disciples as he bids them farewell in the shadow of
the cross: "Peace I leave with you; my peace I give to you. I do not give to
you as the world gives" (John 14:27). On the day of the resurrection, the
risen Lord's first words to his disciples are "Peace be with you." Jesus' greeting of peace is connected with the showing of his wounds, and he repeats
the greeting as he sends the disciples forth, bestows on them the Holy
Spirit, and gives them the authority to forgive sins (John 20:19-23). The
biblical narrative connects the peace that Jesus gives to his death and resurrection, to the apostolic mission, to the gift of the Spirit, and to the forgiveness of sins. The liturgical sharing of signs of peace carries with it
these biblical-theological implications: the peace that is shared is the particular peace that comes from the crucified and risen Lord, and it characterizes the mission of the apostolic community, empowered by the Spirit,
as a "ministry of reconciliation," to use a phrase from Paul (2 Cor. 5:18).

The Old Testament understanding of God's peace significantly en-
larges the framework for interpreting the meaning of the liturgical act.
God's *shalom*, the Hebrew word for peace, entails a comprehensive vision
of God's purposes for humans beings and the whole creation, including
the fullness of life before God, harmony among all nations and peoples,
and the well-being of the entire created order. It is God's shalom that Jesus
offers his disciples and sends them out to extend to the world. The liturgical sharing of the peace mediated by Christ carries with it these cosmic,
eschatological, and missional implications.

In this biblical-theological perspective, it is evident that the liturgical
sign of peace does in fact "bring together, within one symbol, the three
levels of Christian faith and life"—church, world, and kingdom.[12] It is a
sign of the peace of God given by Jesus Christ to the community of the
church, a peace that is to characterize the life of the assembly that shares
it and the communion of such assemblies that is the church. This sign of
peace shared within the local liturgical assembly is part of God's larger
purpose for the entire world. It contrasts with the fractured peace that
marks every level of life in the world. It resonates with the world's deep
longing for peace. The liturgical sign of peace points the assembly and the

world in hope to the peace that is God's purpose for all people and the whole created order.

From this perspective, the sign of peace is much more than an indication of something that individuals receive at worship and share with one another. The sharing of peace within the liturgical assembly enacts a whole set of meanings and relationships that have to do with God's mission to the world in Christ, the nature and mission of the apostolic community, and hope for the world in the expectation of God's reign.

In the midst of the contemporary search for an alternative practice of worship, the wellspring of the church's historic patterns of worship will continue to renew and refresh us, if we will but come and drink deeply from this source of life in Christ. And more than that, we will be gathered together into God's mission in Christ to reconcile the world to Godself. In this, there is great joy for God's people and abundant hope for the world.

2

Life Together Is Only in God

The Achievement of Personhood in Community

DUANE H. LARSON

The crucified and risen Christ is indispensable for re-creating communities mired in alienation and divisiveness. How can a congregation resist the temptation to appeal to individualism and consumerism? How does the doctrine of the Trinity help people understand not only the identity of God but the nature of how deeply they are related to one another? How is restored life in community modeled for the world?

When a pastor of a small village church wrote in the early nineteenth century that "a Christian is never lonely," he was either idealistic to the point of pastoral insensitivity or brilliantly against his time.[1] I argue the latter. Furthermore, I believe that this faithful pastor's insight as to what constitutes Christian life together anticipated the "postmodernity" we are coming to know today, which his liberal and modern period had already needed. We need his insight that Christians are meant to belong to one another.

Indeed, we would do well to make his insight a mandate by which to help recharacterize life together in Christian congregations today. For today, at least in North America, the life of congregations is far too characterized by dysfunction and fracture. The interim necessity for pastors and other church leaders to practice conflict resolution often replaces engagement in vision for long-range mission. Church leaders, consequently, find themselves fighting more fires than they would desire. They also find themselves burning out before the fires do.

This chapter is not primarily about practical means of conflict resolution. We are not going to try to find or suggest habits for successful Christian life here, though that may not be a bad exercise at another time. Rather, we need to ask some prior, deeply *theological* questions as to why such conflict and fracture is happening exactly in the place that Christians intuit this should not happen: the congregation. Why is this such a common experience today? Many would answer that churches are not attending to the basics of biblical study and disciplined church attendance. Many others answer that churches—like those just mentioned—have long been irrelevant to surrounding social needs. Others will give many other answers. They may all be right, and no one wholly wrong. My answer is that we have lost hold of the fundamental theological vision—a basic *Christian* way of understanding the character of God and the purpose of humanity—that impelled that faithful village pastor to utter his strange remark, a definition indeed of what it means to be Christian, that a Christian is never lonely.

Differentiation Rather than Division

This fundamental Christian theological vision is intimated in popular culture's hunger for new community, in spite of its consumerist tendencies toward being "niched." The economic engine behind almost everything in public social life today presumes to identify the likes and dislikes of every individual. Then the economic engine, what contemporary journalist Thomas Friedman insightfully calls "the golden straitjacket," assumes it can place individuals into categories and subcategories, all the more "relevantly" and effectively to market its wares.[2] The consumer is thus totally niched from an economic point of view. This is aided, for example, by cyberspace cookies, focus groups, and statistical profiling.

One result of considerable concern for us is that the human person is finally entirely perceived through economic lenses. Even "church growth" advice "economizes" human beings by such practices. Not that the practices in and of themselves are wrong. But the consequences can be negative when unaccompanied by some basic theological thinking. After all, niche marketing—attempting to identify, attract, and then sell to subcategories that are internally homogenous—is in fact a dividing, not a unifying, principle, and an unwary universal practice of such thinking can severely undercut the more important need for people to be social.

To assume the need for certain divisions in order to make *likeness* the most visible and attractive mark of a consumer or church attender can be tragic, especially for the church. Even political slogans that appeal for something better than a "politics of division" capture popular culture's desire for something bigger, better, and more encompassing—something that overcomes our sense of being divided from one another. Popular culture intuits this truth. We Christian heirs of modernism have lost the big vision. We easily glide from healthy and relative differentiation to unhealthy and absolute division. And we hasten from understanding to action. We want, with the commercial for sports gear, to "just do it." But we forget that we cannot very well "do it" (meaning Christian mission and life together) when we do not even know what the field looks like. To just do it, we first must just see it.

And what is it that we must see? We must see that the Holy Spirit of the crucified and risen Jesus Christ has deeply *related* us to God and one another, in spite of our illusion of separateness and autonomy. The point is *relationship* and how we understand that even in terms of the physical nature of reality.[3] Christians are members of the body of Christ in a way more than metaphorical; every act, every thought, every neural energy charge affects (and effects) everyone and everything else. Christians relate to one another as do points on a web. We are not to suppose that we relate to one another as wholly self-contained and self-willing individual beings who might freely and voluntarily group together through a common denominator. This model of relating is much like how spokes of a wheel relate to one another only through the center; they are otherwise not directly impacting on or "neighborly to" each other at all. This is a cool neighborliness, at best.

The Problem of Individualism

Modernism, characterized by the autonomy of individualism, has so affected the understanding of "being church" that our sense of connectedness has been only voluntary instead of essential. It was at the height of theological modernism in the nineteenth century that influential theologians gave us the definition of church as a "voluntary association of individuals." This seems to be a phrase by which we still "do church" today.[4] Were it not for that phrase and all that it means, we would not know the phenomenon of church shopping. When I "shop" for a church, I join finally that congregation which most suits my preferences of class, or lifestyle, or worship style, or politics, and so on. Again, this activity of differentiation is not a negative one necessarily. But notice the omissions from the examples of criteria. When I "church shop," I do not ask what I can do for the congregation and its mission. I do not ask how it needs me. I am a church shopper when I lay claim to the congregation instead of allowing the congregation to lay claim to me. As the individual—as an individualist—I, the church shopper, and I only set the terms.

This phenomenon is related to what some sociologists have called the loss of the "ascribed self" to the "achieved self." It used to be the case, and not so long ago, that a person would know who she or he was and what she or he would do vocationally from a very early age. It was expected or simply understood that Jim would grow up to be a farmer or a salesperson or a pastor because dad and granddad and great-granddad had done likewise. Sociologists have called this the ascribed self because it was simply given from the outset. This may have been a positive practice insofar as some sense of surety and even destiny could be of comfort to the person growing toward and into the future. But we know how tragic this practice also has been, especially for women, who were not offered opportunities to realize their own talents and con-

> ✿ *"I am a church shopper when I lay claim to the congregation instead of allowing the congregation to lay claim to me."*

tribute their unique gifts. On the other hand, the American dream, which was a great promise especially to the immigrant refugee who sought freedom from ascription, was to exercise fully the freedom to achieve one's self. This is the positive side of self-definition or claiming one's self, and we should make every effort continually to celebrate this. It errs, however, when it is only self, for the goodness of the ascribed self lay in the presumption and security of a family and a unique, purposeful community.

Perhaps what we are seeking to celebrate more as Christians is the "gifted self." The gifted self is not simply the ascribed self, subject to DNA, family bonds, and local culture. The gifted self is indeed the self who is claimed by God at baptism as secured for God's future and so is now free to nurture and exercise the gifts God has given uniquely to each of us for the upbuilding of one another. We are gifted to give. And our personhood is not fully realized or achieved unless we realize and achieve it within a community of faith. The congregation helps us to discern and to practice our gifts. We are gifted selves, indeed gifted by and in Christ for one another, so that we can help build one another. It may sound strange to say, but is in a certain sense true, that we literally make one another up as persons. This is why diversity, of course, is a requirement for authentic community and is God's definition for church: one body, many members (1 Cor. 2:20).

If the achieved self or self-defining person is assumed to be the norm, negative consequences abound: as when I try to play out exactly what was called a modern liberal notion of how church is made and done; as when I act as though my will (and my will alone) could and would be done. Does this not make it almost impossible for congregational life to be a full life together? When joining a church is but the vowing to a contract that could be broken by the prior and fundamental authority of the individual will, and when those who lead churches do so on the fundamental premise that the church contract is to be made as easy and attractive as possible so as to get the would-be member to sign and remain a member, rarely can or do such places know strength and endurance. Many church growth principles are founded on just such suppositions of modernism, and many of these same principles, their inherent value notwithstanding, are unreflectively used. It should not surprise one, then, that the oxymoron of "churched individuals" puts conflict necessarily at the core of church life.

So an answer might appear obvious. That is the answer of locating more authority in the group—such as the congregation itself, the head office, or the denomination—or in one leader, be it congregational president, pastor, bishop, or pope. This answer is wrong, too, because it is based on the same supposition of modernism: that it is an individual (group or person) who leads because of the voluntary acquiescence of the other individuals to the leader. Whether it is a group of self-willed and self-willing individuals who work contractually together as a "church," or a group of individual wills who acquiesce to the will of one leader, in either case individuals are self-defined. What misses is that we are defined by others at least as much as we are self-defined. What misses is the original Christian insight, based on the doctrine of the Trinity, that life in communion honors and requires diversity in just such a way that one's individuality is "in-formed" and enhanced by the diverse gifts of others, in even metaphysical ways. The community cannot really be such without the diversity of its members, and the members indeed could not be *persons* without one another. This so-called postmodern way of thinking is not new at all. It is an original Christian insight. It is the Lutheran way of speaking about vocation. And it is a way of life that is steeped in the very life of God the Trinity. To get a clearer understanding of this, we need to look once again at the history of trinitarian theology.

The Doctrine of the Trinity

The doctrine of the Trinity has been assumed as foundational throughout the history of Lutheranism. Explicit consideration of Lutheran doctrine in light of the trinitarian assumption, however, has not been carried through until the twentieth century, as has been the case with most ecumenical Protestant theology. On the other hand, only with recent Luther research has come the recognition that Martin Luther's own Augustinian theological ancestry was basically unquestioned on the point of the dogma of the Trinity. The Lutheran confessions themselves claimed no new insights, nor need they have done so, because the reality and character of God as Trinity was simply assumed for centuries. There was no need to theologize about what was not debated. The very existence and identity of God, as well as the dogma of the Trinity itself, was rarely questioned until the Enlightenment. But under the critical gaze of enlightened, liberal rationalism, as well as the apparent irrelevance of trinitarian dogma to practical life—given the heightened esoteric and formulaic character of most trinitarian thinking that was conducted—the dogma came to be regarded popularly as dissolute and quaint.

The situation called for renewal of trinitarian thinking in the twentieth century, and this came mostly from Roman Catholic and Reformed quarters. In other words, under the influence of ecumenical theology today, Lutheranism has revisited its trinitarian claims and begun significantly to rehearse its doctrine in their light. While we have been given to reading our own confessional history without the shadings of trinitarian lenses, we have learned recently again how to wear the glasses that our Reformation forebears simply assumed, and this makes all the difference in understanding the tradition, as well as all Christian faith, aright. The basic characteristics of contemporary Lutheran trinitarian theology follow. I also will allude to their impact upon other doctrinal-theological themes, such as what it means to be a human being, and the understanding of the church—ecclesiology—itself.

First, the dogma of the Trinity concerns the identity of God. Because the dogma is a compact expression of Scripture's witness to God active in history, "who" God is precedes all narrative and theological discussion on God's existence and nature. "Father, Son, and Holy Spirit" language, then, synthesizes—as well as gives proper signification to—the whole narrative of God's ways with creation. This narrative begins with Holy Scripture; is focused in the life, death, and resurrection of Jesus Christ; extends through the apostolic age with focus on the Holy Spirit and the early history of the church; and continues "beyond" the scriptural witness through the current life of the church until the last days.

There is also a dialectical principle implied by the Christian narrative that subverts much of the Western church's tendency regarding language about the Trinity. Inasmuch as the scriptural witness is to God's activity in history—often called God's economy—that history reveals a threefold nature (or plurality) to God's identity in history. Thus, as Wolfhart Pannenberg and Robert Jenson write, among other significant Lutheran theologians of the twentieth century, God's identity as one must be understood in the light of the communitarian "three," rather than the three somehow derived from God's unity.[5] That God is Trinity means God is communal *and* simple, as well as transcendent *and* immanent, simultaneously. Classic philosophical abstraction about the oneness of God, or even an emphasis upon God's simple unity *prior* to God's threefold nature, leads one to regard God as immune to change and allergic to time. These are the dire consequences of much of the Western tradition's preference for God's oneness before God's revealed "threeness." These consequences include the popular irrelevance of the dogma.

The latter consequence is, for example, so often accented by Trinity Sunday sermons that attempt to explain God as like water-ice-steam (three forms of one substance) or like a triangle (one figure with three sides). Such unhelpful analogies provoke the questions "Who cares?" and "What have these to do with my real, challenging *life*?" When understood relationally, however, we might soon discern that if I am created in God's image, then the character of God as relational has rather everything to do with the challenges and joys of my life. Because God is relational precisely *as* God the Trinity, then the God who created me relates to me even before I might come to know God. Further, I am related to God's people across time and distance even before I come to know them, or even if I never come to know them. This discovery means the end of the liberal "modernist" way of understanding what it means to be a personal human being; I am related before I define my "self." I am given a self through relatedness even before I supposedly choose to relate.

All this suggests, secondly, that the dogma of the Trinity is a complex of expressions, even a dogma about dogmas, which is concerned with no one doctrine (for example, the doctrine of justification) but with the whole set of Christian claims. All Christian doctrine must be informed by and recur to the Trinity if such doctrine is authentically Christian. Thus, if God is the communitarian ground and goal of all life, justification or atonement, for example, cannot end with an individual's being right with a solitary God.[6] One discovers, instead, that justification is a matter of having been put right by God for Christ's sake in and with a whole social community and natural ecology. With regard to the meaning of being and doing "church," we will conclude under the dogma of the Trinity's terms that a church cannot be merely a voluntary organization of individuals (such as with a sheerly congregational form of self-government, again in accord with a contract model of like-minded self-definers). Rather, a congregation will at least also understand itself as a local realization of the universal body of Christ. Even the human person must be understood as a person-in-relation, a being-in-communion. Otherwise or exclusive of relationality, a human being achieves no personhood whatever.

Understood in trinitarian terms, one is not a person without relationship to others, and God intends that personhood is found and modeled for the rest of the world in the body of Christ we know as church. So our village pastor was right after all; understood in light of the character of God, it is simply impossible for a Christian to be lonely. Understood apart from God—that is, under the category of sin and brokenness—we know too well that people who would be Christian, or other, yet often are lonely. This only underscores even more the importance of seeing God's communal character as characteristic of graced life, to be modeled for the world through the church.

The Trinity: Ground of Diversity in Unity

This leads, for our purposes, to a third and final point: that the dogma of the Trinity functions as a metaphysical principle. It accounts for diversity while maintaining the unity and coherence of the cosmos. It solves, so to speak, the problem of the "one and the many" by revealing that the "many" are already grounded in and constitute together a wholistic "one." Thus, as Colin Gunton observes, the common and contradictory options for interpreting the Trinity are revealed indeed to be against the dogma altogether. A hegemonic notion of unity (suggested by classical, nontrinitarian theism) can be only totalitarian, and a simplistic notion of diversity (based on mere tri-theism) can be only incoherent chaos.[7]

When God the Father, God the Son, and God the Holy Spirit are each regarded as but differing forms of the same reality, God is thus only and wholly an "other" who can relate to the creation only by intervention and fiat, being in principle over and against the creation. On the other hand, if the persons of the Trinity are thought to be in fact different from one another in substance, rather like a small three-person club of individuals, there is then nothing about "God" that substantively holds differences together. In the first case, we have a God who cannot relate to historical persons. In the second, we have three persons who cannot relate together enough to be the God in whom is all and who holds all things together (unless one wants to choose another heresy, whereby God is the fourth part one gets when Father, Son, and Spirit are added together!).

To use a musical analogy, when a choir is so well timbred, phrased, and tuned by each member tuning her or his ear to the other voices, something called "overtone" happens. Those who experience this realize that it is when choral music really happens; all else is but potential. For the one "choir" really to be, one perfect diversity in mutual accord must happen. Choir or "music" happens, and therein neither group nor individual is erased; both are fully alive within a transcendent, new reality. Thus also God the Trinity. When the identities of the Trinity are in mutual reciprocity, always "tuning" their lives to one another, God the Trinity happens such that the three never merely "add up" to one and the one never negates the three. And this happens—we are grateful—for eternity, thus holding the cosmos together and bringing it the more into God's own life.

Where diversity relationally constitutes community through the reciprocity of selfless and self-giving love, and where love wholly grounds the community, one discovers indeed the truth and beauty of life in the Trinity, of life biblically known as the image of God (*imago dei*) itself. Does this happen in congregational life? Can it? Yes, indeed. Congregational members intuit this reality, to be sure, when they have concluded together a renewal retreat weekend (like Cursillo or Via de Cristo events); when a whole congregation adopts enthusiastically a vision for outreach and upbuilding of ministry in terms of a challenging budget; when the smiles that surround the introduction of a new baptized child of God in the congregation extend into the giving of shelter to the homeless and provision of prayerful care for the troubled in one's own congregational midst; when hands join in mutual solidarity and purpose after receiving Holy Communion; when the "Thanks be to God" is loud and anticipatory of great things when the congregation is told to "Go in peace, serve the Lord." This can and does happen where differences within congregations are not turned into divisions but are honored—sometimes with civil debate—and sought after as possibilities for every individual's growth in Christian life, whereby the whole of a congregation's life is indeed more than the sum of its parts.[8]

Re-Creation into God's Intended Community

Redemption is re-creation into God's intended community. Humankind was created for communion, but is everywhere divided. God's action in Christ means to restore us into that communal life where diversity enhances community and vice versa. The church is precisely where God intends this newly restored life to be modeled. This life together is centered in eucharistic worship, in which the Word is proclaimed and the body of Christ is re-membered.[9] There, at that specific time and place of re-membering, God in God's strange wisdom communicates us to one another—whether we want one another or not—as the body of Christ, and we are each the stronger and the better even as our suffering is shared. For it is shared by Christ *and* the Spirit *and* the Father, such that God is all the more God and the "church-becoming" is all the more church, the vision of community for the world.

Where modern individualism takes charge, though, this vision of the whole, and even of the profound meaning of real community, is lost and our perception made dim. At this stage, all our self-defining attempts to achieve the community we so inexpressively desire are but secular parodies of the Christian truth. The task then is this: to return and to devote one's own baptized life again to life together in vulnerable ways, centered in Word and Sacrament, beholding and holding the vision of community in God the Trinity. Then we will "just do it"—engage in Christian life and mission—with the larger view of the consequences, knowing that our very personal lives are in fact at stake in what we do. Whatever we do, we will see that it matters, for it is done to one another to the glory of God in Jesus Christ (Col. 3:17).

3

The Psalms

Individual Laments as Communal Hymns

ANN L. FRITSCHEL

Each congregation at some point faces difficulties, even excruciating struggle and grief. How can the psalms be used today to help a faith community name its pain? How can a congregation through biblical study and liturgical use of the psalms grow to more deeply understand the nature of God, the relation between individual suffering and communal care, and the challenge of being in solidarity with suffering in the world?

The importance of community in the psalms is often overlooked. Even the most individual of laments is turned into communal hymns with significance for both individual and community. The nature of community in the individual laments is both evocative and useful for thinking about various aspects of the Christian community.

The importance of community in the individual lament is one of three interesting paradoxes in the lament psalms. The community is often the source of both despair and hope. People encounter both God and their enemies in the community. People can be enabled by the community to give voice to their most intense and personal laments.

Another paradox is that the psalms are among some of the most loved parts of the Hebrew Bible, yet we find many of them uncomfortable and "unchristian." They express vividly anger, despair, hopelessness, God forsakenness, and divine judgment with a rawness that is frightening. They challenge types of piety that suggest faith is an unquestioning acceptance of events or always being joyful before God.

The third paradox is that while the psalms are so beloved, they often have a limited liturgical role. They often are omitted from the worship service to save time, are rarely preached, and are usually so edited that their theological claims are misunderstood. Many laments are excluded

23

from the lectionary.[1] Yet there is a power in these laments that is useful in pastoral ministry and important for congregational reflection.

Psalm 22 as a Model of a Lament Psalm

Psalm 22 provides a model for exploring community in lament psalms and implications for congregations today.[2] Psalm 22 is familiar to most Christians as a part of Jesus' last words from the cross. This psalm challenges the boundaries of life and death and of community. As a general lament psalm, it has much to say to us about the role of laments, particularly for anyone close to death, and the role of the community in the individual lament.

The heart of the lament psalm is the experience of dissonance and disorientation.[3] The psalmist has certain understandings of God and human relationships with God, yet these expectations do not match current reality. The old ways of seeing things, the old securities and assurances, no longer seem to work, yet nothing new has taken their place. Life is experienced as chaotic, while the psalmist looks for firm ground. In Psalm 22, the psalmist has experienced being surrounded by God's life-giving presence from birth. Now the psalmist is surrounded by death-dealing enemies. God, who was always experienced as near, is now distant, and while God is far off, trouble is near. The psalmist longs for the situation to be restored to previous experiences of wholeness, of shalom.

The laments begin with an address to God. Often, this address acknowledges both a relationship between God and the psalmist and God's painful silence, the reality of unanswered prayer. God is experienced as having abandoned and forsaken the psalmist. In Psalm 22, this abandonment is heightened by the cry "My God, my God." This phrase not only emphasizes the special relationship between the psalmist and God but has a communal aspect as well. The psalmist belongs to a community whose center is God, whose identity and life are given by God's gracious acts. And yet this community has failed the psalmist. There is no one reminding the psalmist of God's faithfulness, of God's salvific acts in the past. Where the community is experienced, it is experienced negatively.

The lament continues with the complaint. In many laments, the complaint consists of several grievances. So, too, a congregation today should be aware that several issues might be involved, rather than addressing only one aspect of grief. The psalmist here experiences God's absence, unanswered prayers, shame and mockery, encroaching death, and enemies who both reject and attack. Death is so near that people are acting as if the psalmist were already dead. The scorn of others has led him to see himself as a worm. This imagery suggests the nearness of death and decay (Isa. 14:11; Exod. 16:20), a lowly condition (Job 25:6; Isa. 41:14), and one who is helpless and easily crushed.

This is in contrast to the portrayal of the psalmist's enemies. The use of animal imagery here is suggestive both of the power of predators hunting prey and of a breakdown of social courtesies and relationships. His enemies, as well as himself, have become less than human, mere animals. The focus here is not so much on a physical assault but on the taunts and mockery of the enemy.

The identity of the enemies in the laments has generated much debate.[4] Often, the individual was assumed to be the king and the enemies were foreign nations. However, it is likely that the psalm was generalized to individuals beyond the king. In this case, the enemies' identities become less clear. They are close to the psalmist, so close they can divide his clothes. Other psalms also suggest the enemies are within the community (Psalms 28, 42). It is a clear reminder that the community is more than a group of like-minded individuals. It is a group of imperfect individuals who will hurt one another and betray trusts. It is a challenge for what sometimes today becomes an almost idolatrous search for the "perfect community."

What can make us uncomfortable about the complaint is that the psalmist quite clearly accuses God of causing the problem or being responsible for it. "You lay me in the dust of death" (Ps. 22:15). Other psalms get even bolder. Psalm 88 cries out, "You have put me in the depths of the pit" (v. 6); "Your wrath lies heavy upon me" (v. 7); "You have made me a thing of horror to (my companions)" (v. 8). The laments engage God with the totality of life. They acknowledge that God has ultimate responsibility for what happens in the world. The theology of the lament psalms acknowledges pain, evil, and death as challenges to God's divinity. If God is truly in control, why do these powers seem so powerful? If God's will is shalom, why does not God fight those forces that are against God's will? And so the laments accuse God and cry out for God to be God.

Then comes an appeal to who God is and what God has done in the past. God is experienced in Psalm 22 as holy (v. 3), trustworthy (vv. 4-5), a deliverer (v. 31), and one who does not despise the affliction of the afflicted (v. 24). The community's traditions claim that God had listened to and delivered the ancestors in the past (vv. 4-5). The psalmist has been in an intimate relationship with God from his birth, his life always surrounded by God's presence (vv. 9-10). Both the traditions and the psalmist's personal experiences make the feeling of abandonment more pronounced. And so the psalmist calls upon God to remember God's nature and to act as God has acted in the past.

What is surprising is that in many of the psalms the deep despair of the lament is followed by the confidence of God hearing and responding to the psalmist.[5] This movement from lament to confidence and hope is thought to happen after a priest or a community member has offered assurance to the psalmist.[6] As Kathleen Norris notes, the lament psalms "don't allow us to deny either the depth of our pain or the possibility of its transformation into praise."[7]

In Psalm 22, this transformation begins with verse 21b, in which the salvation is named and God's actions are proclaimed to all generations. The psalmist is a witness to the community, inviting the people to praise the God who shares the suffering of the afflicted and transforms it. The community that hears of God's salvation includes the psalmists "brother and sisters" (v. 22) and all of the "families of the nations" (v. 27). This language, rather than the more familiar "nations of the earth," suggests a familial interrelatedness among the peoples of the world that is unusual in the psalms. The unusual nature of this community continues in verses 29-31.[8] The Greek text, read with verses 30 and 31, suggests that the community includes the living, the dead, and the unborn. It is an eschatological vision of God's rule and God's community in every time and every place. This breaking of the traditional communal boundaries in the laments, and indeed the laments themselves, has important implications for understanding Christian community today.

The Christian Community and Individual Lament

Many of the individual laments have accompanying directions to a liturgical leader. This suggests that these strong individual laments were sung in corporate worship. This is not unusual; many of our communal hymns use "I" language. It also suggests that the community had a role in these laments. Using the acronym of lament, we shall explore the role of the community in the lament, looking at the six themes of liturgy, the all-encompassing community, mission, evangelism, naming, and transformation. The reader may discern other themes.

Liturgy

One important liturgical function of the laments psalms is that they give people permission to lament. People have a psychological need to lament. Yet there are certain pieties and traditions that assume lamenting is unchristian, a sign of doubt or unbelief. The liturgical use of the laments reminds us that these laments are sacred, holy words where God has promised to meet us.

The form of the lament psalm is somewhat parallel to the form of the liturgy. The address, complaint, petition, appeal, and confidence can be seen in the patterning of our traditional, liturgical worship. The confession of sins and the kyrie both acknowledge that we and the world are not as we and it should be. The hearing of the Word in lessons, sermon, and creed remind us of who God is and what God has done for us. The congregation joins in solidarity with all who are in need through the intercessory prayers. This solidarity is expressed concretely in the offerings. The eucharist acknowledges God's work to bring shalom to the world, as it is brought to the congregation in the bread and wine, the body and blood of Jesus. The congregation praises God for God's salvation and receives the benediction and a transformed and eschatological vision of the world. While all of these steps cannot be experienced fully by the lamenter, the liturgical rhythms of both worship and laments offer hope that the situation will change and assures one that lament has a legitimate place both in the Christian life and in worship.

> "One of the first signs of a hurting individual (or family) is that he or she stops attending worship services."

The communal, liturgical use of the lament also allows the congregation at worship to be a place where we can be fully human and where pain is accepted. In our culture of success and optimism, the congregation is often viewed as a place where one must act as if nothing is wrong. We are not allowed to share our hurts and pains. One of the first signs of a hurting individual (or family) is that he or she stops attending worship services. The communal use of the lament suggests that it is human to experience pain and hurts, to grieve, and that laments can be brought before God and the congregation. Rituals for divorces, stillbirths, job or farm losses, and other types of loss or change may begin both the process of communal reconciliation where needed and the reintegration of the individual into a more ordered world.

All-Encompassing Community

The traditional boundaries of community are broken in the lament psalms. The all-encompassing nature of the community is demonstrated by the presence of enemies, all generations including the dead and unborn, and all of the families and nations of the earth in the community.

While the concept is not explicit in Psalm 22, other psalms suggest that community goes beyond the human world. The heavenly hosts and created order are also a part of this community (Psalms 97, 98, and 148, for example). This broad definition of community can help us reflect on our relationship with the land and all of creation. The community consists of more than a single species; Paul suggests that all creation also groans (Rom. 8:22). The call to solidarity and justice implied in the lament psalms must include solidarity with creation and ecojustice. How can this be demonstrated in our congregations and worship?

The all-encompassing community also acknowledges that the church cannot be just a grouping only of similar or like-minded individuals. While homogenous groups may lead to church growth, this does not reflect the gospel. The gospel comes through the particularity of culture, race, and ethnicity.[9] The issues of classism, racism, ageism, and homophobia must be challenged directly as opposing the gospel. Similarly, congregations must be places where other voices and other ideas can be heard. There must be room for moral deliberation and discussion in which all sides can be safely considered.[10]

The all-encompassing community also calls the community to be in solidarity with those who are lamenting. It is thought that the movement in the laments from lament to confidence came when a priest, a family member, or a member of the community reminded the psalmist that her lament had been heard and God would act. Today, this progression can be understood in two ways. First, the community can be seen as the embodied presence of the absent God, reaching out incarnationally to one who feels abandoned. Often, the perceived abandonment by God is exacerbated by the real abandonment of friends who "do not know what to say" or are unable to handle the lamenter's pain. The corporate presence both incarnates God's presence and enables individuals to find ways to relate to the lamenter.

Second, the community also "believes in God" for the lamenter. During the lamenter's faith struggles, the community sings the hymns and prays the prayers to which the lamenter may not be able to give voice. This includes voicing the laments for one whose piety makes such expression difficult. Paradoxically, the upholding of these faith traditions may exacerbate the feeling of dissonance. In Psalm 22, the experience of the ancestors is contrasted with the psalmist's. The ancestors' trust is emphasized, as is God's protection and deliverance. The psalmist also trusts, longing for God's protection and deliverance, which seem denied. Yet it is the reminder of God's nature and actions, by someone within the community, that brings the psalmist to a new understanding. The psalmist then continues the process by lifting up the faith traditions to all of the nations and to all generations.

The themes of mission, evangelism, naming, and transformation are more fully explored in other chapters in this book. However, we find their presence in the lament psalms as well.

Mission

The laments call the community to mission. It is a call to move beyond ourselves and our individual needs, a call that reminds us that the community does not exist for itself or individual fulfillment. The community is reminded that its own center and focus are God. The community's mission is primarily to proclaim the message of salvation, to one another and to the world. This missional aspect is covered in verses 21a-31 of Psalm 22, reaching to every time and every place. Similarly, mission can take pluralistic forms, from conversion to social justice to ecojustice.

While grounded in proclamation of the word, mission also moves to proclamation in deeds and the area of social justice. The psalmist notes that God hears the cry of the afflicted and satisfies the poor. The local congregation, as part of the body of Christ, is called to suffer with the suffering. On one hand, the lament psalms might suggest passivity because the laments acknowledge that all human efforts have failed and that only God can change the situation. Yet the crying out to God, the angry accusations, also suggests that one should not passively accept suffering as God's will. This suggests that the community, in solidarity with the suffering, can move toward social action and justice. The all-encompassing community knows it must look beyond its own interests and needs and see its connection to all people and all creation. The community both liturgically embodies the presence of God and brings God's shalom to the lamenter.

The lament psalms remind the hearer that salvation is more than eternal life; it is experienced as God's shalom, God's wholeness here and now. As the parable of the sheep and goats in Matthew 25 suggests, we can embody that shalom for others. Unlike Matthew 25, we are called to do so on both individual and structural levels.

Evangelism

This missional aspect then leads the community toward evangelism. The lament psalms always proclaim boldly who God is and what God has done, crying out that God be God. This bold proclamation is seen through the dual lenses of suffering and rejoicing. The community reminds itself and others of what God has done. The all-encompassing nature of the community suggests that this proclamation is to be shared with those not currently in the community. It is a call to reach out to all who are in need of hearing the good news. The community does this through evocative language.

The language of the psalms is poetic and evocative. Poetic language cannot be tied to any one meaning. It pushes at boundaries, resists final definition, and stimulates different images and understandings in different hearers. The evocative language of the psalms suggests that the fullness of meaning can be discovered only through the entire community bringing their voices and insights to the task of interpretation. The reality of many meanings and many voices suggested by the psalms' poetic and evocative language challenges such methods as historical criticism, which assumes that the biblical interpreter must be an expert trained in several esoteric fields. The community is where all voices need to be heard for God's will to be fully heard. This understanding of biblical interpretation reinforces the idea of the priesthood of all believers. The community is where all—not just the "paid professionals"—are given the missions of interpretation and evangelism.

Naming

Laments also name what is wrong. Understanding themselves as part of the larger community, lamenters name the pain of the world as our own. The importance of naming in the laments has been expressed by Marvin Anderson in the area of ecojustice.

> As both an antidote to cynicism and despair, as well as a catalyst for social and political action, . . . *lament* offers promise in countering the pervasive denial of earth's suffering, as well as real hope in demanding divine and human justice in the restoration of the earth's healing.[11]

The power of naming to move beyond despair to action and justice is one of the most powerful aspects of the lament psalms. This naming also challenges individual, social, and cultural idolatries. Laments are offered at the point when all individual and social attempts to provide meaning and wholeness have failed and are shown to be powerless. The time of lament becomes a time for total dependence upon God alone. The recognition slowly comes that there is only one God, and any other offers of trust and security are named as idolatries.

Transformation

The laments recognize the transformation of pain and lament. The laments remind us that such transformation comes not by thinking positive thoughts or by mere human effort but as a gift from God, a gift from outside of us. God, the source of life, can bring new life and new creation to individual and communal situations. This transformation reminds us of the mystery of the cross, of the Good Friday transformation to Easter Sunday.

This transforming, life-changing, life-renewing power provides more than comfort and assurance to the individual lamenter. By naming injustices and idolatries, by acknowledging the all-encompassing community, the transforming power of God may lead to communal acts of reconciliation and the redistribution of power. The congregation, mired in grief or conflict, can be changed and given new life for itself and the communities it serves.

Lament is a natural part of the Christian life. The liturgical use of the laments as well as the lament form of our liturgy may help people to lament. The congregation should be a place where laments are welcomed and given full expression. Congregations are also a place to help lamenters begin to see God's reordering of their world. The theology of the laments brings forth a bold witness about the nature and acts of our God. It lifts up God's salvific actions while recognizing the mystery and hiddenness of God. The laments acknowledge the finitude of human life and efforts to provide meaning. They call for a total dependence upon God, a rejection of false cultural idolatries, and a bold evangelistic proclamation about God to the lamenter, the congregation, and the world. The role of the community suggests an interweaving of mission, evangelism, the naming of idolatries and injustices, and God's transforming power in the all-encompassing community's liturgical life.

4

The Well-Being of Individuals
and the Health of the Community

DANIEL L. OLSON

What if that which is good for the mental health of the individual—having some control over one's life—makes life in community difficult? How does a leader handle people who bring their control issues into the congregation? Wholeness of individuals may come not through an inward journey toward personal fulfillment but through individuals experiencing themselves as valued members of a community with a mission.

I am riding in a subway in Oslo, Norway. A cell phone rings, and the man next to me fishes a phone from his jacket pocket and starts to talk. I do not mean to eavesdrop, but he is talking loudly and speaking English, and it becomes apparent that he is talking to a friend in the United States. I sit in the subway car and ponder the degree of control that we, as individuals, have acquired for achieving our goals, meeting our needs, and fulfilling our personal desires.

I am sitting in a symphony concert in a medium-sized U.S. city. The orchestra is playing a Haydn symphony. Two rows behind me, a cell phone rings. People mutter softly in helpless anger. The orchestra is clearly distracted. I sit and ponder the degree to which we are losing the power to make our common life take the form of genuine community.

"Man Shoots Neighbor in Argument over Meaning of Bible Verse!" The story behind that headline did not happen in my congregation, but it really did happen. There is compelling evidence that people have increasingly strong control needs these days and that they bring these needs with them into their lives in the church. I have not seen anybody shot in a Bible study class, but I do know people who have quit the church in disputes over more trivial things—the choice of color for the new carpet in the worship sanctuary, for example. I also have seen the life and mission of congregations undermined by bitter control struggles among members of more than one pastoral staff. When Walter Cronkite retired from a forty-two-year career of broadcasting the news to Americans, he commented that he had never seen a time when people were as obsessed with control as they were at the time of his retirement. That was in the early 1980s. Cronkite could hardly have predicted how much the phenomenon that he was describing would grow over the following decades.

Here is a paradox to ponder at the beginning of the twenty-first century: The average American experiences more options, fewer constraints, and less coercion than anyone else in history. That, by definition, is *freedom!* Yet the psychological disorders that are increasing among us are those associated with *loss of freedom*. And these disorders are increasing at epidemic rates.

Here is another paradox of our time: The average American exercises more real power in relation to more really important things than anyone else in history. That, by definition, is *control!* Yet the psychological disorders that are increasing among us most rapidly are those that are associated with *helplessness*.

Our relationship with control lies somewhere between preoccupation and obsession. "Take Control!" has become one of the most successful advertising themes. First, it was a tire company appealing to our concern about the safety of our children and the unpredictability of highway conditions: "*Take Control! There's Too Much Riding on Your Tires!*" Then it was an antiperspirant, appealing to our desire to conceal our anxiety in social situations: "*Take Control! Never Let Them See You Sweat!*" When portable computers became truly portable, it was "*Being Out of Town No Longer Means Being Out of Control!*" Presently, hundreds of products are being pitched for their control-enhancing features, many with the simple invitation "*Take Control!*" Something within us is stirred by those words and responds with a resounding yes!

When it comes to Super Bowl Sunday, advertisers need to be a bit more creative. After all, they are paying for these ads at a rate of nearly eighty thousand dollars a second. But the theme is the same: "Life Spans without Limits," "On the Road of Life, There Are Passengers and Drivers," "Use Your Power Wisely," "No Force Is More Potent than Self-Expression." You must refuse to be constrained by either personal inhibitions or social constraints, the ads proclaim. Express yourself! Take risks! Control your own life!

From more scholarly circles, we receive evidence of the high priority of personal control motives for twenty-first-century Americans that is equally compelling and, perhaps, somewhat more enlightening. Social psychologist Ellen Skinner, surveying professional journals of psychology, found literally thousands of articles under dozens of topic headings, all converging on the theme of personal control: *"personal control, sense of control, control motivation, perceived control, locus of control, cognitive control, agenda control, vicarious control, illusory control, outcome control, primary control, secondary control, action control, decisional control, predictive control, informational control, and proxy control."* Numerous studies that did not use the word "control" were actually studying the same thing: *"helplessness, efficacy, agency, capacity, mastery, effectance, effectiveness, autonomy, self-determination, competence, contingency, causal attribution, explanatory style, responsibility, blame, probability of success, and outcome expectancy."* Skinner's dedicated foray through this tangled jungle of research led her to conclude that "a sense of control is a robust predictor of physical and mental well-being and perhaps even longevity across the life span, from earliest infancy to oldest age."[1]

Those of us who have witnessed or experienced the painful consequences of control struggles in families, congregations, and communities may need some convincing about the positive effect of personal control for life together. Three true stories may illustrate that a sense of control is a valid and fundamental human need from earliest infancy to oldest age. A significant dimension of the ministry and mission of the church today is a ministry of empowerment.

Primary Control and the Well-Being of the Individual

We begin with a story from the cradle—literally! The main characters in this story are eight-week-old infants. The setting is a crib mounted with a crib mobile. From the end of each rod dangles a colorful toy. With a gentle nudge from the hand of a passing adult, the whole apparatus springs into lively action, much to the fascination and delight of most infants. "What would happen," wondered one researcher, "if infants learned that they could control the crib mobile themselves?" The researcher put a pressure-sensitive device in the pillows of several infants, who quickly discovered that there was a connection between the way they moved their heads and the way the mobile moved. The infants who controlled their own mobiles showed more sustained interest and delight in the moving objects than did other infants. Even more importantly, the infants who controlled their crib mobiles were generally more alert and significantly less fussy than those who experienced no such control.[2]

The other end of the life span provides equally impressive evidence for affirming the importance of a sense of personal control for the well-being of individuals. Social psychologist Ellen Langer reasoned that elderly nursing home residents' massive experiences of loss of control might be contributing to their rates of depression. She introduced small but meaningful experiences of personal control. Friends or family members will often select and bring a plant as a gift to an elderly loved one and then arrange for the nursing home staff to make sure it gets the right amount of water and sunshine. That thoughtful gesture undoubtedly helps to brighten the lives of nursing home residents. Langer decided to see what would happen if elements of choice and responsibility—of personal control—were added to this experience. A group of nursing home residents were given plants but with the following differences: (1) they were asked to choose the plant they wanted from among several options, and (2) they were given instructions on how to care for the plant and were expected to play an active role in its care. On every measure of depression, the people who made these choices and took these responsibilities were less depressed. For example, if a movie was shown, they were more likely to attend to the story on the screen and less likely to drift off. When seated next to other residents, they were more likely to interact and less likely to withdraw into themselves. When given opportunities to go on outings or engage in special activities, they were more likely to take advantage of those opportunities. And eighteen months later, they were more likely to still be alive![3]

A final story involves people at a time of their lives when they have more personal control. College students were recruited to participate in a study of the stressful effects of pain under a variety of circumstances. They agreed to receive a moderately painful electric shock while being measured for a variety of physiological stress responses. Tested individually, half were given a switch and were told, "If you decide you want to call this off at the last minute, or if you want to cut it short in the middle, just flick the switch." The others were not given a switch to throw. None of the people with the switch threw the switch. Both groups received the same shock, but the difference in stress level was remarkable. Those without the switch registered a much stronger stress response. The difference? At every moment, those who had a switch felt they had a choice.[4] Countless studies have related destructive stress, burnout, and depression in the workplace to a lack of control and choice. Having little control is not only harmful to the health and well-being of individuals but highly dangerous to the communities in which they live.

Personal Control and the Biblical Message

Essential to a healthy sense of personal control are (1) a sense that one has options and the freedom to choose among them, and (2) a sense that one can act effectively and appropriately in relation to one's social and physical environment. Does the biblical message address those needs? Luke shows Jesus beginning his ministry by reading a passage from Isaiah about the promised one who would come to set captives free and empower helpless people; Jesus then identifies himself as that one (Luke 4:16-21). At the end of Luke's Gospel, he entrusts a mission to his followers and promises that they will be "clothed with power from on high" to carry it out (Luke 24:48-49).

As leaders of local congregations, our task is clear: to proclaim that the God whom we worship and serve is the God who frees and empowers the church for a mission. It is to help every member of the congregation find a place in the congregation's mission to the world that will be valued and affirmed by the whole congregation.

Major trends in the church today undermine this fundamental task of ministry. The focus on spirituality can become merely a retreat into ever deeper, ever more private inwardness and thus an act of despair about the world and the mission to the world for which God calls, liberates, and empowers the church. The conception of the church as a provider of religious goods and services to religious consumers is an even more serious distraction from the fundamental task: identifying the mission for which God has liberated and empowered the congregation in the midst of the larger community. Wholeness comes to individuals not through a journey inward or from the consumption of religious goods and services but through the individuals' knowing and experiencing themselves as liberated, empowered, and valued members of a community with a mission. Mission, then, is not a response to good news; it *is* good news.

Biblical authors are not strangers to conditions of captivity and futility or to the yearnings of captive people to be free and of helpless people to be empowered. From start to finish, the Bible describes the experience of people whose lives are controlled by alien rulers. In the Hebrew scriptures, one foreign captor takes over from another. Deliverance from captivity in Egypt and Babylon forms the two central events, apart from which nothing in the Hebrew scriptures can be understood. From the pharaohs of ancient Egypt to the empires of Assyria, Babylon, the Seleucid Dynasty, and Rome, the people of God struggled with external coercion, domination, and constraint, and with utter helplessness in the face of it all. Psalm 137 begins with the lament of humiliated captives as they weep "by the rivers of Babylon" and ends with fantasies of violent revenge of such intensity that they are almost too painful to read. The story of God's dealings with humans in the Bible is of a God who not only intends freedom and empowerment for human beings but acts persistently toward that end.[5]

Secondary Control and the Health of Community

Primary control is a fundamental, "universal human need."[6] When people have it, they relate to the world with zest and energy and to themselves with high self-esteem. When we lose our sense of freedom and personal effectiveness, the ordinary challenges of life cease to be interesting and, instead, become sources of acute distress. The loss of a sense of personal control may undermine the immune system and is a principal cause of depression.[7] Depression is widespread where important things are out of control, where there is social chaos, where the infrastructure has largely collapsed, and where people do not trust their leaders to be able to bring things back under control.[8]

Depression is the normal human response to the perception that the important things in life have become uncontrollable; people will engage in "secondary control" strategies to regain a sense that things are controllable. Secondary control strategies can threaten the health of any community, whether congregation, city, or nation. The following representative actions may be recognized in the local congregation.

Create Chaos

If people feel powerless, they may cause an uproar. A person with a few computer programming skills can become the most powerful person in the world for a few hours or days by creating a virus destructive enough to immobilize major international corporations and government organizations. One can recognize the "create chaos" strategy on a trip to the supermarket. Through the threat of chaos, toddlers learn to control their parents to get their own way.

Blame Someone

If something goes wrong, someone must be blamed so the situation can be "understood" and control restored. The one who is blamed can be punished or excluded. If an illness cannot be explained, doctors must be blamed and sued. In dysfunctional families, it is common to identify and punish a scapegoat. If the coach, the quarterback, the CEO, or the pastor can be considered at fault, they can be replaced. The widespread conviction of innocent people for crimes that they have not committed is evidence that the human mind recoils against the unpredictability, unreliability, and uncontrollability of its world.

Act Violently

Major acts of domestic, school, and workplace violence are reported in the news every day. In less than a month in three different locales, men who felt humiliated and helpless stockpiled weapons and went on shooting sprees in the workplace. The increase in domestic violence is now seen as a widespread adoption of a control strategy relative to other family members, rather than as an increase in anger control problems. The increase of disorders associated with loss of control coincides with the increase of incidents in which people exert control through violent means. People often choose a few moments of violent power, even if they know that the inevitable cost will be their own lives.

Narrow Down Your Life to Controllable Dimensions

The decline in civic engagement in America in recent years has been striking and rapid.[9] Membership and attendance are down sharply in organizations ranging from Lions Clubs to Parent-Teacher Associations to block associations to churches. But like other secondary control strategies, this one is self-defeating. By withdrawing one's commitments from such organizations, people bring into the nuclear family all of their relational needs, and the family is forced to bear more weight than it reasonably can. So the family collapses, and people experience isolation and a loss of control in relation to their most important need: the need to be connected to other people.

Form Highly Dependent Relationships

When people feel that they are helpless, they are likely to look for someone whom they believe is strong and good and wise enough to take care of them. It doesn't much matter who or how. Jim Jones will do. And if he asks you to go with him to a remote jungle, you go. And if he tells you to drink the poison Kool-Aid, you drink it.[10] Adolph Hitler will do. Or, you can find somebody strong and marry them. You can look to the local pastor as someone who must be infinitely strong, wise, and good, and infinitely available. This secondary control strategy also is self-defeating. It undermines self-esteem, puts intolerable strains on relationships, and makes people angry at the ones upon whom they are dependent, because they come to feel that those people are controlling their lives.

Relinquishing Control and Taking Charge

Primary control is a sense that individuals can make choices and act effectively relative to the things in life that are important to them. It is a prerequisite for a healthy and energetic life. More and more people are experiencing reduced control and are either resorting to secondary control strategies or succumbing to depression. The loss of primary control is harmful to the individual, and the exercise of secondary control strategies is harmful to communities.

The ability to distinguish between primary control and secondary control is a helpful contribution from social psychology in thinking about the control issues that bedevil us. There is an even more useful distinction implicit in a central biblical doctrine: stewardship. If we can move beyond the trivialization of stewardship that has reduced it to an every-November campaign, we find that it is a powerful concept that defines the whole of our lives. In relationship to God and the whole of God's creation, including our own lives, we are stewards. Two things are required of stewards: (1) they must take charge, and (2) they must relinquish control.

> ✿ *"The loss of primary control is harmful to the individual, and the exercise of secondary control strategies is harmful to communities."*

Why must stewards take charge? Because they have been placed in charge! When Jesus defined the lives of his followers in relation to everything that is, he said, "It is as if a householder has called together the slaves and placed them in charge" (Mark 13:34). Since taking charge means making decisions, stewards must experience themselves as free. Since taking charge means acting effectively when action is required, stewards must experience themselves as able to act effectively. Since taking charge means bringing order out of chaos, stewards must experience themselves as creative. And since taking charge requires caring passionately about that which has been given into their charge, stewards must be fully engaged.

But stewards also must relinquish control. Control belongs to the one who has placed them in charge. Throughout history, humans have not done well when they have taken control. The earth and its inhabitants have suffered. The intentions of God for creation have been undermined when people have taken control. The wheel and writing were both invented between 3500 and 3000 B.C.E. This gave strong tribal leaders the means to take control of other tribes and form nations, and they did so. National leaders now had the means to take control of other nations and form empires, and they did so. By the time Jesus was born, Israel had been annexed to five empires. And during the brief interlude that it was not annexed to anybody else's empire—the golden age of David the king—it did not do very well under its own control. Israel started annexing other nations and making its own empire. By the beginning of World War II, only two out of sixty-four nations in sub-Saharan Africa did not bear the name of a European nation that had come down in the last half of the nineteenth century and claimed it as its own. There were the Belgian Congo, the Spanish Sahara, Portuguese Mozambique, German Southwest Africa—the list goes on and on. Control over other people was not unique to Western civilization, however. In the East, Japan claimed Korea and China as its own.

Human beings have not done very well with control. Control is a fundamental human need, as we have seen, a need that reflects not only the intentions of God for human beings but also the image of God in human beings. But it also is a need that dramatizes the reality and power of human sin to distort the image of God in us more than any other of our needs. It is the best of life and the worst of life.

An eight-week-old controls a crib mobile and experiences delight and satisfaction. Does life have better moments for those who look on with pride and joy? Napoleon controls the world and experiences delight and satisfaction. Does life have worse moments for those who look on in horror and fear?

Stewardship means to take charge and to relinquish control. It is the way to a faithful church and a sane world. The biblical message calls us to do so in three areas of life:

1. Relinquish control of the outcome; take charge of the process.
2. Relinquish control of other people; take charge of your response to them.
3. Relinquish control of your circumstances; take charge of the decisions you make within them.

Relinquish Control of the Outcome;
Take Charge of the Process

When personal control takes the form of expecting to control the outcome of our every endeavor, we drive ourselves crazy. You can take a perfect swing at a golf ball and send it straight down the fairway. But it can hit a sprinkler head and bounce off into the woods. The swing is the process; the final location of the ball is the outcome. When athletes get distracted from the process of playing the game by concern for the outcome of winning or losing, they often "choke." You can do careful research on investment strategy and seek the best advice, but the market can change in some unpredictable way at some unpredictable time, and your retirement fund suddenly loses much of its value. You have taken charge of the process; the outcome is beyond your control. The biblical authors knew that with regard to the mission of the people of God. Paul made that point when he wrote, "Paul planted, Apollos watered, but God gave the growth" (1 Cor. 3:6). Isaiah, Ezekiel, and Jeremiah got that word from God when God told them that their responsibility was to proclaim the Word and that from that time on the outcome was out of their hands (see Isa. 55:10-11).

Jesus said that the kingdom of God is like a farmer who goes out and plants seed in the field and day and night nothing seems to happen (Mark 4:26-27). Faith is believing that God is tending to the outcome and that our part is to take charge of the process. The most deeply committed mission effort of the local congregation may produce no apparent results. Nobody should be blamed and no responsibility for failure assigned. As stewards, we engage in life-giving mission and relinquish control of the outcome.

Relinquish Control of Other People;
Take Charge of Your Response to Them

The motivation for control becomes tyranny, domination, and dictatorship when people feel that being in control of their lives requires them to control the way that other people think and feel and act. In my life as a clinical psychologist, I have worked with people who not only demanded perfect behavior from their children but monitored every facial expression and every tone of voice to detect unacceptable feelings and then punished their children for feeling the emotion they felt. Beyond that, they monitored every utterance for unacceptable thoughts. Dictatorships always do that. That is why you cannot trust anyone in a dictatorship. Your neighbor might report to the authorities that you are having unacceptable thoughts. Your neighbor might be angry at you and report some unacceptable thoughts that he or she makes up, just to get you in trouble. During the Terror, following the French Revolution, everyone was scrutinized for unacceptable thoughts, and the chief architects of the ideology behind the revolution itself eventually went to the guillotine.

In its worst chapters, the church has done the same. Stewards need to be creative to respond effectively to brand-new situations, and brand-new situations are why stewards are there. Ultimately, community itself is a casualty of the need to control other people. If I successfully control the way that other people think and feel and act, they will either hate me or become depressed and totally dependent on me.

We must relinquish our need to control the way that other people think and feel, even if those people are members of our family, even if we are teachers and they are students in our class, even if we are teachers of the Scriptures or preachers of the gospel and they are our parishioners. Relationships are a lot more fun, and a lot more fulfilling, if they are a meeting between people who respect each other's rights to have thoughts and feelings of their own. You can enjoy your children a lot more if you realize that you cannot control how they turn out—the mass media and their peer group have too large an influence on them. But you will take charge of the process of witnessing to your own faith and your own values, and you will have done what you could.

Relinquish Control of Your Circumstances; Take Charge of the Decisions You Make within Them

Toddlers become angry if it rains when they want to play outside. They think a combination of their wishes and their parents' power should have prevented that. A six-year-old is inconsolable if not invited to a friend's birthday party. Growing up means learning to accept that circumstances do not always turn out the way you wanted them to—or at least that used to be the case when we had more realistic expectations of the control we could assert. But now we hear of death by road rage in traffic jams and death by air rage when flights are delayed. That does not sound much different than toddler rage when the weather is wrong. Paul wrote that he had "learned in any and all circumstances to be content" (Phil. 4:11).

Paul may have been exaggerating a bit—or maybe he wasn't. Life is going to inflict unpredictable circumstances upon us. Droughts and floods come; a corporation that we work for goes out of business; a friend betrays us. Within each circumstance, we are called, entrusted, liberated, and empowered to make faithful decisions: decisions that are faithful to who we are in this new, often unwelcome situation.

Before Jesus began his ministry, he went out into the uncontrollability of the trackless wilderness and there made three decisions, decisions about what it meant to be faithful to who God had declared him to be at his baptism, just before he went to the wilderness. As stewards of the mission of God in a new situation that seems in many ways to be a trackless wilderness, that is our task. That is the control we must exercise. The only control we have is to ask, "Given the identity that God has declared to be mine, and the mission that God has entrusted to my stewardship, what is the appropriate response to this new situation in this new time and place?" That is what God asks of us, and that is what the world needs from us.

In Mark's Gospel, an unnamed woman breaks an alabaster jar of ointment and anoints Jesus prior to his death. She draws a lot of criticism from onlookers, but Jesus says, "She has done what she could" (Mark 14:8-9).

And then Jesus says that wherever the gospel is told, she will be remembered. She did what she could. That is what we are empowered and freed to do, and it is all we are asked to do. In a world obsessed with control in a way that often destroys both communities and their individual members, this witness itself can be our transforming mission to God's world.

5

Re-Membering the Body of Christ

Creating Trustworthy Places to Be Different Together

NORMA COOK EVERIST

Believing that one is an indispensable member of the body of Christ and believing that the local congregation is an indispensable part of the whole church present difficult challenges. Can one belong to a faith community where people do not like one another? Does a congregation wonder whether other churches know or care about them? What are some specific ways to revitalize our life together in Christ? How can we re-member the church?

Entering a congregation a few years ago to be guest preacher and presider on a summer Sunday, I was greeted at the door about a half hour before services by an usher who said, "Good morning. We're not the church we used to be." "Then who are you?" I asked. Crucial to our life together is our own sense of identity as a church body, and particularly as a local congregation. When we apologize for our present predicament, only remembering the past, we cannot fathom what God may be doing now and as we live together into God's promised future.

The church is not merely the carrier of the gospel, a place to hear the good news preached and taught, an organization to preserve as history. The church *is* good news, the radical, possible impossibility of being joined together with people different from ourselves, even with people we may not like very much.[1] For Christ's sake, the church is the reality of the alienated reconciled, the rebellious returned, the lonely encompassed with love. But on any given day in any congregation, one may experience something quite different.

Across this land, people still gather for worship but with less regularity than in previous generations. One cannot count on mere denominational loyalty to ensure church membership. And while many people—often

45

quietly—engage in caring ministry within the congregation and beyond, such service may carry with it fatigue, frustration, and discouragement. Then there is conflict, whether over issues of church governance or over what color to paint the fellowship hall. Our life together in the community of faith often disappoints us. Membership in the body of Christ is difficult but indispensable.

Ecclesiological Foundations

The church is a human institution that meets human needs. As a community of language, memory, and understanding, given the various backgrounds of congregations within a denomination, the church becomes a community of many communities.[2] It is a political community of belief, interpretation, and action.[3] It is challenged to love in ways similar to but also radically different from other human communities. People expect their church to be a keeper of values, a service organization, a place to belong, even an insurance policy for eternal life.[4] But how can we be a congregation when we do not hold shared memories, when we interpret the world and the Scriptures in a variety of ways, when we differ on our goals for justice advocacy? Even though the church can be viewed sociologically as a community, it remains a communion of alienated strangers. The church itself is pluralistic and is often seen not only in its diversity but also in its disunity.[5]

> *"The church is good news, the radical, possible impossibility of being joined together with people we may not like very much."*

We as congregations may spend much energy trying to prove ourselves to the bishop or to other congregations or critiquing one another. The church is not so much to be admired or criticized as believed.[6] Believing that one's congregation is the church—with dwindling membership, secrets and grudges, and budget problems—is often very difficult. A congregation with membership increases may also face conflict in the midst of change, not recognizing itself as the church it used to be.

Our identity is always partial. The church is both local and universal. Where two or three are gathered in the name of Christ, Christ is present; also present are all others in whom Jesus incarnates himself. Christ is never present without the company of all of the members of the body of Christ. The localized church implies the universal; the universal implies the local.[7] When a congregation denies its identity either in a false concept of humility or in shame, guilt, or frustration, it may look to other expressions as the "real" church, deprecating itself in unbelief. Or, when a congregation in a posture of self-sufficiency or through myopic vision does not recognize the church universal—ecumenically, historically, and globally—it thinks more highly of itself than it ought to think. In disbelief, it doubts that God cares as much for other Christian communities as for itself. Congregations need to constantly *remember* one another, believing that although we differ in so many ways—and our differences may cause difficulties—our unity is in Christ.[8]

During a time of doctrinal or political struggle within a church body, one faction may be tempted to think another is dispensable. When a congregation experiences financial or membership struggles, it may worry that it is dispensable to others. Do other congregations know or care? At those very times, we need others to remind us who and whose we are, members together of the body of Christ. When one is in pain, the whole body aches. We need to believe that together we are the church. Even though congregations and church bodies wax and wane, sometimes even ceasing to be institutions, every member of Christ's church is indispensable. We matter to one another, even when we don't know the other exists. Trusting the unity of the body of Christ, especially in the midst of heated debate or abject despair, we can remember to celebrate the churches that were and are and are to come by the power of the Spirit.

A Diverse and Open Church

The church has many expressions, vastly different according to geography, history, and economic reality. In my recent travels, I visited a congregation that would be closing its doors permanently on Pentecost Sunday and another that was growing by an average of one member a day. I saw a little church tucked back into the hills that has both an outhouse and a Web site—and needs both. I felt the anticipation of an urban congregation redeveloping its outreach potential in a changing neighborhood, and the hesitancy of a mature church that had been deceived by its most recent leader. In congregations across the land, large and small, rural, urban, suburban, and edge city, I saw that mission matters. However, sometimes the tensions and tragedies—and even the challenges and celebrations—of a congregation can distract it from significant interest and engagement in the church beyond itself. There is a paradox here. I do not suggest that we focus less on the local congregation; rather, in seeing the local church as gift, with clarity of identity and mission in Christ, it can become not more self-sufficient but more open to see and learn from other congregations, even those younger, smaller, or more troubled than itself.

Christ, incarnate in a body that was broken and raised from the dead, is now continually re-membering the body of Christ in the world, putting us back together again. But faith in the holiness of the church is no more a justification of its unholy condition than the justification of sinners means a justification of sin. It is key to remember that the church is *simul justus et peccator*.[9] The church is the community of justified sinners, the community of those liberated by Christ who experience salvation and live in thanksgiving, the community that keeps its eyes fixed on Christ, taking its place in history.

When we become alienated from one another, either by "forgetting" one another or through misunderstandings, we need to re-member Christ, who reconciles us in the midst of our differences. When we feel lost, wandering away from the church for a while, God waits with open arms and empowers us with patience to wait for one another that we might rejoice when we return to Christ and to one another. This is good news. God has created us for interdependence, re-membered the body of Christ, and spiritually empowered us to empower one another. We can trust Christ, who makes the members of the body indispensable to one another.

The church is called to be and to become inclusive. We have begun to ask in recent years, "Who is not at the table?"[10] This means asking not only who is not gathered at the altar for eucharist but some other challenging questions: Who is not on this task force? Whose leadership gifts are we not calling upon? Whose vision for reshaping the table are we not seeing? We need not only to make room for diverse people in our congregations but to welcome all people's participation in redesigning structures that fully appreciate and utilize their presence.

Not only our congregational doors but our attitudes and hearts need to be wide open. When we who may be very involved in the church move beyond our fatigue and frustrated attitudes toward "inactives," we may be able to share new conversations. When we believe that the place of Christian vocation is where members live and serve all week long, we may see Christ at work there. When we go out into the neighborhood, whether that be a few city blocks, a rural township, a subdivision, or a high-rise, we may establish new relationships and be challenged by diverse worldviews. When we interact with and learn from diverse ecumenical and interfaith communities, we may find that we are indispensable to one another as we cooperate in working toward a just society. Together, we need to create and sustain trustworthy places to be different together, retaining our particularity while participating in a healthy pluralistic society.

Living the Epistles

The New Testament presents numerous images of the church. Paul Minear's classic work presents more than eighty.[11] Minear is not as much troubled by the challenge of unity in diversity as he is awed by the mystery of God. No one model, no one polity, is supreme; each contains flaws, and all hold potential. The richness of God is reflected in the New Testament gallery of pictures of the church.

Four major and a multitude of minor images emerge in the New Testament. Minor images include "salt of the earth," "letter," "fish," "sign," "net," and "boat."[12] The four major images are "people of God," "the new creation," "the fellowship in faith," and "the body of Christ." The body of Christ image is used in three key epistle passages: 1 Corinthians 12, Romans 12, and Ephesians 4.

1 Corinthians 12

In the ancient world, Stoics used the body metaphor to say that individual members must be subordinated to the whole body (the state), but Paul uses the metaphor quite differently. He is not developing a hierarchical notion of the church; rather, the body functions only when all members play their roles. No one member can be the whole body or do without the others.[13]

In 1 Cor. 12:4-6, Paul builds a trinitarian formula: there are varieties of gifts (*charismata*), but the "same Spirit"; varieties of services (*diakonia*), but the "same Lord"; and varieties of activities (*energemata*), but it is the "same God" who activates all of them in everyone. Individual gifts, service, and work all are from God, "for the common good" (v. 7). Gifts of the entire community are never to be stored up but are to be used by God in *active* service. Then, and only then, comes the list of "membership." This is a different list than in Romans or Ephesians, but that is not significant because it is not the specificity or rank ordering that should concern us but the importance of all members in the body. In 1 Cor. 12:8-10, we see utterance of wisdom, knowledge, faith, healing, working of miracles, prophecy, discernment of spirits, various tongues, and interpretation. All are "activated by one and the same Spirit" (v. 11). Three times (vv. 12, 20, and 27) we hear that there are many members but one body of Christ. All are joined in baptism and at the table (v. 13). "If the foot would say, 'Because I am not a hand, I do not belong to the body,' that would not make it any less a part of the body" (v. 15). "If the whole body were an eye, where would the hearing be?" (v. 17).

In congregations today, many members, even the most loyal and active ones, may feel, "I don't belong" or "I don't belong *here* anymore." In the midst of such discouragement—not just when we have emerged from the difficult times—all are still significant parts of the body. Likewise, congregations need to resist the urge to turn new members into people just like themselves.[14] Because Christ's body is resurrected, never to die again, and because we live in the spirit of Pentecost, we need not fear losing "our" church to those "others." A radical body of Christ theology is life-giving for all.

In 12:21, Paul becomes even more pointed: "The eye cannot say to the hand, 'I have no need of you,' nor again the head to the feet, 'I have no need of you.'" Two examples, so we don't miss it! Most of us today think we would never say that, but of course we do, either with words or with the avoidance of words, by actions or by inactions. We also disregard those with seemingly inferior roles in favor of those who consider themselves to have superior gifts. From this biblical metaphor, we begin to realize that we simply cannot say, "I have no need of you" when we believe the body of Christ. We cannot believe *in* the church for we will forget and deny and betray one another, just as Jesus was denied, betrayed, and abandoned on the cross. Rather we *believe* the body of Christ, that, by the power of the Spirit, Christ has re-membered his very body in and through the church.

One needs to note that 1 Corinthians 12 stands between chapters 11 and 13. Chapter 11 has often been used to keep people from the table; however, the phrase "discerning the body" (11:29) refers not so much to lack of correct doctrine as to the divisions, factions, and classism exhibited when some eat and others go hungry. When we partake of the loaf and cup, we are to do it in *remembrance* of Christ. Similarly, in chapter 13, Paul makes clear that no matter what our particular gifts, the very best work is nothing without love, love that is patient, kind, not envious, boastful, arrogant, or rude, or irritable or resentful. And this love, which is of God, never ends (13:1-8).

Romans 12

After Paul has fully developed in the earlier chapters of Romans the themes that none is righteous through the law, that justification is in Christ by grace through faith, and that salvation is for all, he describes the new life in Christ in chapter 12. Justification by grace through faith must be manifest in practice. He challenges brothers and sisters in the faith to present themselves as living, holy bodies (v. 1). This communal body is radically different from the world's concept. It is a transformed, renewed, perfected body (v. 2). Paul addresses individuals and also urges "everyone among you not to think of yourself more highly than you ought to think" (v. 3) because, just as the one body has many members, "so we who are many, are one body in Christ and individually members one of another" (v. 5).

Believing this is a challenge for members of a Christian community for we are prone either to think ourselves more important than others or to discount ourselves in guilt or shame.[15] A biblical theology of the congregation provides a foundational understanding that membership describes not people who all simply happened to have joined the same organization. We are members *of* one another. When one is tempted on a Sunday morning to wonder whether it is "worth it" to go to church, one needs to recall our common membership. My attendance is not merely for my self-edification but *for* others. My absence affects the body. When we "volunteer" someone for a committee job when he or she is out of the room, we need to recall that living, holy members of the body of Christ should not be motivated by goading, guilt, or manipulation but through discernment of gifts, volition, and mutual accountability.

We have gifts that differ. In Romans 12, one's role in the community is in relation to gifts (vv. 6-8), for example, "the giver, in generosity," "the leader, in diligence." It is tempting to try to glean from Romans 12 an exact ordering of ministry categories. One must remember that in the list, the number of gifts is unlimited. Gifts and roles are not ranked. The list is open, not closed. Central to all is the gift that we who are many are one body in Christ.

Ephesians 4

The passage begins with the call to live the life that never ends, in community as a resurrection people. Earlier in chapter 2 (vv. 1 and 5), Paul addresses people who once were dead through trespasses but are now alive *together* in Christ. It is these resurrected people whom Paul begs to lead the life that they have been given and to which they have been called. We hear the same theme as Romans 12: one body, one Spirit, one hope in the calling, one Lord, one faith, one baptism, one God; but in Ephesians the image highlights that no one individual, only Christ, is the head of the body.

In Ephesians 4, the distinct gifts (vv. 11-12) relate to how people will serve: apostles, prophets, evangelists, pastors, and teachers. But once again the roles are not ordered hierarchically, nor are they ends in themselves. Pastors are not pastors for the sake of being pastors, nor should we as pastors ever say, "my ministry," "my pulpit," "my church." The various forms of ecclesial ministry are "to equip" the saints for their works of ministry, and all of this activity is "for building up the body of Christ" (vv. 15-16).[16] In the midst of conflict, uncertainty, and even "deceitful scheming" (v. 14) or a church broken apart, we are called to grow up into Christ so that the whole body joined and knit together promotes the body's growth in building itself up in love (vv. 15-16).

The Ministry of Re-Membering the Body of Christ

These three epistle texts not only image who we are as people joined together in Christ but also challenge us to become living letters to one another (e-mail, if you will), face-to-face, side by side, even if we live worlds away from one another either literally or figuratively. We cannot on our own minister effectively enough to avoid dissension, disunity, or dissatisfaction. But the Spirit empowers us to believe that Christ's body has been given for us, resurrected and whole. Each time the congregation welcomes a new member into the congregation through the baptismal waters and is fed together at the eucharistic table, Christ's body is present. Each of us has been joined to Christ's baptism into his death and resurrection and is called to serve in the world.[17] We together hear "Do this in *remembrance* of me." We are commissioned to "go in peace, serve the Lord." We need to become what we already are in Christ.

So what does powerful servanthood in God's world mean for us whom God intends to re-member as the body of Christ? We are called to create and sustain a trustworthy environment within congregations for us to be different together in *membership, identity,* and *companionship,* through our *worship, education, care, stewardship,* and *decision making,* even our *conflict.* Through remembering our *history,* reaching out in our *ministry in daily life* for *mission* and *justice,* we can participate *ecumenically* in a *pluralistic* world. What follows are a few specific implications. Congregations will discover many more.

Membership

Although membership in many congregations and church bodies has been steadily declining in recent decades, people still seek spirituality; even though it is a privatized search, they deeply long for meaningful community. People today are simply reluctant to join, commit, and become a member of an institution. Congregations, rather than lowering expectations and hesitantly asking people if they might "consider" membership, would do well to reclaim the word "member" in its radical body-of-Christ sense. Those keeping their distance from the institutional church may need to be taken not less but more seriously, unconditionally welcomed with their questions and their wounds, and given opportunity to serve in significant ways.

Identity

To reach out to the community, congregations may be tempted to lessen—or not even name—their denominational identity. They may omit the institution-sounding word "church" altogether, calling themselves merely a "community gathering place." Threatened by the phenomenal growth of a nondenominational group down the street or defensive about one's minority status in the area, congregations may be tempted to define themselves by what they are not. Why not befriend one's heritage, clearly claiming who we are and what we believe, and reach out with vigor to seek and to love, to listen to and to learn from all kinds of people?

Companionship

Is a congregation that can no longer afford a pastor no longer a congregation? Rather than resort to competition with one another for members, or even for survival, we need to dare to believe that when we are tempted to "go it alone" we still are knit and joined together as the body of Christ. How can we use conferences and the clustering of churches to suffer with, rejoice with, and support one another? We may feel overwhelmed by the scope of the universal church, but we can become partners and companions with specific congregations that are different from ourselves, across town or around the globe, not in neocolonialism but to genuinely share needs and gifts.

Worship

The church (*ecclesia*) gathers to be a worshiping assembly—literally assembling the members of the body. But people too easily prefer to remain merely spectators, an audience to a few performers; their only remaining role is critic. If a congregation resorts to providing "the best show," it will discover that people will always be looking for a better one. Rather than just a few on stage in the chancel, why not view all members (yet with clarity of gifts and roles) as actors in the great, living, ever-new drama of God and God's people?

Education

We mistakenly assume that Sunday school is for children and "church" is for adults. Many congregations still configure services so that children are never in worship and adults neglect their own lifelong educational ministry. Why not provide communal worship and education opportunities for all? Youth need not be only passive recipients of a chancel-step story but can lead as lectors, ushers, musicians, and artists. Even though the one adult class is underattended, why not start two or three more, providing a variety of adult learning styles?[18]

Care

In an era saturated with time-saving devices, people feel overworked, time locked, and stressed out. Rather than despair that people are too busy to work "at church," we can begin where Jesus always did, where people are in their need. How can we create trustworthy places to come as we are—with our pain, stress, depression, and wounds of abuse (even perhaps by the church)—and offer God's reconciliation and healing? We can trust that the Spirit is able to make the body of Christ whole, even when it is less than knit and joined together.

Stewardship

Mission seems limited by money but may simply be inhibited by a lack of imagination. God created us for interdependence, not to dominate the earth but to be stewards of resources, working toward a just global economy. Many of us live lives of insatiable consumerism, and we are sick from it. When I dare to pray the petition "Give us this day our *daily* bread," might I not be asking for less on my plate today so that "our" can mean that all God's people are fed today and tomorrow?

Decision Making

The church is not a democracy; neither is it a kingdom. We need to create trustworthy places that encourage all to speak—places where we can be different together. While voting may settle an issue for today, people remember who won or lost for years, even generations. We can learn leadership skills that help a faith community work toward consensus. Consensus does not and should not mean we totally agree, but it does mean all have been heard.

Conflict

People are surprised, becoming defensive and reactive, when conflict erupts in the church. Mired in intimidation and veiled threats, we learn and teach skills of manipulation. We kill one another nicely. At such times, how can we dare to re-member one another as the body of Christ, still belonging to one another—even if we can't stand one another? Clarifying issues and roles, we as leaders need to create and sustain arenas of trust in which people feel safe enough to listen and to speak. When the issue *is* leadership, we need to call on mentors from beyond the conflict to help establish safe boundaries to work through the problem.

History

Rather than living in the past, with nostalgic judgmentalism or apology, or negating the past by ignoring our history and its stories, why not create congregations as healthy places to remember together? We can use video and digital cameras to gather oral history of saints of the congregation and to keep in touch with those who have moved away. Youth can learn interviewing skills in asking to hear the stories of the elders; elders, in turn, can learn to inquire about the visions of youth.

Ministry in Daily Life

Rather than urging people merely to remember what they learned "in church" in order to apply it to daily life (and feeling guilty when they fail), why not begin where the church is on Tuesday afternoon? We can walk with one another in the arenas of our daily lives. The members of the body of Christ, with different gifts and callings, go forth to vastly differing challenges. Can we do theology in the many languages that members speak: technology, medicine, education, real estate? Members, having served at many kinds of tables all week long, return to the Lord's table to be nourished once again.

Mission

Christ never intended the church to be planted only where growth patterns indicate that economically upwardly mobile, ethnically homogeneous people can assure a new congregation will be able to go off mission support per a set time line. How can we afford to start new congregations that might "fail" or that primarily comprise teenagers off the street who surely can't pay the mortgage? How can we afford not to? We need to reach out in every neighborhood, even when it seems no longer to be a neighborhood.

Justice

To engage in mission is to seek to serve. All of our ministries as the baptized *laos* of God need to be ministries of healing and reconciliation. There can be no health in the body of Christ and no peace on the earth without justice. Social ministry needs to include advocacy for justice. Even though congregation members work in diverse places, perhaps *because* they do, members of the body of Christ can become powerful servants of those who suffer and change agents who make a difference in the world.

Ecumenism

Instead of merely debating ecumenical activities, we can remember that our unity in Christ—globally and in the local community—is a given and a "not yet." We are called to live into God's promised future eschatologically, as though we already were one, because we are. Rather than worrying about what we might lose in ecumenical cooperation, why not use our gifts to equip the saints for all kinds of ministry, confident that while engaged in mission together, Christ is building the church?

Pluralism

We live in a diverse world. Rather than building fortresses to protect people from the secular world or trying to compete with its attractions, why not claim our identity and voice so that we can speak clearly in the public world? The United States is not now and never has been a "Christian" nation. The goal is not to make everyone in this nation just like us, but to help create safe places to listen and learn from one another in interfaith dialogue. How could congregations lead a whole community to create hospitable places to be different together?

The challenge is large, but the gift is ever greater. By God's grace, we have become the body of Christ, and we can trust that God holds us lovingly together, in the midst of our differences, to serve faithfully in God's world.

PART TWO

The Church's Heart:
The Indispensable Power of Christ

With part 1 having considered the relationship between individuals and the community, this section of the book goes to the heart of the church, examining foundations of faith in Christ. It also raises some provocative challenges. The authors of this book—as well as the readers—bring different viewpoints to our understanding of these foundations. Members of a congregation—all using the same liturgy, confessing the same creeds, and reading the same Bible—manage to come to opposing stands on the issues they face. Christ provides power for the community to trust their unity in the midst of difficulties so that they are not petrified in stalemate but are able to study and discern and to speak and act in the world.

James Bailey explores faith practices that reflect the gospel, using 1 Thessalonians as a prototype. While in no way negating justification by faith, he presses Christians to move beyond asking what Paul says. Instead, we are challenged to ask what Paul invites the recently converted Thessalonians, still struggling with what it means to be a community, to *do*. Bailey gives specific suggestions: practice a language of belonging, revive a communal memory, serve as living models, respond to communal imperatives, and practice eucharistic prayer. Such practices enhance our functioning as Christian congregations and empower us for outreach.

The reader next approaches the subject from the standpoint of systematic theology. Duane Priebe presents a premise that is simple yet profound: if we are justified by grace alone through faith alone, the gospel of Jesus Christ claims us absolutely in all the people we meet. We believe in God's redeeming love for them in Jesus Christ, regardless of whether they believe that for themselves or not. What does this mean for the way we view other faith communities, people we say are "outside the faith"?

Priebe believes the gospel claims us so that we speak and act toward them as people for whom Jesus died.

Ralph Quere is concerned that in trying to make sure Christian community includes all, we could be in danger of tacitly assuming universal salvation. He grounds his position in a historical look at confessional foundations, including the Augsburg Confession and the Formula of Concord. He explores the human predicament and divine intervention, drawing conclusions about what is necessary for salvation. Quere believes people need not just information *about* Christ but also faith *in* Christ, and that this is crucial for a congregation's evangelism efforts.

David Lull takes us once again to Scripture, raising the deeply difficult issue of how various parts of the community read the Bible differently. Historical and contemporary church bodies are filled with examples of church divisions over biblical authority. Lull helps congregations redefine categories for discussion of scriptural authority, providing helpful suggestions for leaders. Can we become one church, one congregation, when we differ so greatly from one another on issues that we debate on the *basis* of biblical interpretation, such as sexuality?

James Nieman's chapter moves us to one significant use of biblical interpretation: preaching. What are conditions for good preaching? He emphasizes the importance of reading differing contexts, practicing the art of proclaiming with attention to where we are. But he also questions that if preachers speak only what people already have heard, or what could be said in the complete absence of the Bible, of what significance is that? Good preachers learn to collaborate with their various hearers, listening to what Scripture continues to say that is applicable for diverse people in even the most difficult times.

Karen Bloomquist explores the church's voice from the perspective of theological ethics. Ethics tends to be at the periphery of the church's attention, rather than arising out of the center of ecclesiology. Bloomquist says that ethical reflection and action are intrinsic to the nature of life in community: its worship, educational ministry, preaching, and pastoral care. The term *communio* expresses the unity of the church across time and the relationship within and between local, regional, and global churches. She challenges us to become a mutually supportive communion, so that in our decision making we live our faith in the light of God's all-inclusive vision for the world.

6

The Pauline Letters
as Models for Christian Practice

1 Thessalonians as a Case Study

JAMES L. BAILEY

How can the Bible, specifically the letters of the early church, provide a vision for life together and mission for congregations today? Although the struggles the church faces seem so different from two thousand—or even fifty—years ago, Scripture provides foundations in the power of Christ for faith and for practice. What social pressures do Christians face? What courage does it take to face them? To what commitments are Christians called?

Most Christians today are extremely practical in their approach to the Bible. They want guidance and inspiration for daily living, and as a result much biblical scholarship seems esoteric and remote to their concerns. Whereas recent publications on "the historical Jesus" have generated wide interest in church and society, studies on the Pauline Letters have gone largely unnoticed. The apparent neglect of Paul in the church's preaching and teaching is an embarrassment since scholarly study of the Pauline Letters over the past fifty years has yielded significant results with quite practical implications for the theology and life of Christian communities.

In past generations, the church has studied the Pauline Letters mainly to determine the apostle's *theological teaching* (for example, regarding God, Jesus Christ, and the human predicament). Recent Pauline scholars have helped the church focus on what Paul did as well as what he taught, on both his *practices* and his *theological convictions*. Thus we ask: what insights for congregational life might flow from study of a Pauline Letter when attention is given not only to the theological vision expressed by the apostle but also to his ways of shaping community?

We shall focus on 1 Thessalonians as a model for faith and life in today's church by exploring the *practices* recommended in this earliest letter of Paul (about 50 C.E.). What does Paul *do,* and what does he invite the recently converted Thessalonians *to do?* Further, we shall consider how these *practices* reflect the gospel and offer evocative models for ministry today.[1]

Paul's Concern for Community

The itinerant Paul dispatches this letter to the believers in Thessalonica at a critical moment in their struggle to survive as a new community. This small group of believers, probably evangelized and gathered in an urban apartment complex where they worked and resided, has evidently been in existence only a few months and misses Paul, its founder, who hurriedly left the city under difficult circumstances (see 2:17).[2]

Now, in the absence of the apostles, these new gentile believers in the important city of Thessalonica are probably pressured by family members and former associates not to withdraw from familiar patterns and relationships.[3] Paul undoubtedly has urged such a withdrawal upon them since conversion to Christ demanded a new way of living. They were no longer to participate in activities and festivities associated with temples of "idols" (see 1:9). Paul's reference in 1:6 to the Thessalonians' receiving the gospel "in much affliction with joy inspired by the Holy Spirit" likely alludes to the social pressure they are experiencing since their distress is linked to the period immediately after their conversion (perhaps, once Paul has left) and is later described as suffering at the hands of their fellow citizens (2:14). Their conversion resulted in social isolation and stress.[4]

Staying in Athens and worried about his communal experiment in Thessalonica, Paul sends off his coworker Timothy "to strengthen and encourage" the inexperienced Christians "for the sake of [their] faith, so that no one would be shaken by these persecutions" (see 3:1-3).[5] After Timothy returns with "the good news of [their] faith and love" (3:6), Paul dictates this letter to address the community that continues to face a time of distress and whose changed circumstances present critical questions (for example, the fate of believers who died before the coming of the exalted Lord, noted in 4:13-18). Paul obviously is concerned about the character and viability of this new community composed of believers recently converted from pagan life. By means of the letter, a substitute for his personal presence, Paul seeks to strengthen and reassure the Thessalonians in their time of uncertainty.

In 1 Thessalonians, five *practices* are worthy of attention: practicing "the language of belonging," reviving communal memory, offering living models for imitation, responding to communal imperatives, and practicing eucharistic prayer. In each instance, we shall look at the textual base for the practice, demonstrate how the practice expresses the gospel, and reflect on its significance for today's church.

Practicing a Language of Belonging

Paul employs carefully selected terms to shape new communal identity and link the recent converts to the scriptural promises to Israel; he uses "the language of belonging."[6] Already in 1:4, Paul clusters three significant indicators of the Thessalonians' conferred identity—they are "brothers and sisters" (Greek *adelphoi*), "beloved by God," and "chosen." This third term (literally "your election") resonates with the scriptural language of election and invites them to view themselves as members of God's chosen people—Israel.

The apostle addresses the Thessalonians as "brothers and sisters" sixteen times, more frequently than he does in his much longer letter to the Romans. This repeated use of "brothers and sisters" reinforces a *new* familial identity for them, one that links them to the larger circle of Christians and not simply to their blood relatives.[7] Later in the letter, Paul states openly, "Now concerning love of the brothers and sisters [*philadelphia*], you do not need to have anyone write to you, for you yourselves have been taught by God to love one another; and indeed you do love all the brothers and sisters throughout Macedonia. But we urge you, brothers and sisters, to do so more and more" (4:9-10). Paul's comment highlights their concrete expressions of love within their community and for other Christians throughout the region; it not only clarifies that their love is not self-taught but also seeks to motivate them to continue such acts.[8] Paul knows that these recent converts are in the critical process of redefining their primary identity in terms of a new set of relationships.

In the first half of the letter, Paul employs three other "familial" terms that convey deep affection for the Thessalonians. First, Paul depicts himself and his coworkers as "gentle . . . like a nurse tenderly caring for her own children" (2:7). This maternal image emphasizes Paul's gentleness, his caring and nurturing relationship with the congregation.[9] Next, Paul switches to a paternal image to underscore the individual attention he gave as he counseled and exhorted them:[10] "As you know, we dealt with each of you like a *father with his children*, urging and encouraging you and pleading that you lead a life worthy of God, who calls you into his own kingdom and glory" (2:11-12; emphasis added). Finally, in 2:17, the apostle uses a Greek verb that depicts being orphaned, the emotionally painful process of children being separated from their parents. Although the Thessalonians clearly feel "orphaned" by the apostles' sudden departure, Paul surprisingly takes up the term to convey his own sense of loss.

Hence, Paul juxtaposes the metaphors of nurse, father, and orphan to communicate his intense, emotional bond with this new community. Mutuality of identity and affection binds them together in Christ. He longs to see them again, a desire he suggests is mutual (see 2:17—3:10).

The "language of belonging" signals and reinforces the identity they share in Christ. Paul concludes (5:25-28) with a threefold use of "brothers and sisters" (*adelphoi*), directing the converts to practice their new identity as siblings in God's family in three tangible ways—"Brothers and sisters, pray also for us"; "Greet all the brothers and sisters with a holy kiss"; and "I solemnly command you by the Lord that this letter be read to all the brothers and sisters."

Praying for Paul and his coworkers strengthens the Thessalonians' relationship with the apostles and through them with other communities of faith. In Greek, Paul's use of the present tense of the imperative verb suggests a repeated practice—*continue* to pray for us, thereby binding them into a practice of mutual prayer.[11] With the "holy kiss" greeting, Paul is

> *"The language of belonging reminds Christians of their changed identity and the new set of relationships bestowed by their baptism into Christ."*

likely introducing a new practice, one designed to express divine love that binds all together in Christ. He intends this public ritual to enact visually and strengthen their community as Christian brothers and sisters.[12] The public reading of Paul's letter *to all the brothers and sisters* would also do much to shape their communal bond. In the presence of one another, they would hear the apostle's affectionate words for them and strong encouragement to treat one another as beloved siblings in *God's extended family*.

Language has power to shape identity and behavior. The intentional use of the language of belonging by ordained and lay leaders reminds Christians of their changed identity and the new set of relationships bestowed by their baptism into Christ, identity and relationships that are beyond their family of origin. Such language is a language of grace and can exercise surprising sway in today's world, in which people are measured by achievements and possessions and are sometimes rejected by their biological family for not measuring up. Every sense of identity built only on achievement, biology, or ownership is extremely fragile and always in peril. In contrast, our membership in the family of Christ, graciously bestowed, will not be taken away. Yet this gift of identity, with the new set of relationships it brings, is not readily accepted or trusted. A purposeful use of a language of belonging in the congregation is crucial as is the practice of public rituals that express and reinforce this gift of *God's* community.[13]

Reviving Communal Memory

Paul knows the importance of remembering. His frequent reminders seek to create a communal memory of how the gospel has transformed the Thessalonians' vision and situated them in a new way of life. Nine times Paul employs either the phrase "just as you all know" or the phrase "for you all know."[14] He wants them to *remember!* In particular, he wants them to remember moments of God's grace and power among them and how the apostles gained courage from God to speak the gospel to them despite a great deal of opposition (see especially 1:4-5 and 2:1-2). Remembering God's powerful and sustaining work and the apostles' sacrifice will empower the Thessalonians as they experience insecurity and social pressure.[15]

As is already implied in 1:5 (*"just as you know* what kind of persons we proved to be among you for your sake"; emphasis added), Paul later reminds them explicitly of the apostles' work among them: "You remember our labor and toil, brothers and sisters; we worked night and day, so that we might not burden any of you while we proclaimed to you the gospel of God" (2:9). His willingness to work long hours as a leather worker—while with them—not only expressed solidarity with them as artisan workers but also demonstrated in practice his love for them, his not wanting to become a burden by claiming long-term hospitality.[16] Thus, remembering how Paul and his coworkers "labored" among them becomes another reminder of the mutuality of the gospel.

In 3:1-4, Paul returns to the subject of the converts' current struggles by recalling other past activities. He indicates his reason for sending Timothy and then reminds them of his repeated mention, while with them, of the likelihood of suffering: "And we sent Timothy . . . to strengthen and encourage you for the sake of your faith, so that no one would be shaken by these persecutions. Indeed, *you yourselves know* that this is what we are destined for. In fact, when we were with you, *we were repeatedly telling you beforehand* that we were to suffer persecution; so it turned out, *as you know*" (3:2-4; emphasis added).[17] The apostle recognizes that the

Thessalonians' current harsh reality provides a context for appropriating his earlier instruction, but that without his reminder they might neither remember nor discover courage in God to sustain their faith and the life of the community in tough times.

In 4:2 and 5:2, Paul recalls other previous instructions pertaining to their ethical conduct and the timing of the "coming of the Lord." Hence, in multiple ways the letter acts as a reminder of Paul's stay with them when the gospel was dramatically reshaping their lives.

Remembering past moments of God's grace and the Spirit's transforming power is important for any congregation, especially as a cue of God's sustaining activity in tough times. Public worship is the primary arena for a gathered community to remember, largely because the liturgy *re-presents* God's redemptive action both in word and ritual. Liturgical action has the power to *re-member* those persons gathered into a community and to *reconnect* their community with other communities of faith. The Pauline phrase "as you all know" suggests a pastoral and rhetorical strategy for emphasizing what congregational members should know, and do know, yet fail to grasp fully for their existence together: the astonishing power of the Spirit to create and maintain community by means of Word and Sacrament. Paul's persistent use of reminders can become a helpful model for ministry today, both in good times and in bad.

Serving as Living Models

Paul, like others in the ancient world, is keenly aware of the potency of the living voice and the human need to imitate.[18] In 1 Thessalonians, Paul makes use of "imitation" language in the following two passages:

> For we know, brothers and sisters beloved by God, that [God] has chosen you, because our message of the gospel came to you not in word only, but also in power and in the Holy Spirit and with full conviction; just as you know what kind of persons we proved to be among you for your sake. And you became imitators [Greek *mimētai*] of us and of the Lord, for in spite of persecution you received the word with joy inspired by the Holy Spirit, so that you became an example [Greek *typos*] to all the believers in Macedonia and in Achaia. For the word of the Lord has sounded forth from you not only in Macedonia and Achaia, but in every place your faith in God has become known, so that we have no need to speak about it. (1:4-8)

> We also constantly give thanks to God for this, that when you received the word of God that you heard from us, you accepted it not as a human word but as what it really is, God's word, which is also at work in you believers. For

you, brothers and sisters, became imitators [Greek *mimētai*] of the churches
of God in Christ Jesus that are in Judea, for you suffered the same things from
your own compatriots as they did from the Jews. (2:13-14)[19]

In these two texts, Paul associates three key notions: imitation, suffering, and reception of the gospel.[20] Both passages appear within the apostle's *thanksgiving*, which extends for much of the letter (1:2—3:13).
Unlike later letters in which Paul uses the imperative to exhort hearers to
"imitate" him (see 1 Cor. 4:16, 1 Cor. 11:1, and Phil. 3:17), in 1 Thessalonians he uses the indicative to describe the fact of their imitation. In both
1:5-6 and 2:13-14, he depicts the Thessalonians as imitators in suffering
("with joy") as evidence that the powerful word of God was at work
among them. Robert Tannehill perceptively notes that "being *mimētai*
[imitators] is less a matter of conscious imitation than the result of the
power of the gospel working itself out in the lives of the believers so that
a certain pattern results."[21]

The new converts in Thessalonica have become imitators of the apostles, of the churches in Judea, and ultimately of the Lord himself by their
joyful experience of suffering (1:6), and they consequently become an example (*typos*) for believers in other places (1:7).

How are we to understand this "imitation language" of Paul? Even in
later letters in which the apostle uses the imperative (for example, "Be imitators of me, as I am of Christ" in 1 Cor. 11:1), he is not offering himself
as a moral example whose detailed behavior is to be copied. Rather, faithful response to the gospel under pressure or willing sacrifice for others is
to be imitated. For Paul, the cross of Christ epitomizes such self-sacrifice
and suffering mixed with deep joy.

Today most Christians, even pastoral leaders, hesitate to invite others
to imitate them, yet this is what Paul risks doing. Paul knew that others
learned to live most effectively by imitation. In contemporary society, in
which many people have little or no experience with the Bible and church,
"living examples" become paramount for those attracted to a faith community. Congregations invite older persons to serve as mentors to youth
during catechism. Often, however, we do not intentionally provide mentors for adults new to the community of believers. Our identity can be
dramatically affected by those with whom we identify and come to trust.
Living examples offer flexible expressions of daily Christian living, modeling for new believers how to live in various circumstances. To avoid re-
ducing "imitation" to simplistic moral terms, mentors need to focus
clearly on the crucified Christ, who sacrificed all for the sake of others,
thus encouraging faithfulness even in the most difficult times.

Responding to Communal Imperatives

Near the end of his letter, Paul clusters several exhortations. Important to the Thessalonians' life together are respecting leaders (5:12-13), exercising patience with troublemakers and the weak (5:14-15), and practicing life in the Spirit (5:16-22).

Respecting Leaders

In 5:12-13, Paul urges, "But we appeal to you, brothers and sisters, to respect those who labor among you, and have charge of you in the Lord and admonish you; esteem them very highly in love because of their work. Be at peace among yourselves."

The leaders, to whom they are to pay proper respect, are described as those who "labor" among them, with two phrases specifying the character of that labor.[22] The NRSV renders the first key word "having charge of you" ("in the Lord"), or it could be translated "caring for/giving help."[23] In either case, it implies a leadership role. The second Greek word can mean "to impart understanding" or "to instruct" but normally carries the notion of "correcting someone's mind" or "admonishing."[24] The responsibility of leaders to correct and admonish would not make them all that popular, yet Paul urges the community to "esteem them very highly in love because of their work." The apostle's next exhortation—"be at peace among yourselves"—may apply to the relationship between leaders and the rest of the community or may serve as a general appeal introducing what follows.

Here Paul is writing prior to the emergence of clearly defined ministerial offices; consequently, his appeal to respect "leaders" applies best today to lay leaders who undertake labors of love for others in the congregation. The phrase "in the Lord" probably designates persons properly selected and recognized as leaders. Then or now, we are not talking about self-designated leaders. Paul views esteem for such leaders as an important ingredient in the community's discipline and health. His plea to "esteem them very highly in love because of their work" is a needed reminder to contemporary congregations when we neglect to show respect and love for those who diligently labor for the good of the community.

Being Patient with Troublemakers and the Weak

In 5:14, Paul's address of "brothers and sisters" suggests that the next four imperatives are directed to all community members, not only the leaders. He writes, "And we urge you, brothers and sisters: admonish the idlers, encourage the faint hearted, help the weak, be patient with all of them."

First, community members are to admonish "the troublemakers." The Greek word *ataktoi* can be translated "lazy" or "idle" but in this case is best rendered as "disorderly," that is, those who disrupt community life in various ways.[25] Second, all carry responsibility for encouraging and cheering up "the faint hearted" or quite literally "ones with little soul" (*oligopsychoi*), suggesting ones easily discouraged. Third, community members are to assist "the weak," the Greek word *asthenoi* pointing to those physically frail and sickly or possessing a fragile faith or a weak conscience.

The final imperative serves as a summary: community participants are "to show patience towards all." Perhaps, as further interpretation, 5:15 specifies avoiding repaying "evil for evil" and seeking to do "the good to one another and to all."

Contemporary congregations are reminded that all members have a special responsibility and ministry in regard to the troublemakers, the fainthearted, and the weak in their midst. Ministry for the "least of the brothers and sisters" appears rooted in Jesus' own ministry as an expression of God's immeasurable graciousness and persistence. Not surprisingly, this ministry requires enormous patience on the part of community members. In light of these Pauline exhortations, although we cannot allow destructive behaviors to continue, we should have second thoughts about our tendency to write off or dismiss from membership some persons we categorize as troublemakers or even "alligators."

Practicing Life in the Spirit

The eight brief exhortations in 5:16-22 are addressed to the entire community and relate to their common life in the Spirit. The first cluster of three imperatives represents fundamental features of Christian living, all prompted by God's all-encompassing graciousness and not dependent on external circumstances: "Rejoice always, pray without ceasing, give thanks in all circumstances" (5:16-18a). Verse 18b offers the explicit reason for these exhortations: "for this is the will of God in Christ Jesus for you."

The succeeding exhortations in 5:19-22 focus on the work of the Spirit in the midst of the community. The first two prohibitions ("Do not quench the Spirit. Do not despise the words of the prophets.") assume the community to be a place for the activity of the Spirit. Literally, the second prohibition states, "Do not despise prophecies," almost certainly implying intelligible preaching or teaching inspired by the Spirit (see 1 Cor. 14:3). In turn, this explains the first prohibition, "Do not quench the Spirit." The community is to be open to continuing guidance from the Spirit. Yet the next three imperatives ("but test everything; hold fast to what is good; abstain from every form of evil") imply that false prophecy is also a constant problem for a community. The community must be open to the activity of the Holy Spirit, but its members must practice discernment to determine what utterances are really from the Spirit and thus enhance and build up the community.

Paul's directives regarding the practice of Christians living in the Spirit hold significance for today's church. The exhortation to continual rejoicing and prayer as an expression of a comprehensive thankfulness invites members of a Christian congregation to reflect on their fundamental attitude toward life together. Our life is a common one prompted and led by the Spirit of God. For all our easy talk about the working of the Spirit, we are often less than open to guidance by the Spirit in concrete situations. What might it mean to take seriously Paul's directives not to stifle words of prophecy spoken by leaders among us while at the same time scrutinize all such words to ensure that they are from God? According to 1 Cor. 14:3, authentic words of prophecy function for the community's "upbuilding and encouragement and consolation." Most congregations need more practice in this process of discernment.

Practicing Eucharistic Prayer

The final recommended practice with paradigmatic potential is really the first thing Paul does in 1 Thessalonians. He begins by engaging in a prayer of thanksgiving or "eucharistic praying."[26] Paul has urged the community to do what he himself does: "Rejoice always, pray without ceasing, give thanks in all circumstances; for this is the will of God in Christ Jesus for you" (5:16-18). Clearly, these three imperatives belong together, and the succeeding "for" clause underscores their significance. A mood of joy, expressed in eucharistic praying, reflects God's will for the community— God's will that was concretely embodied in Christ Jesus.[27]

That Paul himself engages in this "praying without ceasing" and "giving thanks in all circumstances" must be evident to the Thessalonians in light of his opening prayer of thanksgiving. Directly following the salutation (1:1), the apostle launches into a thanksgiving that extends until 3:13, more than half the letter. On behalf of Silvanus and Timothy, he begins, "We always give thanks to God for all of you and mention you in our prayers, constantly remembering before our God and Father your work of faith and labor of love and steadfastness of hope in our Lord Jesus Christ" (1:2-3).

Paul's thanks are directed to God, not to human beings. Our tendency is to thank people directly as though they deserve the credit, but the apostle thanks God for the glimpses of God's work in and through those in community. Yet Paul's words of thanksgiving do sustain members of the faith community, as they too take note of God's work among and in themselves. The apostle's practice also involves offering thanks for *all* in the community, not singling out individuals for specific attention. Paul's egalitarian practice of praying has its focus on God's graciousness, undercutting all competitive tendencies in the community.

The phrase "and mention you in our prayers" implies that Paul and his coworkers pray together on a regular basis, presumably for the new converts in Thessalonica and other Christian communities. In a later letter to the believers in Corinth, Paul adds to his list of hardships: "And, besides other things, I am under daily pressure because of my worry for all the churches" (2 Cor. 11:28). Separated by considerable distance from churches he cared for, the apostle Paul likely committed his anxiety and concern for the churches to God in daily prayer. Yet, when Paul gives expression in his letters to these prayers, he highlights his mood of thanksgiving. This is based on his remembering their "work of faith and labor of love and endurance of hope," all expressions of their being loved by God and now beloved and chosen participants in God's new community (see 1:3-4).

Paul's eucharistic praying demonstrates a principal approach to his ministry with each Christian community. He begins and ends his concerns and particular counsels for a community with the fundamental act of thanksgiving. Moreover, he opens and concludes his letter with the pronouncement of grace on the congregation (1:1 and 5:28), reminding hearers that all is bracketed by the gracious action expressed in the Christ event.[28] Finally, Paul's appeal in 5:25 ("Brothers and sisters, pray also for us") invites these new converts into a partnership of prayer characterized by its tone of thanksgiving.

If today we practiced eucharistic praying tirelessly, surely attitudes and relationships among church members and pastoral leaders would be affected. So also attitudes among pastors, bishops, and other leaders in the wider expressions of the church might become more caring and honest. Regular and rigorous praying focuses us on the amazing grace of God, seen in the work of the Spirit, and invites us into caring for the whole church and taking more risks for the sake of the gospel.[29]

By focusing on 1 Thessalonians as a test case, we have concentrated on practices that embody the gospel and are central to Christians living in community. How can these Pauline practices enhance our functioning as Christian congregations in today's world? How might they authorize new life among us?

Believing in God through Others;
Believing in God for Others

DUANE A. PRIEBE

Where do people meet Christ today? How should Christians re-
gard people who do not believe in Christ? How can one deal
with difference in a pluralistic world? God's word creates a
community of believers. Through the church God creates a cir-
cle of communication of hearing, believing, and speaking and
an ever-expanding communion between people and God and
among the rich diversity of people and cultures in the global
community.

How is faith possible? For Christians, faith is fundamental trust and
confidence in God, which is grounded in Jesus Christ, orients and
shapes our lives, and gives life a sense of fullness. Sometimes faith seems
natural and easy. At other times, faith seems impossible: doubt, fear,
guilt, emptiness, suffering, or a sense that we do not count seems to overwhelm us. How can we trust God when so much deep within ourselves
and in life appears to count against God's care? How is faith possible in
the face of all the experienced reality that looks as if it counts against
faith? Often, the faith we do have feels as if it is shaky and fragile at best.
Even in the Bible, Ecclesiastes says, "The righteous and the wise and their
deeds are in the hand of God; whether it is love or hate one does not
know" (Eccles. 9:1).

Paul says, "Faith comes through what is heard, and what is heard comes
through the word of Christ" (Rom. 10:17). Faith, then, is possible only
through other people who dare to speak to us for God and promise God
to us in the name of Jesus Christ. On the other hand, if people are justified
by grace alone through faith alone, Jesus Christ claims us absolutely in
every person we meet to believe in God's redeeming love for him or her. It

makes no difference whether that person believes that yet or not. The gospel claims us to speak and act toward others and to speak about them as people for whom Jesus died. That one reality matters more than anything else.

Where Two or Three Are Gathered

Where two or three are gathered in my name,
I am there among them. (Matt. 18:20)

According to Matthew, Jesus promised to be present with his followers where two or three are gathered in his name in the practical exercise of forgiveness (Matt. 18:20) and in their mission to go into the whole world (Matt. 28:19-20). Jesus also speaks of his presence in those who suffer: the poor, the hungry, the thirsty, the naked, and the imprisoned. Jesus' presence in those who suffer places a claim on people's attitudes and actions toward them, for what people do to those in need they do to Jesus (Matt. 25:31-46). In Luke, Jesus appeared to the disciples as they were discussing the events surrounding his crucifixion and rumors of his resurrection, and he was known in the breaking of bread. Jesus, in turn, interpreted the Scriptures in terms of his death and resurrection and the message of the forgiveness of sins for all the nations in his name (Luke 24:13-49).

Faith is possible only in the context of a community of believers, because it comes through the message of God's forgiving love in Jesus' death and resurrection. If faith comes through hearing the message of Christ, faith depends on people who communicate that message, whether through speech, writing, actions, art forms, or other forms of communication. But the act of bearing witness to Jesus Christ itself arises from faith. God is present in Christ in a circle of hearing and speaking, in a history of faith in which the word God spoke in Jesus Christ is passed back and forth between people and is passed on from one person to another and from one generation to another.

This circle of hearing, believing, and speaking constitutes the church as a community of believers. The church is "the assembly of all believers among whom the Gospel is preached in its purity and the holy sacraments are administered according to the Gospel."[1] A Christian congregation is a specific, concrete community of people who are called into faith and are sustained and renewed in faith through hearing the gospel. They answer God's saving love with thanks and praise, and they are called to speak in word and deed the message of God's redeeming love in Jesus Christ to one another and to everyone else in the places where they live.

This circle of hearing, believing, and speaking reaches out beyond the congregation and finds other expressions in the life of the Christian community. It creates, or at least should create, an ever-increasing circle of communion among people and cultures and between people and God in a global community of believers who embrace the rich diversity of human life and culture.[2] This communion is mediated through Jesus Christ and moves toward his future through new proclamation in new times and places: "We declare to you what we have seen and heard so that you also may have fellowship with us; and truly our fellowship is with the Father and with his Son Jesus Christ" (1 John 1:3).

Faith depends on hearing because faith depends on Jesus of Nazareth as the one in whom God acts for the salvation of the world. Jesus Christ's presence in all the rich variations of the church's life and message through history is rooted in what took place once for all in his earthly life and the once-for-all apostolic witness to him. This "once-for-all" also serves as the critical norm of the church's life and message. This gives Christian faith an essential relation to a history in which God encounters human beings in judgment and mercy, to a particular person in whom God has decisively acted, and to traditions in which this message is transmitted and interpreted as a message that includes us and our world. Even when a person is alone, the witness of the community of believers surrounds him or her in Scripture and tradition, and in that witness, Jesus himself meets that person. Jesus Christ is not merely a figure of the past; as the risen Lord, he himself is present in judgment and redeeming love in the message of his death and resurrection for us.

Jesus Christ also is present in a way that claims a person's life through other people in their need of words or actions. In the parable of the last judgment (Matt. 25:31-46), Jesus is present in those who are hungry, thirsty, strangers, those who are naked or in prison, and in the little ones who belong to him. What people do to these people they do to Jesus himself.[3] In a similar way, God's forgiveness in Jesus Christ calls us to forgive through those who stand in need of a word of forgiveness (Matt. 18:21-34). Our love for one another, even enemies, is grounded in God's love for all of us. "We love because [God] first loved us" (1 John 4:19; see also Matt. 5:43-48). Those who live in Jesus Christ are called to live in the field of power of God's love for the world in Christ, to hear the claim of Christ on our words and actions in those who need love, comfort, liberation, healing, or forgiveness, and to carry it out in word and deed in Jesus' name.

Believing in God through Others

So faith comes from what is heard,
and what is heard comes through the word of Christ.
(Rom. 10:17)

Faith neither creates nor sustains itself. Even in the ordinary fabric of daily life, faith or trust in other people depends on their reliability and on the words in which they promise help, friendship, love, or faithfulness. Trust must be evoked by the other person if it is not to be illusory. For all his dreams, Charlie Brown can believe that the little redheaded girl loves him only if she tells him so. Words spoken or acted out are essential to relationships of trust. Through words, even in formalized greetings and idle conversation, people present themselves to one another in the way they want to be there for one another. Whether they cut one another off, promise themselves to one another, or simply occupy time together, words, even silent words, create the fabric and texture of relationships between people and with their world. Through the power of words, including symbolic forms such as art or music, people can be present to others and share themselves with them across time and space.

Faith in God depends on God's promise in Jesus Christ being spoken to people in such a way that it touches their deepest longings. Through this promise, God is present to us in Christ in the way God wants to be God for us. Because Jesus Christ is present in the message of his life, death, and resurrection for us, we can stand before God and entrust ourselves to God in every circumstance, as sinners, in suffering and temptation, even when we despair of God's help. God's word calls forth our faith and makes our words possible in prayer and thanksgiving.

God obviously does not speak to us in the direct way other people do. God has spoken in a person, Jesus Christ, and God speaks through people who address the message of Christ to us through words spoken, acted, and written. We believe in God through others who dare to speak to us for God. Faith, which is always the individual's response to the gospel, is possible only within the social matrix of a community of believers who preserve and transmit the apostolic witness to Jesus Christ.

In the fabric of our relationship with God, woven through words in which God speaks to us through other people and in which we answer God, there are important distinctions. We have to say some things for ourselves because no one can say them for us. We are the ones who have to confess our sins and give thanks and praise for what we have received, and we are the ones who have to answer God's promise with the faith that entrusts our lives to God in the brightest and darkest moments. We are the ones who have to call on God in need and relate our gifts and lives to God in prayer.

There are other things we cannot say to ourselves. They must be said to us. We depend on others for words of love and for assurance of friendship or faithfulness if these are to be real for us, rather than an illusory dream. We can confess our sins and apologize, but we have to be told we are forgiven. We may cry out to God or long for God's blessing and presence, but other people have to speak to us for God if we are to hear words of forgiveness, promise, and blessing that address the message of God's love in Christ unconditionally to the reality of our lives. When such words are absent, God is absent, even though God is present to us in hidden and unknown ways. This is why it is essential to life in faith that people live within a community of believers who dare to speak to one another for God.

In the dialogue between God and people, God's word makes our words possible; our words do not make God's word possible. We call on God as Father because God has spoken to us in Jesus Christ and because our prayers have been taken up into Jesus' prayer to the one he called Father. The message of God's forgiveness makes it possible for us to recognize the depth of our sin and need of God's mercy in confession. We must speak to God for ourselves in prayer, but the courage to call on God in our deepest need, even when God seems to have withdrawn or to be absent, depends on the word God has spoken in Jesus' death on the cross. The social framework of the community of believers, in congregations or other forms of Christian community, in which people speak to one another for God, is the context within which a person's life can become a conversation with God.

A Universal Witness to a Universal Message

God our Savior . . . desires everyone to be saved
and to come to the knowledge of the truth. (1 Tim. 2:4)

The possibility of speaking for God also is grounded in hearing and faith: "We declare to you what we have seen and heard" (1 John 1:3). The message of Jesus' death for *sinners* makes it possible for Christians to proclaim the forgiveness of sins in Jesus' name to those who are sinners. His care for the lost, the poor, and the suffering makes it possible—indeed necessary—to live out that message toward others in his name. The gospel authorizes Christians to speak for God to others, because the good news of Jesus Christ speaks of God's extravagant, unconditional mercy and saving work for *all* people.

The unconditional character of the gospel is expressed in a variety of biblical formulations: people are justified by God's "grace as a gift" (Rom. 3:24); God is the one who "justifies the ungodly" (Rom. 4:5); "while we were enemies, we were reconciled to God by the death of [God's] Son" (Rom. 5:10; see also vv. 6-10); righteousness is a "free gift" (Rom. 5:15-17). Furthermore, this message has universal, even cosmic scope: "Therefore just as one man's trespass led to condemnation for all, so one man's act of righteousness leads to justification and life for all" (Rom. 5:18). "For in him all the fullness of God was pleased to dwell, and through him God was pleased to reconcile to himself all things, whether on earth or in heaven, by making peace through the blood of his cross" (Col. 1:19-20). "For the creation waits with eager longing for the revealing of the children of God; the creation itself will be set free from its bondage to decay and will obtain the freedom of the glory of the children of God" (Rom. 8:19-21).

In Paul's Letter to the Romans, equally universal statements about God's judgment (see Rom. 3:19-20, 23; 11:32) highlight the issue of sin and the need for redemption. They also underscore the universal, cosmic scope of God's gracious love for lost sinners in Jesus Christ, the universal effect of Jesus' death and resurrection, and the universal intent of God's saving will. God desires "everyone to be saved and to come to a knowledge of the truth" (1 Tim. 2:4).

Within the horizon of God's redeeming love for all in Jesus Christ, Paul speaks of the person in Christ as a new creation (2 Cor. 5:14-21). This can mean both that the person in Christ is already a new creation and that those in Christ see the world around them in a totally new way. Both are true. When they know God's love in Jesus Christ, Christians become a new creation: controlled by Christ's love, they live for Christ, not for themselves. They also see all people, those who do well but also those who are lost, despised, and count for little from a new perspective, in terms of Jesus' death for all. They can no longer think of others from a "human point of view" (Greek: "according to the flesh," v. 16), in terms of their achievements or failures or the many ways people value or discount one another (see also 1 Cor. 1:26-31). The fundamental difference between the Christian and an "unbeliever" is that the Christian sees everyone, even the unbeliever, in the light of Jesus' death for all, and the Christian is called to speak and act accordingly.[4] The question of whether or not the other person believes in Jesus Christ does not alter the Christian's perception of that person or the validity of the gospel for that person. Faith is not the basis of God's grace, but faith arises from the message of God's mercy in Christ (see Rom. 10:17). The universal scope of the message, "in Christ God was reconciling the world to himself," provides both the basis and the necessity of the Christian community's ministry of reconciliation to the whole world (vv. 18-20).

Believing in God for Others

For the love of Christ controls us,
because we are convinced that one has died for all;
therefore all have died. (2 Cor. 5:14 RSV)

The good news of God's love in Jesus Christ authorizes and empowers Christians to hope on behalf of those who are without hope, to believe in God on behalf of those without faith, and to love on behalf of those who live without love. This is a matter not of ideas but of words and actions that arise from the experience of God's mercy and correspond to God's love in Christ. Christians are to forgive others because God has forgiven those others through Christ. Christians are to seek the lost because Jesus Christ has sought the lost; they are to have mercy on enemies and to be reconciled with them because God has shown mercy to their enemies and has overcome the dividing walls of hostility in Christ; they are to help the poor and feed the hungry because God has blessed the poor and hungry and identified with them in Christ. Christians are to live in the light of Jesus' death and resurrection for all, and they are to communicate that message in words and in their lives. That is the indispensable role to which God calls the church and individual Christians, and through that task people and congregations participate in the mission of their Lord.

The good news that God's salvation in Christ is offered freely and without condition to all people places a universal and unconditional claim on the words and actions of those who believe in Christ.[5] Through Jesus Christ, God has drawn near in love to those who are lost, to the sinners, despised, and suffering as well as to the pious and upright. God calls those who believe in Jesus Christ to speak and act in a corresponding way. If another person is lost or is a sinner, or if that person counts for little in the eyes of society, those who believe in Jesus Christ know that that person is one whom Christ came to seek, for whom Christ died, and to whom the gospel is to be spoken, both in words and in deeds. The more radically the gospel is characterized by such formulas as "grace alone," "justification of the ungodly," "giving life to the dead," and "creation out of nothing," the more radically God's claim on our words and actions is present in *all* other people. There are no mitigating circumstances that allow us to evade the claim of God's love in the other persons we encounter in the fabric of daily life.

This issue is reflected in Jesus' parable of the Pharisee and the tax collector praying in the temple (Luke 18:9-14).[6] Jesus portrays the Pharisee positively as a model of Jewish piety. The Pharisee does more than the law requires; he also gives God all the glory in thanksgiving, taking no credit for himself. Pious Jews knew they lived entirely from God's mercy and that they could find forgiveness in God when necessary.[7] The Pharisee in the parable saw his life as evidence of God's grace. The problem was that, like many Christians, he thought the difference between his life and the tax collector's meant he could think of himself in terms of God's mercy and the tax collector in terms of his sins. That is the double standard the New Testament condemns as hypocrisy.

When they pass judgment on others, Christians reject the basis on which they affirm their own standing before God. Such judgment is excluded throughout the New Testament, and judgment always falls back on those who pass judgment on others (Matt. 7:1-5; Rom. 2:1ff.). When I think of God's judgment on sinners, I always have to think first of myself. A person can believe in God's love in Jesus Christ for oneself only by including others, who are godless and sinners, in the effective field of that saving love by believing in God on their behalf and by communicating that love through word and action. It is through believing in God's love for others that we discover the power of God's love in our own lives.

In the New Testament, Christian faith entails an understanding of the world, and within that horizon it is also an understanding of oneself. Christian hope is a vision of a new future for the whole world in God's promise. In an individualistic culture, the Reformation's important insight that it is necessary for a person to believe Christ's work is "for me" risks becoming isolated from the affirmation that Jesus Christ is the savior of the whole world. As a result, an emphasis on grace seems to make love toward others optional, while an emphasis on love seems to make grace conditional. Apart from motivation, there seems to be little internal relationship between God's love toward us and our love toward others.

Yet the message of salvation in Jesus Christ is a message about all humanity and all creation. God's mercy and forgiveness in Jesus' death is effective for the sinner and the lost before they believe it. Their faith does not create God's mercy; faith is created by God's mercy in Christ through the message of the cross.

> "The gospel calls us to believe in God for others, whether or not they believe in God for themselves."

Those who receive the gospel in faith know that the message of Jesus' death and resurrection is true for others as well as for themselves. The gospel calls us to believe in God for others, whether or not they believe in God for themselves. Hearing the message of Jesus Christ in faith creates a new understanding of other people and the world, and it thereby shapes a person's relationships, words, and actions.

When people see their world in the light of Jesus' death and resurrection, they are called to live and speak in a way that communicates that message to other people. In Christ, God builds people up, even the lost and sinners; God does not tear them down. God's love frees people to live in the power of that love. In his 1519 commentary on Galatians, Martin Luther elaborates this in terms of how we talk. He says that spiritual people do what the Holy Spirit does. Like the Spirit, they protect and comfort people before God. They excuse, extenuate, and completely cover over the sins of others and magnify their faith and good works. Satan is imitated by those who "exaggerate, enlarge, and expand the sins" of others and "minimize, find fault with, and disapprove of their good works."[8] God's claim on us in others includes not only our words but everything about us.

> If there is anything in us, it is not our own; it is a gift of God. But if it is a gift of God, then it is entirely a debt one owes to love, that is, to the law of Christ. And if it is a debt owed to love, then I must serve others with it, not myself. Thus my learning is not my own; it belongs to the unlearned and is the debt I owe to them. My chastity is not my own; it belongs to those who commit sins of the flesh, and I am obligated to serve them through it by offering it to God for them, by sustaining and excusing them, and thus, with my respectability, veiling their shame before God and [people]. . . . Thus my wisdom belongs to the foolish, my power to the oppressed. Thus my wealth belongs to the poor, my righteousness to sinners. For these are the forms of God of which we must empty ourselves, in order that forms of a servant may be in us (Phil. 2:6), because it is with these qualities that we must stand before God and intervene on behalf of those who do not have them, as though clothed with someone else's garment, . . . even before [people] we must, with the same love, render them service against their detractors and those who are violent toward them; for this is what Christ did for us.[9]

The same can be said of faith, which is a gift, worked in us by the power of the Holy Spirit through the message of the gospel. My faith is not my own. It is to be used on behalf of those who have no faith, to include them in Christ's love, to cover over their unbelief, and to intervene on their behalf before God.

Christians pray that God's love will prevail in the world, that in mercy God will make their words and actions part of God's love toward others, and that in forgiveness God will redeem their misdeeds by making them vehicles of God's love toward others. When our words and actions direct people away from ourselves to God in Christ, they become the vehicle of God's presence. This parallels Jesus' relation to the Father: "The Son can do nothing on his own, but only what he sees the Father doing; for whatever the Father does, the Son does likewise" (John 5:19). Because the Son does what the Father does, the Father's work is the subject matter of the Son's activity. By directing people away from himself to the Father, the Son reveals the Father and is one with the Father.[10] So it is with Christians who do what they see the Father doing in Christ and speak what they hear the Father say in Christ, making God's saving work in Jesus Christ the subject matter of their lives.

When Christians believe in God for others, they hold a place for those people in God's love, including them in God's saving word through word and deed. By doing so, they make faith possible by communicating the message of God's redeeming love in Jesus Christ, through which God's Spirit works faith in people. When Jesus ate with tax collectors and sinners, he was the one who believed God's rule was near and meant salvation for them. Because Jesus believed God's rule brought salvation to the lost, he made its saving power present to those who were with him. Conversely, Jesus' presence became judgment for those who wanted to draw their life from some other power (John 3:16-19). God's rule was present for people through Jesus' faith in the kingdom on their behalf. In a world filled with darkness and unbelief, in which people search for the power that gives hope, meaning, and life, the church is called to be a community through which God is present to create new life. This takes place through the gospel, which calls people into faith in Jesus Christ on behalf of the world and to live and speak that message to the world.

The Office of the Keys

Receive the Holy Spirit.
if you forgive the sins of any, they are forgiven them;
if you retain the sins of any, they are retained.
(John 20:22-23)

The office of the keys is the church's authority to forgive sins and to withhold forgiveness. The phrase derives from Matthew, when, following Peter's confession, Jesus says: "I tell you, you are Peter, and on this rock I will build my church, and the gates of Hades will not prevail against it.

I will give you the keys of the kingdom of heaven, and whatever you bind on earth shall be bound in heaven, and whatever you loose on earth shall be loosed in heaven" (Matt. 16:18-19).

For all the controversies about the interpretation of this passage, some things are clear. First, it reflects Peter's position of leadership in the early church. Second, Peter's authority has its basis in his confession of Christ. Third, while the language was originally linked with the administrative or interpretive authority of the ruler of the synagogue, it was very quickly associated with the forgiveness of sins. This is explicit in Matt. 18:15-20 and John 20:22-23.

At first glance, these passages seem to authorize the Christian community to withhold forgiveness as well as to forgive. In different ways, however, both Matthew and John take back the authority to withhold forgiveness and place the emphasis on the authority to forgive. In Matt. 18:15-35, Peter, to whom the "keys" were given, asks how often he must forgive before he can withhold forgiveness. Jesus' answer, "seventy times seven," indicates that forgiveness is to be without limit. Then Jesus tells the parable of the servant who was forgiven a huge debt by his master and refused to forgive a small debt owed by his fellow servant. The experience of forgiveness requires us to live in forgiveness, and the sin we refuse to forgive is always smaller than the sin God forgives in us.

In John, the risen Jesus appeared to the disciples, breathed the Holy Spirit into them, and said, "If you forgive the sins of any, they are forgiven them; if you retain the sins of any, they are retained" (John 20:23). But John also qualifies this. Jesus told the disciples that he is sending them into the world in the same way as the Father sent him (20:21). The Father did not send the Son "to condemn the world, but in order that the world might be saved through him" (3:17). Like Jesus, the disciples are sent as messengers of God's mercy in Christ, not of wrath and judgment. Nevertheless, judgment does take place around Jesus Christ, who is the content of their message, through the way people receive the message: "This is the judgment, that the light has come into the world, and people loved darkness rather than light because their deeds were evil" (3:19).

The office of the keys is not a matter of extraordinary power. It describes a reality. Those who confess "Jesus is Lord" and bear his name in fact represent Christ and his saving work in the world, whether they intend to or not. Sinners and outcasts who are received into the forgiveness and communion of the Christian community experience God's forgiveness. Conversely, people who are excluded from the communion and care of the Christian community, whether because of sin, unworthiness, or race, experience exclusion from the healing power of Christ's love. If

Christians expect others to change and become something else before they are welcomed into communion with Christ and his people, those people experience a conditional gospel. Many conclude that the God known in Jesus Christ has nothing to do with them, because they are excluded or condemned in the community that bears Christ's name.

This is not a trivial matter. When the Christian community passes judgment on the lost and the hopeless for whom Jesus died, or when it withholds Christ's forgiveness from those who need it, the Christian community itself falls under judgment. Jesus warns that there are those who claim his name whom he will send away as people he never knew (Matt. 7:21-23). The office of the keys does not give the church or Christians power over the gospel. It places them under the power of the gospel and calls them to be the vehicle of the Lord's presence and mission in obedience to God's love. Forgiveness does not belong to Christians for their own benefit. It is God's weapon in the struggle to free God's lost creation from bondage to the destructive power of sin and death and to overcome hostility and alienation through the reconciling power of God's love in Jesus Christ.

The Community of Faith
as a Confessional Norm

Universalism and Evangelism

RALPH W. QUERE

In a desire to appreciate all the diverse faiths of the world, what becomes of evangelism? Does the Christian faith become dispensable in a pluralistic culture? Congregation members, in an effort not to offend their neighbors, find it difficult to give an explicit verbal witness to Christ. The historic confessions of the church provide an opportunity to explore the meaning of sin and bondage and of justification and faith.

Life together in community becomes a problem when we forget that the church is primarily a community of faith and secondarily a community of love. Martin Luther's seven signs of the church add loving service as an often ambiguous sign. "They will" *not* always "know we are Christians by our love" unless we name and proclaim the name of Jesus. "They" may just think we members of a congregation are "nice people." And then we can be proud of our niceness.

Evangelism is in trouble in mainline churches despite all the programs and slogans developed in recent decades. What has undercut Lutheran efforts at evangelism? Lutherans long have struggled to translate their clear theology of proclaiming the Word into a theology of mission or evangelism. The state-church and folk-church mentality complicated mission. The Christendom mentality assumed everybody baptized was still a believer. Most Lutherans have applauded "repentance" as the return of the prodigals or, more problematically, they think "repent" meant simply feeling guilty enough to be slightly miserable. Instead of understanding conversion as the Holy Spirit's work of drawing the impenitent or unbelieving to Christ, Lutherans have sometimes fallen into revivalist decision theology, in which human choice, cooperation, and action are emphasized.

Often in reaction to such synergism, other Lutherans have shied away from the theology and practice of evangelism. We remain suspicious and even fearful of explicit verbal witness to Christ to outsiders.

Without German or Scandinavian pietists and their American descendants,[1] it is a moot question whether Lutherans would ever have gotten into world mission or "home missions."[2] But what accounts for the decline in the number of missionaries in the Evangelical Lutheran Church in America and many other mainline Christian church bodies today? Has all the world been reached with the gospel?

"*We remain suspicious and even fearful of explicit verbal witness to Christ to outsiders.*"

And why the decline in mission congregation starts in America, given the rapid rise of our non-Christian population? Finances are a factor but hardly an excuse. Is it a question of priorities or theologies?

I fear that a part of the explanation for our current crisis in evangelization is the assertion or assumption (or both) of universal salvation. Among members of a local congregation, one may find a range of beliefs and opinions on the issue of salvation. Christian universalists teach that through Christ, in whom God has reconciled the world, God will save all people, even those who in unbelief reject the gospel.[3] Dante's *Inferno* makes that view all the more attractive, but it is interesting that unbelief is not one of the sins for which Dante judges anyone damned. The doctrine of justification by or through faith, as well as the doctrine of the church as a community of faith ("communion of saints" or "assembly of believers"), is central to the Lutheran confessions and definitive for an understanding of the issue of universalism.

Sixteenth-Century Issues and Confessional Answers: Universal Salvation

The kind of answer Luther had given earlier in the mid-1520s to the "fanatics" such as Andreas Karlstadt in "Against the Heavenly Prophets" is summarized in the ecclesiology of his Large Catechism.[4] There Luther defends Cyprian's unpopular dictum, *extra ecclesiam nulla salus* (outside the church there is no salvation). Luther argued that there is "no Christian Church" where Christ is not believed as Lord: "For where Christ is not preached, there is no Holy Spirit to create, call, and gather the Christian Church, and outside it no one can come to the Lord Christ."[5] In his 1528

If so, why did Luther not promote global mission?

"Confession concerning Christ's Supper," Luther had said: "In this Christian Church, wherever it exists, is to be found forgiveness of sins. . . . Moreover, Christ and his Spirit are there. Outside this Christian Church there is no salvation or forgiveness of sins, but everlasting death and damnation" (LW 37:368). Luther reiterates the point as good news in the Large Catechism: "in this Christian Church we have the forgiveness of sins, which is granted through the holy sacraments and absolution, as well as through all the comforting words of the entire Gospel" (BC 417.54).[6]

Rejecting "Pelagians and others" who deny original sin (AC II, BC 29.3)[7] and bondage of the will (AC XVIII, BC 40.8), Philip Melanchthon attacks the positions of nominalists, Zwinglians, and Anabaptists. Those Protestants who reject baptismal regeneration are corrected by sacraments as "the signs and testimonies of the will of God toward us, intended to awaken and confirm faith [in those who use them]" (AC XIII, BC 35.1). That leads Melanchthon to the strong assertion that "Baptism is necessary for salvation" (AC IX, BC 33.1). In Melanchthon's later *Loci*, he defends *extra ecclesiam nulla salus* by linking ecclesiology with God's presence in the visible church and his doctrine of God's election and call. Since baptism is a means of grace by which God inserts persons into the community of faith, the church must *necessarily* baptize infants. This becomes a polemic against Anabaptist doctrine and practice.[8] Life together in community means taking responsibility intergenerationally—not just parents and godparents but biological and surrogate grandparents—for nurturing the faith of the baptized. This has significant implications for congregational life today.[9]

Seventeenth-century Lutherans taught that this did not imply the *absolute* necessity of baptism if an accident or fatal illness prevented such baptism. Rather, it was the despising or rejecting of baptism that was condemned. The later Melanchthon seemed to be arguing that the "necessity of baptism" was something necessary for the church's ministry—a ministry it dare not withhold from children.

In his 1528 "Answer to the Anabaptists," Melanchthon makes a point similar to Luther's: "since the promise of grace relates to infants and there is no remission of sins outside the church, it follows that the sign which witnesses that remission of sins relates to them must be applied to them."[10] The doubly deadly condition of original sin and enslaved wills forces us to acknowledge the prevenient grace of baptism (and even predestination) where God alone can work to free and forgive us through faith.

The Augsburg Confession's teaching regarding Christ's return for judgment asserts eternal life for the godly and condemnation for the ungodly—a position the Roman Catholic confutators accept. Anabaptists such as Hans Denck—eventually excluded also by the Anabaptists—are condemned for teaching that hell's torments will end (AC XVII, BC 38.1–4).[11]

In some ways, the rejection of universal salvation that is most complete and most clear emerges in the doctrine of predestination of the Formula of Concord. It is set forth as a *comforting* doctrine (BC 494.1)[12] because it places our salvation in God's hands (John 10:27-30) but places the source or cause of evil, sin, and damnation in the devil's hands and the wicked and perverse human will (BC 494.4; see also 496.11). The Solid Declaration expands on this point: God has ordained "that he would harden, reject and condemn all who, when called through the Word, persistently resist the Holy Spirit who wants to work efficaciously in them through the Word. In this sense 'many are called, but few are chosen'" (BC 623.40; see also 41–42).

An interesting interpretation of Rom. 9:22f. reinforces human responsibility for condemnation and undercuts double predestination: God alone prepares "vessels of honor" and "man, who, through the instigation of the devil and not of God, has made himself a vessel of dishonor" (BC 629.79). The formulators note that Paul says, "God *endured* the 'vessels of wrath' with much patience. He does not say God *made* them vessels of wrath" (BC 629.80; emphasis added). Again, the confessors make clear that it is the work of Satan and humans themselves that prepares and causes their condemnation "and in no way God. Since God does not want any[one] to be damned, how could [God] prepare [one] for damnation? God is not the cause of sin, nor is [God] the cause of punishment, damnation" (BC 629.81). The formulators assert that damnation is our own "damn fault" just as salvation is God's "fault" alone.

Original sin and human bondage notwithstanding, we are "free" enough to be responsible for continued resistance to the Word and Spirit who would bring us to faith. In their rejection of double predestination, the formulators clearly teach that continued unbelief or impenitence leads to condemnation. The Formula's single predestination is not the universal predestination to salvation of some of the radical reformers.[13] The formulators assert that "there is no basis for the assumption that those might be the elect who despise God's word and who reject, blaspheme, and persecute it . . . who harden their hearts . . . resist the Holy Spirit . . . do not truly believe in Christ . . ., or [who] seek other ways to righteousness and salvation outside of Christ (Romans 9:31)" (BC 622.39).

Confessional Affirmations: Evangelization

The Augsburg Confession is a source for a theology of Christocentric evangelism, empowered and made effective by the Holy Spirit's work through Word and Sacrament.[14] Melanchthon asserts that God the Son became human and thus had two natures united in one person who was truly God and truly human. In Christ, God was reconciling the world (2 Cor. 5:19). There is a twofold direction in all reconciliation: not only is the world brought back, like the prodigal, to God through Christ's willing self-sacrifice, but God's wrath is turned away from the world—God is brought back into "full communion" with the world by Christ's atoning death (BC 29f.).[15]

The *Christus Victor* theme, so important to Luther and the early church, is only hinted at in Article III: the risen, ascended Lord is ruler and defender of believers (BC 30.4). When combined with Luther's Small Catechism on the second article of the Creed, we have a full picture of the Lord redeeming, purchasing, and freeing us from sin, death, and Satan. In the Large Catechism, Luther simply defines Lord as "Redeemer" (BC 414.27–31).

As if to show that he was not exclusively tied to *Christus Victor* language, in the Large Catechism, Luther explains the *payment* Christ makes in terms of making "satisfaction for me" (BC 414.31).[16] Melanchthon in Augustana Article IV, in the Latin text, also uses the language of St. Anselm: Christ's death made satisfaction for our sins. In the less theological German text, Melanchthon simply says, "Christ suffered for us" (BC 30.2).

Article IV continues the Christocentric theology of the cross that Hordern (see note 14) recommends. I would suggest that the Christology of Ephesians 1 is summarized by Melanchthon with the Latin phrase *propter Christum*, that is, because of or on account of Christ (sometimes it is translated with the more ambiguous phrase "for Christ's sake"). To this christological soteriology, Melanchthon adds to the definition of justification "by grace, through faith" from Ephesians chapter 2. In our doctrine of justification and our understanding of evangelism, it is necessary to balance and sometimes even to juggle these three: Christ, grace, and faith. Without "Christ *alone*," a relativistic pluralism proposes other saviors. Without "grace alone," Pelagianism proposes human freedom unaffected by original sin or bondage of the will. Without "faith alone," various synergisms add merit or works or even love to faith. More subtly, we turn faith into a decision *we* make. There is also the danger of "cheap grace" without repentance and "cheap faith"—vague intellectual beliefs or "mere historical knowledge"—without trust in God's promises in Christ (see BC 114.45, 53).

One way of tying these three necessary dimensions together would be to describe justifying faith as reliance on the grace of our Lord Jesus Christ. Grace can never be separated from Christ, and salvation cannot be promised apart from faith in Christ. The frequently heard assertion that the Reformation was about "grace alone, period" is simply wrong. The issue in the sixteenth century was "faith alone" (BC 115.61—117.74). To be sure, there were different definitions of grace, but nobody denied it or seriously questioned "grace alone."

Article V of the Augsburg Confession makes the centrality of the issue of faith quite clear and also advances a theology of evangelization: "To obtain such faith God instituted the office of the ministry." Protecting that from a clerical interpretation, Melanchthon explains, "that is, provided the Gospel and the sacraments." The Latin text continues with a clear soteriological *ordo salutis*: "For through the Word and the sacraments, as through instruments, the Holy Spirit is given, and the Holy Spirit produces faith, where and when it pleases God, in those who hear the Gospel" (BC 31.1f.). The centrality and necessity of faith for salvation are clear. "Grace" is present in the discussions as prevenient in Word and Sacrament and instrumental in creating faith via the "means" of grace; it is reintroduced into the restated definition of justification: being "received into favor for the sake of Christ" by a "gracious God" (BC 31.3).

The other significant issue about Augsburg Confession, Article V, is that Melanchthon backs away from the double predestination musings of Luther in *The Bondage of the Will*[17] and in the articles the Lutherans and Reformed had agreed upon at the 1529 Marburg Colloquy. Those Marburg Articles read that the Spirit works faith "where and *in whom* [God] wills."[18] Rejecting the possible implication that God does not will to call all to faith through the gospel, Melanchthon substitutes "when," allowing for the Spirit's freedom to move, like the wind on the waters of chaos, to create faith "when it pleases God."

If there is any doubt that "faith alone" was the issue at Augsburg, the Apology's nearly seventy-page expansion of the approximately seven-line article in the Augsburg Confession should end all doubt. The Roman Confutation had responded that the "ascription of justification to faith alone is diametrically opposed to the truth of the Gospel, by which works are not excluded" (BC 107n. 8).[19] Perhaps the most significant development in connection with the Joint Declaration on the Doctrine of Justification with the Roman Catholic Church comes in the Annex: "Justification takes place 'by grace alone' (JD 15 and 16), by faith *alone*, the person is justified 'apart from works' (Romans 3:28, cf. JD 25)" (emphasis added).[20]

One of Melanchthon's chief arguments for the necessity of faith is that the gospel is a promise (BC 114.53–56) and the promise of Christ "can be accepted only by faith" (BC 116.70). This argues for the necessity of faith on the basis of the efficacy of faith; indeed, only faith can deal with God's promise effectively. Unbelief excludes one from the benefits of the promise. As Melanchthon argued: to know Christ is to know his benefits (see 121.101).

The Human Predicament and Divine Intervention

A central dimension of a Lutheran theology and methodology of evangelism is the law-gospel dialectic, which takes seriously the issues and questions arising from the human and cosmic context and the divine invasion and intervention into our fallen world and our broken human communities. Probably the Confession's clearest, most concise statement is from Apology XII: "These are the two chief works of God in [humans], to terrify and justify and quicken the terrified. . . . One part is the law, which reveals, denounces, and condemns sin. The other part is the Gospel, that is, the promise of grace granted in Christ" (BC 189.53). The practical implication of this is starting with the bad news of sin and death. In the 1970s, many theologians felt everybody had and knew too much bad news already and we should skip the law and start evangelizing with good news: God loves you! But "I'm okay" soon matured into the "me" and "greed" decades, with self-love and self-esteem as the highest goods. This does not mean we should begin with the law as a club. Careful listening to others can reveal the brokenness of original sin and the exclusion from God and other humans it produces.

Experiences of addiction are but symptoms of the enslavement of the will in relation to God, who created humans with freedom. The burden of guilt and shame from our sins, transgressions, and trespasses in loveless thoughts, words, and deeds turns us and our children into "encultured" and lost sons and daughters—prodigals whose only hope is the Father's outstretched arms.

In our bondage from which we "cannot free ourselves," the law identifies our captors and names the demons: "Sin," "Death," and "Satan." From these enemies, Christ liberates for the freedom of service in God's kingdom. Concerning the congenital disease of original sin, it is the law that does the diagnosis, prognosis, where necessary the euthanasia, and finally the autopsy on our sinful "flesh." Christ comes to heal and resurrect us through the gospel's power. Regarding the sins we commit, the law uncovers the "world's" deception and "enculturation" as well as humans' responsibility for yielding to the culture's temptations. Christ forgives the sins of those terrified by law's warnings and judgments and promises new life and salvation in Word and sacraments.

But along with the law's bad news, the promise of the good news needs to be proclaimed: reconciliation for our alienation, redemption from our bondage, remission of our sins. Because of the complexity of our human condition, the manifold promise needs to be unveiled in its many-splendored goodness: forgiveness of sins, deliverance of death and the devil, and eternal salvation to all who believe (SC, BC 348f.). These benefits, like those given to believers in the Lord's Supper (BC 352.5–10), offer the wholeness and holiness that begins now and is fulfilled in God's future.

Because baptism links believers to Christ's death (Rom. 6:4), we can draw connections between the different word pictures describing the cross, the human condition, and divine correctives: Christ's cross as atoning sacrifice reconciles the alienated and saves and includes the excluded world; Christ's cross as glorious victory redeems and delivers enslaved captives of "sin, death, and the devil"; Christ's cross as satisfaction is a substitution of his innocent suffering and death for ours, bringing us "pardon, remission, and forgiveness of all our sins" (Lutheran Book of Worship, 155). But the Word of promise is always directed toward faith, calls us to faith through the gospel, gathers us into the community of faith, and enlightens, sanctifies, and preserves us in true faith, for only faith can receive the promised benefits.

The Importance of Justification through Faith for Evangelism

The church must be careful not to undercut the doctrine of justification or the doctrine of the church by *promising* salvation apart from faith. Such universalism undercuts justification *through faith,* when it proclaims a possible alternative to *trust* in Christ or, even worse, trust in some other *name* than Christ for salvation. The latter was characteristic of the Unitarian and Universalist churches in the nineteenth century, as well as Protestant liberalism and current postmodern pluralism. All of these contend that there are other saving *self*-revelations besides Christ, and thus that other world religions are *valid ways of salvation.* From this point of view, evangelization of non-Christians is rejected as inappropriate, if not harmful.

It is the former, the firmly christological, form of universalism that I am primarily addressing. For though Christ is affirmed as *the* self-revelation of God and humanity's *only* savior, faith is ultimately unnecessary for final salvation. Catholicism—from Trent to Vatican II—veered dangerously toward works-righteousness when it resisted "faith alone." Protestants have also steered this dangerous course by making faith a human decision or a good work. The contemporary temptation is to overemphasize Gustav Aulen's *Christus Victor* and deduce from it God's final triumph even over those who, with their dying breath, continue to reject the gospel of Christ. A Reformed version of christological universalism picks up on Karl Barth's creative adaptation of John Calvin's untenable doctrine of double predestination. Barth argued that Christ was both the elect and the reprobate human and has taken into himself God's decision to damn some. Barthians (but not Barth!) have concluded from this that God *will* save all people. For Barth, it was at most a prayer and a hope that hell would be empty.

I fear that it may be only a short step from this christological inclusivist universalism to a relativistic pluralist universalism without Christ as the only savior. That kind of pluralism is represented by John Hick in his works on the myth and metaphor of God incarnate.[21] He acknowledges the roots of his views in Schleiermacher and nineteenth-century liberalism. Hick rejects the church's historic doctrines of the Trinity, Christ as God the Son incarnate, and almost any doctrine of atonement beyond "at-one-ment." Dismissing these truths that neoorthodoxy rediscovered leaves his neoliberal theology open to the devastating judgment H. Richard Niebuhr made concerning liberal theology: "A God without wrath brought [humans] without sin into a kingdom without judgment through the ministrations of a Christ without a cross."[22]

God's love for and reconciliation of the whole world in Christ is the primary motivation of a congregation's evangelism efforts. Evangelism is not simply telling people that they are already reconciled as if as if it were an important bit of information they happen not to know: that they are already children of God—"OK as is"—needing nothing but that helpful knowledge. People need new birth through water and the Spirit, new life rescued from death, forgiveness of sins—all this through faith. When Paul proclaims the reconciliation of the world through Christ and announces the *ministry* of reconciliation committed to us, he ends the *message* of reconciliation: "Be reconciled to God" (2 Cor. 5:14-21). Our task is not finished until that part of the good news is also heard. And the Holy Spirit keeps working until the good news is believed and confessed.

The church is *the* community of faith because to it are committed the instruments of the Holy Spirit—Word and sacraments—by which faith is created. Membership in the church through the audible and visible Word received *by faith* is necessary for salvation.

He never deals w. those who have not heard!

Living Together Faithfully
with Our Different Readings of the Bible

DAVID J. LULL

Church bodies and local congregations historically and today have been torn apart over debates about the authority of Scripture. It remains a most difficult issue. What Bible should one read? What is the difference between canons and versions, manuscripts and translations? How can a congregation affirm the unity of the church in its diversity of biblical interpretations, particularly when facing challenging social issues?

Debates about "the authority of the Bible" are occurring in unexpected quarters—churches not known, rightly or wrongly, for being "Bible-centered." All of the older established Protestant churches, the Roman Catholic Church, and Jewish congregations are caught up in a painful and divisive debate over homosexuality and the authority of the Bible. Differences over interpretations of the Bible and authority on this and other issues of faith and life frequently divide congregations as well.

After decades of study, discussion, and debate, many Protestant churches entered the new millennium with a "majority rule" but no consensus about the church's teaching regarding homosexuals, homosexuality, "homosexual practice," and same-sex covenant unions. All positions on this issue claim "the authority of the Bible."[1] Members of congregations can have equally "high" views of the authority of the Bible and still hold widely differing positions on controversial moral issues. A consensus around a common view is neither possible nor desirable. Recognition of this dual reality is essential to avoiding schisms over such issues. To put that positively: congregations need to learn how to live together faithfully with different readings of the Bible and its authority as they face the issue of homosexuality and other painfully divisive issues.

Authority

A popular bumper sticker urged those of us who came of age in the 1960s and 1970s to "Question Authority!" "Authorities" in those days told black Americans to take seats in the back of the bus, not to drink from "white only" drinking fountains, not to go to "white only" schools, not to sit at "white only" food counters, and not to even think about applying for "white only" jobs. "Authorities" told women that they were to stay bare-foot, pregnant, and in the kitchen and that their rights were not equal to those of men. "Authorities" defended the pursuit of corporate profits at the expense of fair wages; the health and safety of workers; clean water, air, and land; and endangered species. "Authorities" still permit or allow racism, sexism, militarism, and economism to flourish today. These "authorities" give authority a bad name, so some people today, even some who participate in congregational life, have an allergy to "authorities." Nevertheless, some recent voices in the church have used their authority and the authority of the church, its Scriptures, and traditions to challenge racist, sexist, militarist, and economist "authorities." These are signs that "authority" might recover its good name.[2]

In the debates about homosexuality in some denominations, "the authority of the Bible" has had almost exclusively a juridical, forensic, or litigious function. Church "authorities" are called upon to charge and try violators of "the authority" of the church, its Scriptures, and traditions. We need to be concerned about standards for the church's life and work, especially

> 🕊 *"We assert the 'authority of the Bible' too often* against *'them' and to* support *'us.'"*

for the life and work of church leaders, but we assert "the authority of the Bible" too often *against* "them" and to *support* "us." Too often, we appeal to "authorities" to deal with our *opponents* and too infrequently to examine *ourselves, our* teaching, and *our* behavior. A helpful corrective would be to meditate on Rom. 2:1.

Moreover, juridical, forensic, or litigious uses of the Bible tend to reduce it to propositions—"doctrines" or "rules" that can have only one true meaning or application—and to treat it as a mere quarry to be mined for propositional, prescriptive content. The Bible does include such materials, but it consists mostly of stories that we cannot reduce to propositions and prescriptions. Propositional and prescriptive uses of the Bible, therefore, are too limiting. A different use of the concept arises from the root meaning of the word "authority," namely, that of "authoring." The Bible has authority in this sense when it is formative of or foundational for Christian identity, community, or spirituality. Moral precepts are only one aspect of this authority; however, this chapter is limited to a discussion of the propositional and prescriptive use of the authority of the Bible so that we can reorient our thinking about the use of the Bible, which is dividing our congregations and churches.

The Making of Bibles

The phrase "the authority of the Bible" refers to something more elusive than we think. Actually, we need to use the plural form, "Bibles." An examination of the making of Bibles will give us a sense of the diverse forms: (1) canons, (2) versions, (3) manuscripts, and (4) translations.[3]

Canons

Throughout the ages, religious communities have compiled or constructed "Bibles" in multiple forms from the wealth of sacred scriptures of ancient Israel and the early Christian church.[4] The Jewish Bible[5] is different from the scriptures of the Samaritans[6] and from the Septuagint, which consists of Greek translations of Hebrew writings plus other writings originally written in Greek.[7] The Old Testament in Roman Catholic Bibles[8] differs from that of Protestant Bibles,[9] which in turn differ from the various Orthodox canons,[10] which include additional apocryphal books.

Which "Bible" are we talking about? Any answer to this question is a confessional answer, founded on tradition, reason, and experience. The answer itself cannot appeal to "the authority of the Bible." No answer to the question is the only true answer. No answer to the question is merely an individual preference; rather, all answers are rooted in a particular community that understands itself to be formed by a particular form of "Bible." At the most fundamental level, communities of Bible readers participate in the Bible's very formation by how they choose, define, interpret, and apply the concept of authority.

Versions

Bibles, in addition to consisting of different canons, exist in different "versions," which are ancient translations of both Testaments from original

Hebrew and Greek texts.[11] By extension, all modern English translations, as well as other vernacular translations, are versions of the original Hebrew and Greek texts.[12] All such translations, whether ancient or modern, presuppose or imply the authority of the original Hebrew and Greek texts. These versions, however, also gain an authority of their own and, for most Bible readers, replace the original texts.

If all appeals to "the authority of the Bible" had to be to the original Hebrew and Greek texts, or to the Latin Vulgate, then only experts in ancient languages could participate in debates about homosexuality and other contemporary moral issues. Responsible use of Bibles in framing church moral teachings will take account of the best scholarship by experts in biblical languages, but few members of congregations—and, alas, few clergy—debate issues concerning homosexuality or other moral issues with copies of the Hebrew, Greek, or Latin texts in hand. Even if they did, they, like experts in biblical languages, would disagree about two additional aspects of the making of Bibles before they even reached the debate.

Manuscripts

The original Hebrew and Greek texts also exist in multiple forms.[13] A casual glance at the footnotes in any modern English edition of the Bible leads to the discovery that at many places "other ancient authorities" have a different text, because all Bibles are based on manuscripts and fragments of manuscripts that are copies of earlier copies that no longer exist.[14] We have no "autograph" copies of biblical books.

As Bart D. Ehrman has shown, in emerging orthodoxy's opposition to so-called heresy, early Christians altered texts in what became the New Testament to make Scripture conform to their "rule of faith" (*regula fidei*) and to preclude opposing views.[15] So-called heretics did the same thing. The result is a rich and varied manuscript tradition that already illustrates the circular path of interpretation. Once the emerging "orthodox" church formulated its "rule of faith," which it claimed is the one true interpretation of Scripture, it defined not only "the authority of the Bible" but also what constituted Scripture itself—which texts were in, which texts were out, and how the texts that were in should read and be read.

Although few significant variations may appear in the texts relevant to the debate about sexuality, it is important to remember that at the most basic level confessional traditions, reason, and experiences of communities construct not only biblical canons but also the biblical texts themselves.[16]

Translations

English-speaking congregations, at least since the appearance of the King James Version at the beginning of the seventeenth century, have read translations of community-constructed canons of Hebrew and Greek texts.[17] When those who are not trained in the biblical languages think and debate about the Bible, they do so in the language of a translation. English-speaking Protestants today use at least eighteen different translations of "the Bible." All translations are "confessional" and community based.[18] One example is the New International Version, whose translators were required to sign a confession of faith. The members of the Standard Bible Translation Committee of the National Council of Churches, which produced the Revised Standard Version and the New Revised Standard Version, were not asked about their "confessions," but their "confessional" stance places a priority on history, philology, and contemporary linguistics over traditional church doctrine.

The authority to which the translator is accountable, however, is not one but many, just as the translator's scripture is not one but many. The translator is accountable to two quite different authorities: the ancient text and the language into which it is translated (the receptor language). The responsibility of the translator is to be faithful both to the words and meanings of ancient text and to the receptor language. Moreover, languages consist not only of words but also of meanings that cannot be taken out of their own thought—and social—worlds. That means that the translator must attend to the *cultures* of the ancient text and of the receptor language. Any translation, therefore, is a combination of the authority of the ancient text and its culture, on the one hand, and the authority of the receptor language and its culture, on the other. A couple of illustrations from the RSV and the NRSV will illustrate the point.

When the RSV appeared, a firestorm of controversy surrounded its translation of Isa. 7:14.[19] Whereas the KJV reads, "Behold, a *virgin* shall conceive, and bear a son, and shall call his name Immanuel," the RSV reads, "Behold, a *young woman* shall conceive and bear a son, and shall call his name Immanuel."[20] Some critics claimed that the RSV eliminated, or at least obscured, the prophetic voice of the Old Testament's foretelling of the coming of Jesus as the promised Messiah. The RSV, however, followed the original Hebrew, whereas the KJV, under the influence of church doctrine and tradition, followed the Septuagint, the Old Latin Bible, and the Vulgate. Critics of the RSV regarded the Hebrew text as "inspired" and, on that basis, criticized the RSV where it follows one of the Syriac, Aramaic, Latin, or Greek "versions" instead of the Hebrew. When it came to Isa. 7:14, however, they argued that Matt. 1:23, which quotes the Septuagint, shows the Septuagint also is "inspired"—or that this one verse of the Septuagint is—and, therefore, is the basis for translating the Hebrew as "a virgin."

In this debate, Christian doctrine about the mother of Jesus, or one form of it,[21] influenced the translation of a Hebrew word[22] that means "a young woman," not "a virgin," for which Hebrew has a different and perfectly good word.[23] RSV critics allowed their Christian doctrine to overlook that Isaiah was talking about his own wife, already the mother of his first son (7:1-9) and now pregnant with a second son and then with a third.[24] These critics blamed the translation of Isa. 7:14 RSV on the committee's only non-Christian, Harry Orlinsky, a Jew.[25] They criticized Luther Weigel, the chair of the translation committee, for failing to require its members to adhere to an "orthodox" statement of Christian faith. For the committee, however, the translation of Isa. 7:14 was a matter not of Christian faith or doctrine but of Hebrew philology. Records show that the committee hardly debated the translation of Isa. 7:14 and that they had no clue that their translation was inviting controversy.

What this criticism of the RSV shows is that translations play a big role in defining what views Scripture authorizes.[26] Doctrines formulated in the course of church history shape Bible translations, and then people who invoke "the authority of the Bible" have in mind those translations. The original biblical text, however, is actually open to different, competing doctrinal formulas. Bible translations alone cannot solve these doctrinal matters; neither can the original biblical texts. A confessional community's tradition, reason, and experience enter these debates alongside Scripture.

From beginning to end—the construction of canons, versions, manuscript traditions, and translations—all Bibles are products of confessional communities. However, even if we agree on a version, a manuscript tradition, and a translation, we would not yet have reached a basis for consensus about the authority of the Bible. The reason is that texts require *interpretation,* an activity that both shapes and is shaped by different canons, versions, manuscript traditions, and translations.

Reading Scripture against Scripture

Even when the church has agreed on an interpretation of specific texts, the church throughout its history has taken positions contrary to passages in the Bible. Although the Bible contains passages that accept divorce and remarriage, the church is not of one mind.[27] The Bible contains stories that accept slavery, but the church was divided over the question of slavery.[28] Although the Bible contains passages that restrict the role of women in the leadership of the church—which, however, are loaded with text-critical and translation problems—the church has increasingly come to affirm the gifts of women and their right to leadership in the church.[29] In a similar way, many churches today do not require that wives be "submissive" to their husbands.[30]

These examples teach at least three lessons to those who seek to warrant or authorize ethical norms or moral rules based on the authority of the Bible. First, once-secure moral judgments have not passed the test of time. In each case, proponents of a moral judgment were sure that their moral judgment rested securely on the authority of the Bible only to have their church change its mind. Second, they demonstrate that scriptural authority is not one but many. Churches based earlier moral judgments on the authority of *topically specific texts*. Judgments on those matters changed when the authority shifted from texts bearing moral precepts to the witness of the Bible as a whole or to its "kerygmatic core"—that is, the proclamation of God's redeeming love in Jesus Christ.[31] Third, scriptural authority is relational, not absolute. Other authorities—for example, a confessional community's tradition, reason, and experience—do not just interpret scriptural precepts. They also shape judgments about their validity and application in contemporary situations.

These lessons are worth keeping in mind in the current debates about homosexuality and other controversial issues as we turn now to a further complication in "the authority of the Bible." Some Christians might agree on what constitutes the one true *Scripture*, which contains the norms that would then authorize the common faith, life, and work of a particular church or congregation; some might also agree on the one true form of *authority*.[32] Neither of these agreements, however, would ensure that Christians would agree on the one true *interpretation* of the relevant passages of the Bible.[33]

Interpretation

Scriptures, as forms of communication and expression, are open to different interpretations. Texts allow for, and even require, multiple interpretations. They are, as it were, pregnant with multiple meanings. In the debate about homosexuality and other contemporary moral issues, however, debaters privilege one interpretation among several plausible, good, and faithful interpretations as *the one and only* true interpretation.

To take the so-called ban on homosexuality in three New Testament texts as an example, scholars do not agree on the translation and interpretation of key terms in 1 Cor. 6:9 and 1 Tim. 1:10 and about the interpretation of Rom. 1:26-27. Even if scholars did agree on these matters, we would still need to ask what the relationship is between the ethical norms and moral rules in these texts and the assumptions about sexuality and gender ideologies on which they depend. We also have to ask whether we can give the former the authority of the Bible without also giving that same authority to the latter.

First Corinthians 6:9 and 1 Tim. 1:10 illustrate the difficulty of establishing a consensus at the most basic level—namely, about what the text says.[34] The problem begins with the ambiguity of the Greek texts. The wide range of English translations reveals the translators' sexual ideologies. At issue are two Greek words, *malakoi* and *arsenokoitai*.

It is difficult to bring order to the array of translations, but they seem to fall into two categories. Some presuppose or imply that these words have to do with sexual behavior; of these, some refer specifically to *homosexual sex*, and others to *sex more generally*. Others presuppose or imply that they have to do with *perversion in general*. Some translations render the first term as "effeminate," but is that intended in some sexual sense or more broadly to male and female social conventions and, if so, to which conventions?[35]

So much is at stake in the translation of these two Greek words! The translations differ widely, and their differences make a big difference in the moral import of this key verse in the debates over homosexuality. How many families and congregations have split over these two words, and how many denominations will divide over them?

These Greek words are open to a wider range of meanings than their English translations are. In the debates, authority rests in the different translations and interpretations instead of in the more ambiguous ancient Greek text. Instead of acknowledging that the text is uncertain and open to a range of interpretations and translations, even conflicting ones, and that consensus is not possible, a privileged translation/interpretation is granted authority as "the one true translation/interpretation."

A traditional interpretation translates the first Greek word as a term that refers to so-called passive males penetrated in same-sex intercourse. In this interpretation, the first Greek word refers either to callboys in pederasty[36] or to male prostitutes.[37] Another interpretation translates it with the word "effeminate."[38] The New Jerusalem Bible translation, "the self-indulgent," is consistent with the view in the ancient world that a man was "effeminate" who engaged in various activities in excess, performing certain sexual acts, and moving his body in ways associated with females.³⁹ This term, which can denote "soft" or "luxurious" in general, can also convey a sense of weakness, such as when it refers to someone who is sick.⁴⁰ Aristotle also pairs this term with the lack of self-control and discipline concerning "pleasures and pains," as opposed to being self-controlled, being capable of patient endurance, and having control over sensual pleasures.⁴¹ For Aristotle, being "self-controlled" and "able to endure" are *manly* virtues, so that a man who pursues pleasures in excess and avoids even moderate pain, therefore, is "soft, weak, effeminate."

Nothing in 1 Cor. 6:9, however, indicates which aspect of this range of meanings is intended. This suggests that the first Greek word is used in 1 Cor. 6:9 not as a specific condemnation but as a "malleable" or "blanket" one.⁴² When we invoke "the authority of the Bible" in the debate over homosexuality, to be faithful to *this text*—and to be honest with one another—we need to remember that this Scripture passage allows or "authorizes" more than one interpretation.

A traditional interpretation of the second Greek term, which appears in the Greek language for the first time in 1 Cor. 6:9, translates it as a word for the so-called active male who penetrates another male in anal intercourse.⁴³ This interpretation traces this compound Greek word to the holiness code in the Septuagint version of Leviticus because it consists of the word for "the male sex" and a euphemism for "intercourse."⁴⁴ That interpretation confuses the parts of a compound word with its meaning. Usage, however, is "the real determinant of meaning."⁴⁵ Another interpretation interprets it as "exploiting others by means of sex."⁴⁶

Perhaps we should admit that we simply do not know what the second Greek word means.⁴⁷ One thing is certain: the claim that it *obviously* has to do with "active" participants in homosexual sex flies in the face of the difficulty of determining this Greek word's meaning.⁴⁸ Nothing is "obvious" about the translation of this term—nor about the first Greek word. The honest thing to do under these circumstances is to admit that the scholarly community is not of one mind about what this text says and to resist absolute claims about the ethical norms and moral rules that this text authorizes.⁴⁹

Nothing in this text excludes same-sex sex from its view, but good reasons exist for questioning the *limitation* of its view to same-sex sexual activity. Whether these Greek terms refer to *same-sex* sex or to immoral sexual activity *in general*, they presuppose or imply a variety of warrants for the condemnation of a range of behavior—namely, notions of excessive pursuit of pleasure, honor and shame, justice, and self-control. These notions are also related to the notion of "nature" in Rom. 1:26-27.⁵⁰ Whatever meanings these warrants convey, they are not limited to one interpretation but are "pregnant with meaning." Jews and gentiles in Paul's culture would easily understand them because they are common among Jewish and gentile moral philosophers.

The primary warrant for excluding from the kingdom of God those who exhibit the behavior listed in 1 Cor. 6:9-10, however, is the specifically *Christian* understanding that members of the community belong to—and *are*—the body of Christ, so that they should judge all they do in relation to the body of Christ.[51] Paul informs the Corinthian believers that, in Christ, they are not simply solitary individuals but, rather, are connected with one another and with Christ.[52] That standard is what ties this verse to the preceding verses about lawsuits and with the following verses about engaging in sex with prostitutes.[53] It would be un- and even anti-Pauline to invert the relationship between this major theme and the minor details of this commonplace list of vices, and to turn this text into a legal text. Paul's method of handling the problems in the Corinthian community of believers is not to hand down laws but to engage in discernment about what is consistent with love, the body of Christ, and the Spirit.[54]

What lessons can we learn about the authority of the Bible and living together with our different readings of the Bible from this examination of one controversial text? First, translations make all the difference in the world! We can and should debate the differences among the translations but then remember that the underlying ancient languages authorize more than one translation. That recognition alone could lower the temperature of the debate over the Bible, homosexuality, and other controversial issues. Second, congregations and churches will avoid schism if they honor the range of interpretations to which the text is open, the distinction between the text's moral judgments and its range of warrants, and the distinction between its general cultural warrants and its specifically Christian warrants. Those who honor these dimensions of moral judgments in the Bible will acknowledge the following range of applications of this text to sexual ethics as differing and yet faithful readings of this Scripture passage:

- Same-sex sex *of any kind* is contrary to God's "kingdom" (realm or rule).[55]
- Same-sex sex is contrary to God's "kingdom" (realm or rule) *if and when it is motivated by excessive sexual pleasure, shows a lack of self-control, or violates codes of honor, shame, and justice in the community of believers* (the body of Christ).
- *Sex of any kind*, whether between people of the opposite or same sex, is contrary to God's "kingdom" (realm or rule) *if and when it is motivated by excessive sexual pleasure, shows a lack of self-control, or violates codes of honor, shame, and justice in the community of believers* (the body of Christ).

This text, however, does place limits on the range of interpretations and applications. For instance, we cannot make this passage answer questions that are alien to it. Paul directs his statements about sex with prostitutes toward *males*; he says nothing about the experience of *female* prostitutes. He is also silent about persons born with a homoerotic "orientation."[56] If it deals with male same-sex sexual activity, however we understand that, it is silent about monogamous homosexual same-sex relationships based on mutual love.[57] Whatever we say about these matters, we will move beyond anything Paul or the rest of the Bible says about human sexuality.

One place to begin exploring this issue is with a discussion of whether such biblical stories as the relationship between Ruth and Naomi, Jonathan and David, and Jesus and the "beloved disciple" in the Gospel of John could serve as models of same-sex *love*.[58] Although these relationships include forms of affectionate contact, they are common in Mediterranean cultures and do not qualify as "sexual" contact in the normal sense of the term.[59] Another fruitful place to look for biblical standards to apply to same-sex relationships is 1 Corinthians 7. Homosexual persons who have a "gift" for abstaining from sexual activity could find support here for "celibacy in singleness" or for same-sex relationships without sex. Others, however, might find Paul's standards for marriages between a man and a woman helpful—namely, fidelity to a single partner (7:2), mutual and reciprocal respect for each other's sexual needs (7:3-5), and celebration of their sexuality as a "gift of God" (7:7). In the end, unless we find only condemnation in the Bible, we need to admit that biblical boundaries for same-sex relationships remain elusive and that, if we think we see them, we can see them only "in a mirror, dimly."[60]

Another limit on the use of this text comes from its context within Paul's letter. When Christians use this verse to bring lawsuits against clergy and laity, that ignores its context. Paul chastises the Corinthian church for taking one another to court and says, "In fact, to have lawsuits at all with one another is already a defeat for you. Why not rather be wronged? Why not rather be defrauded?" (6:7 NRSV). Paying attention to the literary setting and rhetorical situation of this text within Paul's letter undermines appeals to the authority of the Bible in support of its litigious use.[61] A more faithful reading is that it authorizes a process of moral discernment grounded in the faith that, in and as the body of Christ, by God's grace we might learn ways of living together faithfully, even with our different readings of the Bible when it comes to difficult moral issues.

10

Practice *Where* You Preach

Conditions for Good Preachers

JAMES R. NIEMAN

If dealing with the difference in biblical interpretation is an on-going challenge, congregations face the issue directly in the sermons they hear each week. The Bible is a difficult book. How does one judge a sermon as good? How does one avoid preaching merely to amuse? Preaching is hard work. The preacher holds a symbolic office that is to be exercised responsibly with care and with utmost attention to knowing the community.

Preaching gives rise to reactions. Those who submit to it every week, speakers and hearers alike, are neither indifferent nor short of opinions. Only good preachers are desired, I am told, ones who tell the truth and stir the soul. The real challenge comes in sorting out what this all means. One person's pulpit orator is another's tiresome bore. The folksy storyteller who charms many is a homiletical abomination to at least a few. Beneath these differences in style, however, rests a basic question of how one cultivates good preachers in the first place, the conditions in which they might thrive. Fortunately, we possess some rather helpful guidance about this in two remarks from long ago. In substance, they are actually about as different as can be, but both are absolutely true. Not surprisingly, they also belong to Luther.

The first was uttered by the reformer a few years before his death. Weary and embattled, health failing, Luther feared that all he had done was for naught. So on an April evening in 1542 when asked once again his advice for preachers, he repeated something he had said a score of times before: a list of attributes. This list was just six items long—six, an incomplete number, like the days of creation but without any sabbath. It's a clue that something is missing. Indeed, it fairly dripped with ironic, flowery words that betrayed preaching's deeper corruption.

What is required for preaching that is loved by the world? Six things make the world want to listen to a preacher. First, you should display considerable agility. Second, you should be ever so learned. Third, you should be quite eloquent. Fourth, you should be so beautiful a person that servants and the unmarried love to be in your company. Fifth, you should demand nothing of worth from hearers, but rather always give them sweet treasures. And sixth, you should speak only of what people have already heard.[1]

A decade earlier, however, the scene was quite different. With the bold confession at Augsburg just behind him, the challenges of the Smalcaldic League just ahead, Luther was in the midst of a raging storm. The evangelical cause needed pastors who could preach the pure gospel with conviction. So in 1532, Luther shared with Conradus Cordatus, his hometown pastor and persecuted colleague, another list. This one, later frequently copied, was ten items long—ten, a perfect number, complete and whole. Even so, the tone in this case was spare and no nonsense, like urgent instructions during a battle when time is of the essence.

Conditions for good preachers: One, can teach. Two, a good head. Three, able to discuss. Four, a voice. Five, good memory. Six, knowing how to stop. Seven, hard working. Eight, risking life and limb, goods and honor. Nine, willing to be mocked by everybody. Ten, bearing patiently the fact that nothing is more easily and quickly seen in preachers than faults.[2]

Two remarks from the same person, about as different as can be, but both absolutely true. It takes no rocket scientist to tell the difference between preachers who make a flashy show of education—and those who know how to think, who have a "good memory" of Scripture, and who then can share that insight with others. Most listeners in the pew can distinguish between preachers who have a way with words—and those who have a "voice," who have something worth saying that sounds like the truth. We are quite able to discern between attractive yet undemanding preachers, full of sparkle and charisma—and those who are realistic about fickle crowds and their stunning resistance to a message of grace. Ignore all else about Luther's contrasting statements, but notice at least this haunting fact: both are absolutely true. Both of them speak accurately of preachers. Only one, however, suggests what makes them *good*.

It is easy to overlook that Luther spoke in the form of a *list*—an orderly arrangement to clarify and guide. Preachers do not arise from some haphazard collision between native ability and dumb luck. We can name what is needed to become a preacher, and these things develop in a certain order. Some, like the ability to think and discuss, are *gifts* with which preachers begin. Others, like voice and memory and even how to stop, are *skills* to be learned. Congregations need preachers who know what to say, how that relates to the memory of the church, and how to arrange it so people can follow. Beyond both of these is a *wisdom* that can be gained only over time, such as the fact that this is hard work and people won't always love the preacher for it.

These gifts and skills and wisdom do not just develop in an order. They also have an aim. Luther expressed that aim in a single, disturbing contrast between "speaking only of what people have already heard" in the one list—and "risking life and limb" in the other. If preachers simply repeat what could be said in the complete absence of the Bible altogether, then whatever they utter will be of small account.[3] Then they are merely consumed with waffling words, sounding smart, and gathering groupies. When, however, preachers aim to risk life and limb, goods and honor,

> "*Most listeners in the pew can distinguish between preachers who have a way with words—and those who have a 'voice,' who have something worth saying that sounds like truth.*"

it can be for only one reason: because they point to the Crucified, whose life and limb, goods and honor, were emptied for our sake. Then they are not surprised to be found in such holy company, mocked by everybody and patiently bearing the faults that others so quickly bestow.

How do good preachers know they are seeking this aim instead of its counterfeits? What safeguards them from self-delusion or self-pity? Luther's earlier and more urgent list offers us a subtle clue. Supporting it are a few foundational practices that typify good preachers, habitual behaviors that keep them on the right list and aim them in the right direction. To be sure, these practices are only the basics, but even those should not be underestimated. Inattention to the basics, whether for musicians, romantics, or preachers, can turn the initially delightful into the eventually unendurable. For now, therefore, consider four basic practices that become the ground on which good preachers stand.

Holding a Symbolic Office

Leaving aside the relatively rare phenomenon of the street-corner preacher, we usually think of preaching within the setting of worship. Moreover, the preacher is not just amid the congregation at worship but is one of the assembly, part of them and yet set apart for a special function. We hardly ever stop to think about why this is so or what the church is saying through the symbolism of being set apart. Of course, at one level it is simply a question of the recognition of special gifts. Some people (allegedly) can preach, and others can listen (which, I assure you, is also a gift). There is, however, much more at stake than this.

The overwhelming majority practice of the church in various times, distant locales, and even its diverse factions has been to treat preaching as an office tied to one person. Do not misunderstand me on this. I am not saying "one congregation, one preacher." Indeed, the very idea of one preacher preaching one time during worship has never been the uniform practice of churches, even in America. Yet, even in places with several, occasional, or visiting preachers, or having multiple sermons during worship, it has still been typical to call upon one person specifically to be responsible for overseeing the preaching in that place. Often, that person has also been a regular preacher there, but not always. In any case, orderliness seems to have demanded this arrangement. Assemblies want to ensure that preaching is done by those with the requisite gifts and training. They also want local controls upon the preaching, with one of their own deciding on their behalf who will speak and who will not. In some groups, this orderliness is also tied to the order of worship, expressing a consistency between who preaches and who presides at meal and bath, prays for the gathered, and receives the collection for the poor.

There is more involved here than just orderliness, however. Regardless of how many sermons or how many preachers appear during worship, preaching has a surprisingly solitary core. One person is bid to speak, and that is a profound symbol. Again, do not misunderstand me on this. Of course there are collaborative, dialogue-type sermons, and of course various traditions rely upon give-and-take for effective preaching. My point, however, is that one voice has been called upon as the catalyst to get all of this under way. Preaching is not like a hymn or a group recitation. One person is bid to speak, a solitary voice at a particular moment becomes the catalyst, and that itself is the symbol.

Plainly put, this solitary voice symbolizes something daring, even dangerous. The worshiping assembly at its best seeks someone to break in with a bracing word of truth and hope it might not otherwise hear if left to its own devices. These "other" voices—really, *any* different voices—hold the possibility of bringing a creative and challenging word that might not otherwise be heard by a self-enclosed assembly. There is danger in that symbol, of course. Consider, for example, the level of resistance to certain kinds of preachers on the basis of their gender, race, or sexual orientation. Good preachers realize that along with the solitary, catalytic voice comes a symbolic authority that can make the church quite nervous. They therefore exercise it with care, knowing at the same time that what the church has given is intended to be used.

Knowing a Particular Community

When you stop to think about it, it ought to be almost impossible for preachers to connect with anyone in the congregation other than themselves. There's a good reason for this. Contemporary sociolinguistics and, before that, the tradition of classical rhetoric have long known that the language of a message and the language of a community must somehow fit together if understanding is to result. Whatever is said must be conveyed in terms a community can accept and understand, lest it be treated as something alien and worthy of rejection. This is the barrier that all preachers face. Especially when good preachers try (as they ought) to confront certain evils and name various distortions, won't their words immediately be perceived as alien and thus automatically be rejected? Human defenses against any form of critique are quick and sophisticated. So how can the message one hopes to preach ever be listened to long enough to have its intended impact?

A major part of the problem is that we are shaped by Enlightenment views of "critique." Westerners operate with the modern assumption that discerning analysis and effective solutions require distance and objectivity. It is the scientific view of things in which the expert makes shrewd observations and proposes testable changes. On this basis, then, really good preachers obviously would need to stand apart from all the messy institutional attachments that pastors usually have. They would come from the outside, so the theory goes, free from constraints and pressures to conform.

Nice as this sounds, however, it fails to fit the picture of arguably the most potent preachers in Scripture: the prophets of ancient Israel. Those preachers instead found themselves mired in the cause of the nation they confronted and thus made regular appeal to the tradition already existing there. In the same way, it seems to me that good preachers commit something rather like embezzlement, an "inside job" best done with resources available locally. It is utterly crucial to drop the heroic vision that preachers bring bracing analysis and decisive solutions from the outside into an otherwise foolish community. What the church needs instead are preachers who locate themselves and their message sufficiently *inside* the existing community agenda.

This requires from preachers first the humility to recognize their own social placement that both strengthens and limits what they are able to proclaim. We all speak from a particular perspective, and good preachers honestly claim that perspective for what it is and is not, for what it cannot see and what it can. Next, they dare not try to stand above the fray but rather within it. What preachers say will only matter to others insofar as they hold themselves under the same promise or indictment they dare to announce. Finally, these same preachers realize that they enter into a conversation that began long ago and will continue long after they have stopped speaking. By noticing the conflicts and debates and languages already at hand, they can become invested and concerned in these for the sake of the whole community. Good preachers know the local scene, becoming committed to and invested in the life of a community.[4]

Bearing a Pastoral Integrity

Stephen Carter's recent discussion of integrity interests me because it offers provocative insights about how preachers can contribute to transformation.[5] The term *integrity* is rooted in the Latin word *integer*—a term of wholeness (like whole numbers). The integrated person is whole and complete, not necessarily perfect or flawless, but certainly with nothing seriously lacking that would detract from full and healthy living. This is why we admire people of integrity. They seem really to be living, and in ways that enrich and enliven others.

At its heart, integrity is really a perpetual dance between three elements. The first is *discerning* what is right and what is wrong—a matter of what we *know*. Second comes *acting* on what we have discerned, even at personal cost—a matter of what we *do*. Third is the work of *saying*, clearly and openly, that we are acting on our understanding of right and wrong—a matter of what we ultimately *speak*. It's a nice little package, but the real challenge is to attend to all three of these, and all of the time.

How easy it is for people to become stalled at any one of these three moves. Moral reflectiveness never leads to genuine amendment of life or new forms of speaking. Frenzied action is never held in check by reflection or accounted for through our words. Or, perhaps most typical for preachers, bold speech lacks the cognitive grounding or practical implementation to make it worth hearing in the first place. All of this suggests a challenging little formula for pastoral integrity, as well as a sound practice for making preaching that is genuinely good. Have preachers thought adequately about what they are about to say? Are they already doing something about it in their own sphere of influence before urging it upon others? Are they able to hold a further, extended dialogue with others about what they have first said only in the relative safety of a brief pulpit monologue? The point is not to restrict what is uttered in sermons but instead to let those words resound with still greater impact.

There are also important things to say about what integrity is *not*. Integrity is not the same as single-minded zeal or obsession with a cause. It is neither compulsively attentive to following the rules nor forever seeking new and flagrant ways to break them. It knows the value of compromise and the insufficiency of mere honesty. Most of all, integrity involves profound personal risk. For all these reasons, good preachers who are able to utter a daring call to repentance and transformation can only do so because they first embody pastoral integrity.

Reading a Difficult Book

Remarkably, Scripture still serves as the central, incontestable warrant for most Christian assemblies. This is true even when congregations don't know the treasures the Bible contains, and perhaps especially because they don't! By grounding proclamation in this warrant, good preachers speak in a distinctive language that the church at least claims it wants to hear and must somehow bump into if it is to be church. Ernst Käsemann once told the story of a fundamentalist Reformed congregation in the Netherlands in 1952 whose town was threatened by a raging storm and the imminent collapse of the local dike. Since it was a Sunday when work was prohibited, the elders of the church argued endlessly about whether they should repair the collapsing structure. The exasperated pastor quoted Scripture to remind them how Jesus had declared that humans were not made for the Sabbath, but the Sabbath for humans—whereupon one of the elders snorted, "Ach, I always thought he was a liberal!"[6] The point is that even in choosing to ignore Scripture, the church still has to account for why it will violate its own deepest values and thus bring judgment upon itself. That is something for preachers to remember.

Good preachers draw from Scripture not simply as the church's warrant but also because it is deeply cross-cultural. Despite our best efforts to make texts seem normal or up-to-date, the fact is that they preserve an ancient and alien world with a theological perspective often wildly at odds with our own. Through that encounter with difference, the church is forced to reckon with two things: first, our ancestors who claimed the same God as do we, and second, why we are as stubbornly faithless as were they. Put in perhaps a more positive frame, the promise of Scripture is that through it, preachers bid us to enter another world for a time and leave our own behind. We are given, if only briefly, a glimpse of a place we might inhabit—and then are thrust back upon our own reality to ask questions about why we persist in our old and death-dealing ways. Granting this unexpected vision of God's reign is what good preachers do.

Beyond these two remarks stands another reason for appealing to Scripture, and it begins with an odd observation. Have you ever wondered how Scripture can continue to be applicable for our day (or any other)? Why should a text written for one people have any binding power on any-one else? Why wasn't its meaning and usefulness exhausted at the time of its origins? The reason is that Scripture offers something like an official story, a comprehensive world with a place for everyone and everything. All effective narratives do this. As part of its credibility, Scripture retains many stories and points of view, even those of marginal figures, alternative opinions, and outright losers. Despite the tendency of official stories to portray what has sometimes been called "history without wrinkles,"[7] Scripture still preserves other, secondary perspectives. These other discounted voices, such as women, peasants, and the conquered, whisper the message that things might have been otherwise and still could be.

In this way, Scripture gives preaching a powerful new perspective. Good preachers read biblical accounts carefully for their suppressed features and initiate a process of shifting the relative weights of primary and secondary elements in a text. The critical edge comes from taking those other voices, ones found in the official warrant of the church, and marshaling them toward an inescapable yet confrontational conclusion. When those little ruptures are heard to the fullest extent possible, then by means of indirection and even surprise, preachers have the means to sidestep human defenses against what they dare to announce.

One especially effective strategy for reading against the grain of Scripture has been to be public during the period of sermon preparation, before ever entering the pulpit. Good preachers learn to collaborate with their hearers in opening the Scripture and listening for what it might say.[8] Of course, this cannot be used as a way of evading responsibility for what is preached or devaluing the daring symbol of the catalytic preacher. The real gift of collaborative approaches is that the limits of any one perspective need not be fatal. Other voices from other perspectives notice other ways the text might speak God's hope for a particular assembly. Justo and Catherine González have affirmed how collaboration, especially with the marginalized, offers a distinctive "metamodern" interpretation particularly well suited to Scripture.[9] Collaborative reading eludes the cool, so-called objectivity of modernity, awaiting instead Scripture's ancient countercultural claim in all its bracing freshness.

Two Lists Once Again

We began with two very old lists: "preaching that is loved by the world" on the one hand, and "conditions for good preachers" on the other. No one can ignore Luther's audacity in presuming to know what makes for good preachers, let alone their worldly opposites. He was not, however, trying to offer a homiletical archetype—a timeless model slavishly to be followed. Luther's earlier and urgent list uttered in the heat of battle was, I believe, meant as a prototype—a gesture in the right direction but ultimately taking many forms. These ten conditions for good preachers are something to be used, like the contents of a toolbox regularly and lovingly employed in a craft. Good preachers are bid by the church to *do* something with the tools they have at hand. When they possess the gifts and skills and wisdom of Luther's list, they then *use* them by holding a symbolic office, knowing a particular community, bearing a pastoral integrity, and reading a difficult book. "By their fruits you will know them," Jesus once said about false and true prophets.[10] The same might be said of good preachers.

11

Communio as a Basis for Moral Formation, Deliberation, and Action

KAREN L. BLOOMQUIST

Whereas preaching continues to be seen as central to a congregation's life, ethics is often relegated to the periphery. The ethical life is not merely an add-on. It arises from the church's heart. Ethics and ecclesiology go together. The power of Christ leads to indispensable action in the world. How might relationships within the communion be deepened so that difficult questions are asked and actions taken?

When most people hear the word "ethics," they think of problems to be solved, especially in situations where competing moral claims are at stake. These are the difficult questions that tend to be at the edges rather than the center of our daily lives, such as those related to prolonging a life through technological means. Or, they may be decisions facing those in professions such as business or medicine. The concern is with the decision or action such individuals take for the sake of "being ethical," that is, socially acceptable. Ethics in this narrow sense tends to be at the periphery of the church's attention rather than arising out of the center of ecclesiology.

In contrast, much of Christian ethics in recent years has tended to focus less on developing normative guidance for decisions in difficult situations and more on character, on who we are as moral agents. This often has been connected with a focus on how ethics and moral response grow out of the very being of the church, whose teachings, worship, and other practices *form* who we are (that is, our character).[1] We are formed in the ecclesial community by the biblical story such that the people of God called church are to live in distinction from the ways of the world. Biblical narratives cultivate emotions, such as outrage and compassion, that are appropriate to moral action. Much attention also has been given to the relationship between the church's worship and ethics.[2] "The form of liturgy is the way Christian ethics should be enfolded to a community, *and* it is the form of Christian moral reasoning itself."[3] Although some ecclesial-focused approaches might be questioned as to how well they are able to engage those who do not share their faith assumptions, these are communitarian attempts to respond to such factors as individualism, subjectivism, and privatization in the wider society.

Such an ecclesial grounding also has the effect of making Christian ethics more integrated with worship, educational ministry, preaching, and pastoral care. Through each of these aspects of congregational life, we are being formed morally, with the basis for such in God's gracious response toward us. Through congregational decision making, mission, and outreach, we exercise moral agency. We live out our faith, expanding our horizon in light of God's all-inclusive vision for the world.

Moral Formation

Moral formation is a process through which our identity as part of a community with certain attitudes and motivations emerges. It has to do with the beliefs, symbols, customs, habits, and ethos that undergird and shape who we are, our values and priorities, how we live, and what we do. In other words, we are formed morally before we even begin to think about it. This moral formation, as it occurs especially in precognitive ways, is the matrix out of which moral deliberation and ethical action arise. The ordinary is the terrain on which the moral life moves and grows, where we are formed in our relationship with others. Our routine life together in the congregation, how we care for the sick, how we make decisions in church council meetings, how we reach out to help others—all grow out of our being a community of faith. In turn, our witness, mission, and ministry shape the faith community.

We are being formed morally throughout our lives—through the persons, milieu, and events that affect us and through how we see ourselves in relation to others (that is, our moral life). This includes the formative effect of family and the wider community that forms who we are. As an African might put it, "I am because we are": only in and with the community can there be identity.[4] Educational, cultural, and political institutions play powerful roles in shaping us and our perspectives. We are pervasively and continuously being formed morally by social realities, both positively and negatively. As moral agents, we in turn affect or change these realities. What can become especially pivotal are personal experiences or crises as well as congregational events or conflict that dramatically differ from, challenge, and transform how we have been formed in the past. Much of what has formed people morally in past decades can no longer be taken for granted. Families and neighborhoods play less central roles in such formation than they used to, especially in the face of the powerful influences of the market and the media. The church's effect on moral formation in society also is much less than in the past. In the face of this declining influence, some search desperately for *moralistic* answers to the vacuum they feel, but in ways that tend to truncate or instrumentalize what the church is called to be about. This also can result in dangerously self-righteous postures. A more holistic sense of the church's role in moral formation is needed.

Practices of the Communio

In moral formation, the *practices* of being part of a communion are likely to be more influential than formal beliefs. Practices are those shared activities that address fundamental human needs and that, woven together, form a way of life. Christian practices are what Christians do together over time in response to and in light of God's active presence for the life of the world.[5] These include such practices as

- honoring our bodies as worthy of care
- hospitality in response to human need and exclusion
- managing our households for the sake of human well-being
- renouncing what chokes off the fullness of life God intends
- embracing the gift of sabbath keeping
- testimony that speaks truthfully for the edification of all
- discernment that places our decisions within the context of God's transforming activity
- shaping communities of justice for all
- forgiveness that seeks reconciliation
- dying in ways that are continuous with the rest of our lives.

Every Sunday in the wonderfully eclectic congregation to which I currently belong in Geneva, Switzerland, moral formation occurs in and through the liturgy of the whole people of God. Here are gathered people from every part of the globe, who bring their different pieties, practices, and beliefs, gathering weekly around the table, extending hospitality to the constant flow of strangers, shedding tears of grief and compassion with one another, singing songs in languages from many cultures, lifting up the particular sufferings and conflicts in the world, and together praying the Lord's Prayer in the many tongues of Pentecost.

Here God's *communio* is glimpsed and felt, the pulsating life of the Spirit as it flows in and through the people who are the body of Christ, the communion of saints, strangers and sojourners united across bounds of class, race, culture, and nationality. And through this communion, a community is being formed morally. What transpires here makes a difference in *who* we are and *how* and *what* we do during the rest of the week, giving such a deeper sense of meaning and purpose, setting it within God's wider eschatological purposes. "Eucharistic worship renders ecclesial and moral reality one."[6]

> [Liturgy] effects a transfiguration of our lives. It enacts the presence of the Holy Spirit in the church, the human world, and all creation, now understood as participating in the historic economy of the trinitarian life. It invites human beings to participate with Jesus Christ, who has already carried our humanity into the Godhead, in the divine dance. This participation gives us new eyes to see the world and new energy to bear witness to it. Liturgy is thus not something added to moral and political endeavor but its nourishing ground.[7]

This lofty understanding of the liturgy's role in moral formation must not overlook that the church and its liturgy have also led to *mal*formation into assumptions and practices that perpetuate injustice and oppression, such as through the use of patriarchal, androcentric language and imagery. Also, "devotion to the liturgy has sometimes lent itself to an irresponsible ghetto mentality." However, "by connecting the fundamental Christian story with the very presence of the mystery it re-enacts, the liturgy has the potential for overcoming the church's malformation and for transfiguring its view of the world and its capacity for action in the world."[8]

Communio and Ethics

The "Ecclesiology and Ethics" study (1992–96) of the World Council of Churches has been a particularly probing, significant exploration of this relationship between what the church *is* and what it *does*.[9] This study was based on the conviction that ethical reflection and action are intrinsic to the nature and life of the church. The church is a "moral community," that is, it necessarily wrestles, in light of the gospel, with issues of moral import. When we act, it is the church acting through us. Thus, ecclesiology and ethics must stay in close relationship. What a congregation does together on Sunday morning is intrinsically related to its life in its neighborhood and the wider world during the week.

A similar compelling basis for the close relatedness of ecclesiology and ethics is the *communio* self-understanding growing among the 133 member churches of the Lutheran World Federation (LWF). Since 1990, the LWF has defined itself not as a loose federation of churches but as "a communion of churches which confess the Triune God, agree in the proclamation of the Word of God and are united in pulpit and altar fellowship."[10] Through Word and sacraments, every local church is bound into the wider communion of churches. This wider communion—or eschatological *communio*—is called, gathered, and maintained through God's action as we know it through the triune God, the communion within God's self into which believers are brought.[11] *Communio* expresses the unity of the church across all time and space, the nature of life together in the local church, and the relationship between local churches in a regional and global context. The communion with God and one another, based on the Holy Spirit, is manifest and realized in a communion that can be experienced and seen.[12]

Understanding ourselves as part of such a *communio* has significant implications for Christian ethics. *Communio* points to close organic relationships and mutual participation in one another, in ways that defy and transform the usual boundaries that keep us separate and distant from one another. We are bonded together so that when one suffers, all suffer (1 Cor. 12:26). Mere diversity is transformed into a mutually supportive communion. The sharing of spiritual and material gifts, which is implicit in communion, cannot be isolated from examining the causes of inequities in wealth and joining with others in seeking change.[13]

Luther's own explication of the *communio sanctorum* opens up provocative possibilities for the ethical action. For Luther, *communio* refers not only to the gathering of the people of God (*ecclesia*) but also to the dynamic of participation in Christ and with one another. We are changed into one another; the communion is horizontal as well as vertical.

> The sacrament has no blessing and significance unless love grows daily and so changes a person that [s]he is made one with all others. . . . For just as the bread is made out of many grains ground and mixed together, and out of the bodies of many grains there comes the body of the bread . . . so it is and should be with us, if we use this sacrament properly. Christ with all saints, by his love, takes upon himself our form, fights with us against sin, death, and all evil. This enkindles in us such love that we take on his form . . . and through the interchange of his blessings and our misfortunes, we become one loaf, one bread, one body, one drink, and have all things in common. . . . That is real fellowship, and that is the true significance of this sacrament. In this way we are changed into one another and are made into a community by love.[14]

Through the activity of the Spirit, God indwells and empowers inter-subjectivity. The *communio* becomes an embodied sign of the interdependence of all of life. *Communio* is an indicative, not an imperative—a gift, not of our making. We are freed from being obsessed with "doing right," which can work against and destroy community. Yet we are also implicated in a calling or task—to live out this reality in our life together within and beyond the church.

Our ethical horizon and the basis and orientation for moral agency are expanded significantly by *communio*. Faith becomes active in love not only toward those close at hand who are "like us" but also toward those who are most distant and different from us.

Communio is lived out as those within the communion advocate for and act out of this sense of relatedness, responsibility, and accountability to others in the communion and, through them, to the rest of the created world.

Communio Deliberation amid Differences

The first social statement of the Evangelical Lutheran Church in America, "The Church in Society: A Lutheran Perspective," raises up the following commitments:

- Be a community where open, passionate, and respectful deliberation on challenging and controversial issues of contemporary society is expected and encouraged.
- Engage those of diverse perspectives, classes, genders, ages, races, and cultures in the deliberation process so that each of our limited horizons might be expanded and the witness of the body of Christ in the world enhanced.
- Address through deliberative processes the issues faced by the people of God, in order to equip them in their discipleship and citizenship in the world.
- Arrive at positions to guide its corporate witness through participatory processes of moral deliberation.
- Contribute toward the upbuilding of the common good and the revitalizing of public life through open and inclusive processes of deliberation.[15]

Such deliberation is crucial, among other reasons, because of how differently we have been formed. Yet, despite those differences, within the church we are held together by something/someone in common. We together are the body of Christ, formed in him into a New Creation. This ecclesial reality of which we are a part is what makes deliberation in the context of the church significantly different from a debate or an argument in which winning or defeating those with whom we differ is what matters. Here we are called to "put on the neighbor," that is, those different from us, not as abstractions but in all their particularities.

Such an ecclesial-grounded incarnate ethic calls us to pay attention to how people have been formed morally. It calls us to take into account the differences that gender, race, nationality, social location, class, and other factors related to power and access can make. Facing these differences is essential to developing more honest, mutually empowering relation-

> ✿ "Communio *is an indicative, not an imperative—a gift, not of our making.*"

ships between persons and groups. The conflict these differences can raise within and among us is not something to fear or avoid but has the potential to become transformative of unjust relationships. A congregation in the midst of a difficult decision may surface more opposing views than people assumed were present within the membership. But that very moment—as fearful as it may seem—may provide opportunity for genuine conversation, growth, and new, more healthy relationships.

Facing diversity within the church becomes an important aspect of the church's witness in society. Diversity becomes the matrix in which the gift of the catholicity of the church takes shape. This catholicity is appreciated not primarily through theological concepts but through shared life experiences across all that would divide us. The *character* of our communities and the power relationships within them become theologically and ethically significant.[16] Those who are "other" from us challenge us when we mistake our reason and experience as being universally the case for all people.

The discipline of ethics has often relied on universal moral theories. These tend to assume, inspired by Kant, that the pure rational agent can through reason reach an ethical answer for all times, places, and persons. From the standpoint of the generalized other, each individual is viewed as entitled to the same rights and duties we would ascribe to ourselves. What is significant is not what is different from us but what we share in common. Moral categories of rights, obligation, and entitlement and moral feelings of respect, duty, worthiness, and dignity are based on this premise.

In contrast, from the standpoint of the concrete other, each person is seen as having a particular history, identity, and range of emotions, much of which is rooted in community. We must try to understand the other and his or her needs, motives, and desires. Norms of equity and of reciprocity become key. Each is entitled to expect and assume from others responses through which each feels recognized and confirmed as concrete, incarnate persons with specific needs, talents, and capacities. Differences complement rather than exclude. Rather than the assertion of rights and duties, norms of friendship, love, responsibility, and solidarity prevail.

Recognizing the dignity and rights of the generalized other is necessary for there to be a moral viewpoint in society. We have to be able to generalize to some extent. But the concrete other reminds us there are limits to such universal discourse. We recognize the dignity of the generalized other through acknowledging the moral identity of the concrete other— how the other has been formed morally.

It is crucial, therefore, that there be a process of moral deliberation that takes these differences seriously. This will involve changes in how we make decisions about ethical and other matters. Instead of a quest for "impregnable" arguments that will attack others and win, "pregnant" positions are developed for fruitful conversations among different people that give birth to new possibilities, with welcoming postures that invite others in and creatively synthesize.[17] Through dialogical interaction, a kind of universality can begin to emerge, *through* rather than above the particularities.

Communio as a Counter to Economic Globalization

Communio may be key in moral formation and in how we deal with our differences through moral deliberation, but the real test is in whether it can provide a basis for acting in relation to central moral challenges of our day, such as those related to economic globalization.

Economic globalization, driven by institutions and practices of international finance and business and accelerated by new technologies, has become the defining reality in our world today. Under its sway, parts of the world are connected in ways previously unimaginable, even by the church, which has long prayed for the unity of the whole human family. Forces of globalization are bringing enormous benefits to some. However, this overlapping array of connections, when they intensify what are already unjust relationships of power and access, can also increase misery and suffering in much of the rest of the world. For those in a position to benefit, the very word "globalization" evokes the exuberance of unlimited possibilities. But for most people, it evokes fear, panic, and intensified feelings of powerless. It feels inevitable, like a reigning "god," as something that we just must go along with rather than seeking to respond to in light of our faith. Moral agency tends to become immobilized in the face of globalization's overwhelming power.

The effects of globalization and the ways in which different regions and populations can be set against one another pose significant challenges for us as a communion. As a church, we have important theological perspectives, ethical critiques, and ecclesial connections and action to bring to these challenges, especially through the relationships that have evolved, such as companion synod programs that link churches in the United States with those in other parts of the world.[18]

The moral task of holding processes of economic globalization more accountable to values other than highest possible profit suggests the need to mobilize the whole people of God in new ways, beginning with members of local congregations. When one part of the communion experiences negative effects of globalization, how might they hold accountable those in another part of the communion who in their daily lives have access to those responsible for decisions that generate these effects? For example, when people in India are displaced from their ancestral land by a large transnational company that wants to mine the valuable minerals there, the cries of those affected should be *heard* by church members in the United States who work for that company and who may be in a position to challenge such practices.

"Being ethical" in business acquires a much wider scope than is typically taught in business schools. How can members be challenged to think about their decisions and actions in relation to parts of the *communio* impoverished in Africa, in our cities, or on Native American reservations? How might church members who work for a large seed company in the Midwest think about how the profit-seeking policies of their company are affecting farmers in Africa who are dependent on those seeds? How might middle-class congregations learn how to minister among those who are poor from congregations in another part of the world where the majority are poor?

In other words, how might the relationships within the communion be deepened in ways that difficult questions are asked and actions taken in relationship with one another? The horizon, scope, and impact of our moral life expand significantly. When we live deeply out of what it means to be a communion—from its local to global dimensions—we begin to discover new possibilities for countering the negative effects of economic globalization, through our own embodied "globalization" as a communion in society.[19]

What begins to emerge is the possibility of linked discourses, and thus actions, that address the contradictions and failures of systems.[20] These discourses emerge out of particular cultural and personal situations but come together around a common moral concern, through which people begin to understand one another and to act in light of such. This is countersystemic, at times subversive, going against the grain of conventional wisdom. Through the power of the Spirit, there emerge a common recognition and basis for action. This is similar to what caught up and empowered those first followers of the One, whose life, death, and resurrection decisively countered the systems of his day and who calls us, his body, to continue in that same spirit in our day. Those whom forces such as economic globalization tend to pit against one another are brought together in the body of Christ—the whole body, the ministry of all the baptized in their daily lives. And we begin to discover connections that become the basis for effective actions where we least expect them!

PART THREE

The Church of God in Motion:
The Indispensability of Mission

Consideration of the church's voice in preaching and moral deliberation sets the stage for a more direct look at the church's mission in
the world. It dare not be static. Mission is always in motion, but such action—past, present, and future—is subject to varying interpretations. Debating beliefs is problematic enough. Trusting God to be at work in
mission in diverse, perhaps even seemingly contradictory ways, is risky.
But mission is indispensable to the act of being the church. In this part,
we begin with the challenge of one church body to become a church in
mission. Next, we shift our focus to view from a global perspective a
young church engaged in vibrant outreach. The center chapter sets forth
the basic components of mission. Finally, we consider two vital, specific
ways to set them in motion.

Craig Nessan begins with a case study of the Evangelical Lutheran
Church in America, showing how various traditions flowed together. Becoming a new church is hard work and perhaps more difficult than first
imagined. Building on the body of Christ image, he believes each of these
traditions needs to be seen as complementary to one another, each contributing to the whole. A church poised for mission will focus not on its
own structure but on the reign of God in the world. Bishops, pastors, diaconal ministers, and associates in ministry, each in unique ways, support
the ministry of all the baptized on behalf of God's reign.

We move from Nessan's chapter halfway around the world. David
Ramse tells the story of the Church of Nepal, a postdenominational
church. Ramse provides helpful material for any congregation seeking renewal. He begins in the hills of Nepal, in Bir Bahadur's village. We identify
with Bahadur as he encounters the church. Through his eyes, we see the
marks of community: identity, corporate worship, spoken and lived Word,
incarnational ministry, leadership training, and healing. Will established

churches facing difficulties be able to listen well enough to learn from a young church? Such learnings are indispensable.

H. S. Wilson sees the Christian church, even with its difficulties, as vibrant. He defines evangelism as the indispensable ministry of inviting persons to participate in the joys and demands of the discipleship of Jesus Christ. Mission means being active in the affairs of the world with a Christian perspective and zeal. Using the image of an oriental fan, he provides "blades" of mission, distinct but overlapping. When a fan is folded, one sees a limited view, but when it is open, one sees the breadth of the fan and feels the wave of air that is moved. The breadth of mission, open to the world, is broad on all levels: individual, communal, and societal.

Having been challenged by basic approaches to the church in mission, we move to two chapters that focus on issues that are particularly difficult challenges today: youth ministry and rural ministry. Paul Hill notes that every congregation is worried about its youth and wants someone to take care of the difficult "problem." He sees youth ministry as an evangelism and mission task. He challenges the congregation to see youth ministry as their indispensable task as a community. He therefore believes youth ministry is directly related to cross-generational renewal. Citing Luther, Hill both speaks a hard word and offers gracious hope.

L. Shannon Jung, in looking at twenty-six vital town and country congregational ministries, writes that extending the life of discipleship rests in developing a stronger and more profound relationship with God. Spiritual formation and hope are linked to giving ongoing attention to nurturing community. He finds that exciting. Jung provides "marks of vitality," which in many ways parallel those provided previously in James Bailey's chapter on 1 Thessalonians and David Ramse's description of the young church in Nepal. These elements provide hope and direction for congregations in any setting.

We Are the Body of Christ

Ecclesiology for a Church in Mission

CRAIG L. NESSAN

*Core in the church's identity is the indispensability of diversity
and the indispensability of mission. Mission is the church of
God in motion. As the church flows through history, peoples
move apart and traditions also flow together. What are the gifts
that various traditions bring to new church configurations,
whether they be church bodies or merging congregations? What
are the difficulties of establishing trust so that the church can
move forward?*

Becoming a new church is hard work. This is as true for national
church bodies as it is for mission congregations. How can a church
keep its momentum for mission when facing a host of organizational issues, especially establishing trust? This chapter focuses on the formation
of the Evangelical Lutheran Church in America (ELCA) as a case study
that examines the challenges facing a new church. The lessons to be
learned from the early years of the ELCA can assist church leaders in congregations and judicatories in every denomination to become wiser in
building a common ecclesiology that invigorates the mission of the
gospel.

One of the most difficult obstacles in becoming a new church with a
common focus on mission has been the lack of mutual trust. In its first
years of existence, the ELCA encountered many reasons for division: the
doctrine of ministry, representational principles (quotas), diaconal ministry, homosexuality, church growth strategies, contemporary worship
forms, ecumenism, and the place of the historic episcopate. Theological
arguments were presented on all sides of these debates. Tempers flared. In-
temperate words were uttered. Regional differences have been blamed. The
process of learning to live together in one church has been tumultuous.

Wherever one feels one's previous beliefs and traditions are not being honored, one becomes extremely defensive. When we believe it is necessary to defend from attack the identities that we have attained through our respective traditions, envisioning the future together becomes impossible.[1] God intends the ELCA to be an instrument in proclaiming the gospel and making manifest God's reign. How can we become a church open to God's possibilities for us in the future? How can we interpret the traditions of the past in a way that honors the differences each brings to our common life? Such questions prompt us to ask, on the local level, how we can honor the variety of traditions from which congregational members come. This issue becomes increasingly acute as we discover that congregations consist of people who grew up with very different religious backgrounds.

> ✿ *"When we believe it is necessary to defend from attack the identities that we have attained through our respective traditions, envisioning the future together becomes impossible."*

Paul imaged the church as the body of Christ, a metaphor with immense potential. Christ is the head of his body, the church, and the source of its identity and mission. The church is totally dependent on the saving work of Christ for its very existence. Without its head, the church loses its way. To be one church, Christ must be our guiding reality as we pray for one another, study together, and gather together for worship around the Lord's table.[2]

Paul's "body of Christ" metaphor in 1 Corinthians 12 has much to teach each Christian community—whether on the local, regional, or national level—about the gifts each member brings to the one body. "The eye cannot say to the hand, 'I have no need of you,' nor again the head to the feet, 'I have no need of you.' On the contrary, the members of the body that seem to be weaker are indispensable" (1 Cor. 12:21-22). What if the ELCA were to take Paul's body of Christ metaphor seriously as we reflect on the gifts each member brings to our common life as a church?

Frontier Origins

The various Lutheran traditions that flowed into the ELCA have been mightily shaped by the frontier context in which they first were planted on U.S. soil. Each group naturally sought to reestablish an experience of church according to the patterns familiar in its European homeland. This meant not only native language but also ethnic traditions of great specificity. Several Lutheran groups came to America seeking relief from persecution (for example, Missouri Synod, Buffalo Synod, Haugeans, and Austrian Lutherans). This led to necessary suspicion of state churches and the arbitrary exercise of power. Free church traditions sought to maintain a high level of autonomy.

The frontier situation contributed in many places to the development of a highly congregational polity. The relative scarcity of clergy meant stronger congregational structures. American democratic polity shaped congregational self-governance and independence. Church institutions—whether synods, seminaries, or social service agencies—formed in order to support and extend the ministry of congregations, more for pragmatic reasons than out of the desire for unity. All Lutheran groups affirmed their "confessional" commitment, although the interpretation of what that meant varied.

Only gradually did language differences and ethnic traditions give way to the common influence of Americanization and the recognition of how much Lutherans have in common with one another. The history of Lutheranism in America is primarily the story of separate ethnic streams flowing together into a common river. Conflict has become most intense when we have not sufficiently valued one another's family of origin. In the meantime, new members—not of European origin—have also entered the Lutheran church, calling into question the ethnic presuppositions and divisions of the past.

The Gifts Each Brings

The time has arrived for the ELCA as a church to affirm and claim the genuine gifts that different traditions have brought into it. Rather than viewing one another as problems to be solved or voting blocks to be outmaneuvered, what would it mean to our common life to see one another as members of the one body who have unique and needed gifts to contribute to the whole?

The following survey will be far too brief and subject to generalization. It indicates, however, an approach to difference that looks for complementarity rather than contradiction.[3]

From the Missouri Synod (through the Association of Evangelical Lutheran Churches), the ELCA has inherited many gifts: excellence in Christian education (through both day schools and parish educational programs), deep commitment to Lutheran doctrine, an ethos of Christian stewardship as a way of life, a functional view of pastoral ministry (that is, Walther's transference theory), and a tradition of service by deaconesses. Through the English District of the Missouri Synod came a sense of national church, strong liturgical traditions, a theology of "confessing," and a healthy suspicion of centralized authority.

The churches that composed the American Lutheran Church also brought many gifts to enhance our common life. The Danish Inner Mission and Hauge traditions contributed a profound understanding of the church as the ministry of all the baptized. This was accompanied by a focus on the importance of faith, piety, and regeneration among those who belong to Christ. One vital expression of the universal priesthood occurred through social service to those in need. The congregation served as the primary locus of authority. Worship practices were indigenous to a particular place. These traditions shared with Missouri a more functional view of the pastor.

The other partners in the American Lutheran Church, including the Iowa, Ohio, and Norwegian Synods, brought a strong tradition of biblical and theological study. Although cautious about the meaning of such membership, these groups chose to belong to the World Council of Churches. Those influenced by the Loehe tradition combined a profound commitment to mission (including global mission) with solid liturgical understanding. Particularly in controversies with the Missouri Synod, the Iowa Synod allowed for there to be "open questions," that is, that there need not be doctrinal agreement on every point in order to enter into church fellowship. This demonstrated the gift of tolerating a degree of difference. Congregations were the central locus for carrying out God's mission, centered on Word and Sacrament.

The traditions of the Lutheran Church in America (LCA) also offered precious gifts. Because of their strength on the East Coast, these churches brought a long and rich heritage of being Lutheran in America. English had become the common language for a long time, and ethnic heritages became less significant over time. Given the yielding of ethnic identities, liturgy has had great importance as a unifying factor.

Within the LCA, the United Lutheran Church brought together a broad spectrum of Lutheran synods. In its polity, the individual synod bore a large measure of authority over clergy, agencies, and programming. Both home and foreign missions took high priority. The involvement over time of these Lutheran churches with other Christian denominations led to a well-developed appreciation for the importance of ecumenism, with particularly strong connections with those in the Anglican tradition. This ecumenical outlook also meant ready participation in the World Council of Churches.

Among all the various Lutheran traditions, a unique gift derives from the Augustana tradition within the LCA: a long-standing appreciation for the catholic nature of the church. Theologians from Augustana have been at the forefront in articulating a more corporate understanding of what it means for congregations to be church together. Augustana long stood for the ideal of church unity, both among Lutherans and between denominations. Not incidental to this concern for ecclesiology, Augustana derives from the Swedish church that over the generations preserved the historic episcopate as a sign of the catholicity of the church.

One of the greatest challenges facing the various European traditions is the capacity to welcome and be changed by those joining from a great variety of not traditionally Lutheran backgrounds. African American, Asian, Hispanic, and Native American peoples of rich cultural diversity bring tremendous gifts to our life together—social activism, communal awareness, music, and care for the creation, among many others. As long as we continue to remain preoccupied by unresolved conflicts based on European ethnic identities, the capacity to embrace such gifts will be undermined. We must learn to live together in mutual affirmation of gifts within the one body of Christ in order to be prepared for the mission God seeks to accomplish through us.

Constructing a Common Ecclesiology

Based on the heritages that flow into the ELCA, how can we forge an ecclesiology that both honors these traditions and yet moves forward to the pressing issue of living as a church in mission? Whenever we begin to discuss the structure of the church, a hierarchical image soon comes to mind. This image is in the shape of a triangle, with bishops and clergy on top and the laity at the bottom. According to the Lutheran theology of the universal priesthood of all believers, however, such an image of the church is a distortion of what we confess. In contrast to this hierarchical model, let us employ another image to depict the church.[4] (See diagram.) Within the church, members have gifts that differ. But all of these gifts are ultimately for the service of God's reign in the world.

Being church is finally *not* the point. So often we confuse the means with the end. This is most acutely true when we start to believe that God's will has to do with people becoming members of the church. In fact the very word *member* can easily lead us astray. God does not want church members if this is analogous to belonging to a club by attending meetings and paying dues. The great commission sends us instead to "make disciples" (Matt. 28:19). Through baptism, Jesus aimed to build up a community of disciples, those who were taught "all that I have commanded you" (Matt. 28:20).

The real point, the ultimate and eschatological point, is the reign of God. Jesus came proclaiming and bringing the kingdom of God. The kingdom means repentance, turning away from the way of sin and death.

Those who have hardened hearts must be softened up through condemning words of judgment. The kingdom means life, God's life, life in restored relationships that build up and do not tear down God's creation.

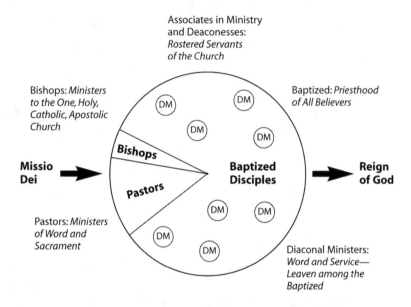

FIGURE 1: The church: the body of Christ in service of God's mission

Jesus used many stories and metaphors to inculcate the way of the kingdom. It arrives by God's power. It is priceless. Those who discover the kingdom make it their highest priority. The kingdom brings God near, breaking into the present to transform experience. God's intervention is merciful. God comes to our aid like a merciful parent or a generous neighbor. Those who have received the generous grace of God's kingdom are sent to go and be gracious to others.

Jesus not only taught about the kingdom but instantiated the kingdom in his own person. Jesus healed the sick, even touching lepers. He cast out demons from those possessed. Jesus fed hungry multitudes. He welcomed all kinds of people into his company: children, women, foreigners, outcasts, even those denounced as public sinners. Jesus forged a scandalous table fellowship. Jesus dared to declare sins forgiven. On the cross, his death became the sign of a new covenant. When God raised this Jesus from the dead, God affirmed Jesus' identity and mission, verifying that the kingdom Jesus brought revealed God's will.

Jesus taught his disciples to pray "Your kingdom come." The church of Jesus Christ continues to have as its authorized mission the furthering of the kingdom of God. This is the aim of Christ's work and the creation's ultimate destiny: the subjection of all things to God's reign (1 Cor. 15:27-28). The church serves as God's agent in the world in faithfulness to the mission of God's kingdom. The church prays and worships in order to be formed as people of the kingdom, and then moves into the world as leaven of that kingdom. Being the church is not the point. The kingdom of God is the point!

The baptized are the priesthood of believers who live at the interface between the kingdom of God and the fallen world. In their homes and at their jobs, on the streets and at the market, the baptized are the ones God sends into the world for the purpose of witnessing to God's living reign. If the church is to be God's church, *its primary focus must be on the mission of the baptized in the world.* This means ministry in daily life, evangelism, and social ministry. Membership must entail formation for discipleship. One of the greatest failures of the church over the generations has been the fostering of the dependency of the laity upon the institutional church and its clergy. Renewal of the church today involves the baptized claiming their identity as Jesus' disciples in all that they do. Among the baptized, the ELCA recognizes associates in ministry and deaconesses as having particular charisms of service within the life of the church. In affirmation of these gifts, these baptized persons are rostered for a rich diversity of forms of service on behalf of the church. Also among the baptized are those who have particular gifts to serve as diaconal ministers, ordained ministers of Word and Sacrament, and bishops.[5] The church fills these positions by affirming the charisms of those who offer themselves for these forms of service.

In this model of the church, *the insistence is on service.* Becoming clergy is not the point. The point is the kingdom of God. Those holding office in the church are to be held accountable as the "servants of the servants of God."[6] The primary orientation of each of the offices in the church is toward the service of equipping the baptized as agents of God's kingdom in the world.

Diaconal ministers serve as ministers of Word and service, demonstrating by their own service the movement between church and world on behalf of God's kingdom. As they carry out their own unique ministries, diaconal ministers also prepare and accompany the baptized in their daily service to God's kingdom. Diaconal ministers are leaven among the baptized, reminding the church that finally it is God's kingdom that is at hand and nothing else. While diaconal ministers celebrate diverse specialties of service—teaching, healing, art, music, and so forth—each of these gifts finds proper expression by empowering the baptized themselves into service.

The office of Word and Sacrament is a unique and necessary service within the church. Those who exercise this office are called to serve based on a charisma for preaching the gospel and administering the sacraments, leading the gathered congregation at worship.[7] If there is an identity crisis today among ordained pastors, it may be because we have forgotten the fullness of what it means to preside over Word and Sacrament. At worship, the congregation gathers to enact the kingdom of God.[8] The pastor is the leader in preparing for this assembly, working in concert with others to shape rituals that feed the hungry imagination.

Many other tasks compete for the pastor's attention, but the office itself is defined by commitment to the things of worship, preaching God's word, and overseeing sacramental ministry. Direct extensions of the office of Word and Sacrament involve teaching and pastoral care. Some priorities must fall by the wayside, however, if the pastor is to remain focused on that which is crucial. Pastors offer their unique form of leadership by proclaiming the gospel of forgiveness and grace in order that the Spirit of God has means by which to set the baptized free for service to God's kingdom in the world. Like diaconal ministers, pastors live as disciples themselves, serving the kingdom in daily life. But their unique gift is proclamation through Word and Sacrament that aims at setting free the baptized for their own service of the kingdom in the world.

The office of bishop supports all of the others in ministry. As thoughts turn to consider the unique contribution of bishops to the body of Christ, it is important to stress from the outset that *this is an office of service to the baptized, diaconal ministers, and the ordained in order that God's kingdom might be served in the world*. Of all traditions, Lutherans need to be properly wary of the possible abuse of power by bishops. A Lutheran church true to its heritage will provide constitutional safeguards that establish checks and balances on the exercise of power by bishops.

At the same time, it simply is not sufficient to define the office of bishop with reference to the one office of Word and Sacrament.[9] While bishops rightly are ordained ministers of Word and Sacrament, the election to the office of bishop needs to be seen as the church's affirmation that these persons have a unique gift and calling among the baptized. These are the ministers entrusted with special oversight and responsibility that the church be and remain one, holy, catholic, and apostolic.

Since the time of the New Testament, bishops (together with creeds and a biblical canon) have been signs of the *unity* and *catholicity* of the church. The office of the bishop represents the whole church, just as the person of the ordained pastor represents a congregation and the person of the baptized represents Christ. Special responsibility belongs to bishops to oversee the church's ecumenical and global responsibilities, those aspects that foster unity and catholicity. Furthermore, bishops are entrusted with the task of ministering to the unity of the church when congregations face deeply divisive conflict. This does not mean that all the baptized, diaconal, and ordained ministers do not have interest in such matters. It does mean that the whole church looks to bishops for leadership in resolving conflict. By virtue of the office, the bishop is a sign of the one catholic church.

Similarly, bishops have special responsibility to care for the *holiness* and *apostolicity* of the church. Clearly, Christ is the one who made the church holy by his death on the cross. But to the bishop is entrusted the oversight of those who serve as ordained pastors, those in congregations who proclaim the justifying and sanctifying gospel. The bishop finally is called upon on behalf of the church to decide if the gospel is being rightly proclaimed, the sacraments rightly administered, and the teaching kept faithful to the apostolic testimony of the Holy Scriptures. This entails stewardship over the candidacy process, the consecration of diaconal ministers, the ordination of pastors, and the administration of the call process.

Lest bishops abuse the authority of the office, each of these responsibilities needs careful constitutional definition and control. It is inadequate, however, to see the service of bishop only as an extension of the work of other ordained pastors. While ordination is a prerequisite, the bishop's calling is unique in its ministry of oversight and attention to the church's character as one, holy, catholic, and apostolic. This understanding of the bishop's work gives clearer definition to the task and should give clearer direction to the church as it discerns the gifts of those who would become its bishops.

For the Sake of Mission

The members of Christ's body need one another's gifts. Congregations can fulfill their mission only by engaging the diverse gifts of their many members. This is also true of the various gifts brought by the different Lutheran church bodies becoming the ELCA. All of the Lutheran predecessor churches shared the focus on mission as the overarching goal. While it is easy to talk about the importance of mission, too often we find ourselves entrenched in machinations that betray our self-interest in maintaining the status quo. If we are to become a church that is for mission, all of the parts must be working properly, promoting "the body's growth in building itself up in love" (Eph. 4:16).

Mission fosters God's reign. Drawing on the free-church traditions, furthering the ministry of the baptized is the primary way in which the church works in the world. The baptized live as Jesus' disciples in society to announce and follow the way of the kingdom. If the church is to reclaim its missionary purpose in a post-Christian age, the baptized will need to reclaim their identity through intentional discipleship. This will mean laity engaged in study and supported by fellowship for the sake of witnessing to the gospel in daily life. Diaconal ministers offer service in equipping the baptized for their calling. Associates in ministry and deaconesses offer their particular gifts that further the church's mission.

True to the Lutheran confessions, the proposed ecclesial structure revolves around the proclamation of the gospel and administration of sacraments in congregations. The assembly of the baptized for worship is crucial for the establishment and nurturing of the church's identity in Christ. At worship, the baptized hear and receive the gospel *pro nobis*. Worship ministers to the heart and feeds the hungry imagination with the good news of the kingdom. This gospel frees the baptized from fear and self-preoccupation for loving their neighbors. The calling of ordained pastors is primarily to care for the Word and sacraments through preaching, teaching, and worship. Pastoral care extends the ministry of the Word to individuals and families. Where salvation happens, energy is released to extend the influence of God's reign.

The charism of a bishop entails concern for the ecclesial character of the whole church. No other office bears responsibility for oversight of the whole body. In particular, the office of bishop is entrusted with the ministry of caring that the church be one, holy, catholic, and apostolic. At the same time as we consider the shape of a reformed episcopate, it is important to stress that the office of bishop be subject to clear constitutional controls. Only so do we honor the experience of those who have learned healthy suspicion of the abuse of power by bishops.

Based on the mutual affirmation of gifts, a church body with this understanding of its inherited traditions would be ready to move forward into the future in service to God's mission of bringing forth the kingdom. Such a church would be ready to embrace newcomers to its tradition as fellow members of the body of Christ whose gifts are to be celebrated. By virtue of its orientation toward the ministry of the baptized, such a church would be ready to promote the service of congregational members in their local settings. There can be no trust within the church without honoring the gifts inherited from the past. Yet there can be no openness to God's future without shaping a common life explicitly for mission.

13

The Church as Organism

Characteristics of a Young Church

DAVID A. RAMSE

Can diverse churches learn from one another? What can large, long-established churches learn from young, vibrant ones? A church that crosses caste or race or class lines gives a clear, positive witness to the nature of Christian community. If one were participating in the beginning of a brand-new church, what would be the essential marks of the Christian community? What would the person who has never known of Christ see and hear?

Come to the Far East, to the mountain Kingdom of Nepal, where there is a growing, young, vibrant church. Listen, ask questions, and draw lessons from the characteristics of the church in Nepal, translating them into your own context. But first, a story.

Bir Bahadur's Story

Bir Bahadur was a farmer in the hills of Nepal. His village was within a day's walking distance from the border with Tibet. Eking out a living from subsistence farming in the rugged terrain was not easy for him and his expanding family. One day, a former neighbor of his who had gone to the capital city, Kathmandu, some months before, came back to the village to visit his aging parents. He brought his parents money he had earned in the city. Bir Bahadur was impressed with the watch that his neighbor was wearing on his wrist. Why was he, Bir Bahadur, working so hard and barely keeping his family alive? Why couldn't he also go to Kathmandu and become wealthy?

It was not long before Bir Bahadur left his family in the village and walked three days to the nearest road, where he caught a bus into Kathmandu. Immediately, he searched for a job. Days later, having been told time after time "No work available," he found a job weaving carpets. He would be paid per carpet completed. Bir Bahadur had never done this kind of work before. There were instructions on the wall, but Bir Bahadur could not read. Many times he became discouraged and wanted to return to his village, but it would be shameful to return with less than with what he had left!

One day, one of the other carpet weavers told Bir Bahadur about a person called Jesus, someone whom the creator God sent into the world because God loved it so much. Imagine, a god who loved people! Bir Bahadur was interested to know more about this god. Thus, Bir Bahadur was invited to visit Immanuel congregation, where a group of about 200 *beswasi* (believers) were gathered.

Worship began with singing. Everyone was sitting on the floor on straw mats, the women on the left and the men on the right, with children wandering on both sides. Some people sang from books; others seemed to have memorized the songs. A person in front began to speak to God as though God was in the room. He spoke of repentance, asked God for forgiveness, and concluded by using the name of Jesus. Then, those assembled stood up. The person in the front began to read from a book he called a Bible and then went on for the next hour to explain what it meant. But to Bir Bahadur's ears, this was good news. Why had he never heard about this loving God before?

After explanation of the Bible text, a bag was passed around and people put money into the bag—mostly coins but also some notes. He noticed a woman across from him took a small gold ring from her ear and put it in the bag. Bir Bahadur had nothing to put into the bag. After talking to God again, mostly giving thanks, the worship was concluded with an announcement that the "baptized" were invited to "the Lord's Supper" after the nonbaptized and those in need of ministry had moved out of the worship area.

Bir Bahadur noticed that a number of people stayed seated on the straw mats. People around them came and spoke to them. Some prayed with them; others put their hands on the heads of those seated. Then Bir Bahadur, not being baptized, slipped out along with the majority of those assembled. He was curious, watching from a side window for a while, and noticed that about one-third of those who had been assembled for the corporate worship had stayed behind for the Lord's Supper. It seemed to him a very solemn ceremony and rather private, so Bir Bahadur left reflecting on what he had heard and seen.

Bir Bahadur could not stay away from Christian worship. His friend at the carpet factory also continued to witness to him about the person called Jesus. Not many weeks later, Bir Bahadur asked Jesus to become the Lord of his life. What a transformation! Now he, Bir Bahadur, could not keep from telling others at the carpet factory about the love of God through Jesus Christ that he had experienced. He wanted to tell his family and his villagers about this new life and the joy he was experiencing. By this time, Bir Bahadur was working about eighteen hours a day at the carpet factory and had been able to save a little bit of money. He returned to his village to bring his immediate family back with him to Kathmandu. However, while in the village, he shared the changes in his life with many of his friends and neighbors. Some listened and wanted to hear more. Others became hostile to Bir Bahadur.

Returning to Kathmandu, Bir Bahadur and his family became active in the life of Immanuel congregation. People observed that Bir Bahadur was good with children, having quite a few of his own. The elders had been concerned for some time about the need for Christian education for the children, the second generation of the congregation. There were a growing number of young people, children similar to Bir Bahadur's own. Yes, Bir Bahadur wanted to teach the young people. However, he was illiterate. Immanuel congregation had recently begun a literacy class for anyone who wanted to be able to read the Bible. Bir Bahadur joined the class and in the meantime began to teach the children, outside under a tree.

A few months later Bir Bahadur sensed a call to return to his home village and share the good news. With some help from Immanuel congregation, Bir Bahadur and his family were commissioned and soon departed to begin a church in his home area. About two years later, Bir Bahadur came to Kathmandu to participate in a short leadership-training course. He visited Immanuel congregation and reported, "There are now three active congregations in my village area."

The Church in Nepal

Squeezed between two giants, India and China, the Kingdom of Nepal has declared itself a "zone of peace." In 1990, after a bloody struggle, it became a multiparty democracy. As the only Hindu kingdom in the world, the country stipulates in its constitution one-year imprisonment for anyone leaving the religion of one's birth and six-year imprisonment for causing others to leave the religion of their birth.

In spite of, or perhaps because of, this religious persecution, the church of Jesus Christ is growing exponentially. In the early 1950s, there were no known Christians in Nepal. In 1959, the Nepal Christian Fellowship was formed, composed of thirty Christians from all over the country. Some members walked fifteen days to come to its meetings for fellowship.[1] The Christian movement grew tenfold in the seven years between 1990 and 1997, from fifty thousand to approximately five hundred thousand.[2] Bir Bahadur's story is typical in Nepal today.

What gives this church vitality? Twelve characteristics mark the church in Nepal: identity, corporate worship, spoken word, lived word, prayer and signs, incarnational ministry, leadership and leadership training, lifestyle, indigenization, witness, persecution, and unity.

Identity

. . . the disciples were first called "Christians." (Acts 11:26)

Christians in Nepal do not identify themselves as "Christians." Neither do they go to "church." They refer to themselves as "believers" (*beswasi*), and the place they go for worship is "fellowship" (*sangati*). Therefore, one may hear Nepali people saying, "I am a believer [in Christ is implied] on my way to fellowship." In the Nepali language, the words "Christian" and "church" do not exist.

The Nepali church identifies very closely with the New Testament apostolic church. Personal lifestyle and worship are patterned after the Acts of the Apostles as well as after other New Testament writings.[3] Knowing and naming corporate Christian identity is important for any congregation.

Corporate Worship

They devoted themselves to the apostles' teaching and fellow-ship, to the breaking of bread and the prayers.
(Acts 2:42)

Sunday is the beginning of the Nepali workweek. Therefore, congregations worship corporately on Saturday, when offices, schools, and many businesses are closed. Some, like Immanuel, meet in rented halls, where hundreds of people gather together. Larger congregations have more than one gathering on a given Saturday. Smaller congregations meet in homes. It is often difficult to find someone who can read the Scriptures. However, many Christians own a Bible, even if they are unable to read its contents.

Corporate worship normally continues for a minimum of two hours. The text for the day may be from the Old or New Testament but quite often is from one of the New Testament epistles. The corporate worship setting is not used as an opportunity for evangelistic outreach; people evangelize mainly through daily personal witness and friendship. During worship, people sit cross-legged on mats or carpets on the floor (there are no chairs or pews), and as others keep coming, those gathered will merely sit closer

> ✿ *"Knowing and naming corporate Christian identity is important for any congregation."*

together. Even within a larger worship building, furniture is sparse, but the leader does use a pulpit to preach and teach.[4]

The eucharist is celebrated about once per month. Ordination is not required for administering the sacrament; rather, the bread and wine are silently passed from one communicant to another. The wine, which is in a small cup containing a small spoon, is dripped into the mouth without the communicant making contact with the spoon.

Musical instruments may include guitars; however, rhythm mainly comes from traditional drums and clapping of hands. People pray aloud, mostly in the Nepali language but some in their tribal languages. The Nepali church leaders will be quick to inform a visitor that they are not "speaking in tongues," as this requires interpretation.

People also worship throughout the week in "house fellowship" groups, where substantial mutual ministry takes place. Normally, there are no distinctions made; however, some groups are divided based on tribal language, gender, or age.

Nepali Christians enjoy eating together. Occasionally, an all-day "love feast" is organized, in which the entire congregation and "daughter" congregations are involved. People pool resources and purchase supplies, including live chickens and goats. The believers—including entire families, all castes, ages, and both genders—gather usually before daylight and spend the majority of the day preparing the food together. Later, while the food is cooking, the people worship. Only after everything is cleaned up, usually after the fall of darkness, do all return to their homes.

Spoken Word

. . . proclaimed the good news . . . (Acts 8:40)

Nepal continues to be mostly an oral society. However, as increasing numbers become literate, the written word becomes more important. The Nepal Bible Society has translated Scripture into the Nepali language. The Christian Arts Association of Nepal encourages Nepali Christians to use the arts, including writing. A considerable amount of Christian written material is now available in the vernacular.

Corporate worship centers on the Word, as do the house fellowships. People study in small groups and encourage one another to personally read the Bible as well. The Bibles of literate Nepalis are well marked up and worn. During the sermon time in a corporate worship setting, most literate Nepalis have pen and paper in hand, with their open Bibles on the floor in front of them, if space permits, taking notes on what is being said and marking references in their own Bibles. They take the Bible as God's Word to them very seriously.

Lived Word

She was devoted to good works and acts of charity.
(Acts 9:36)

The Nepali church understands "holistic ministry" as care and concern for all people—body, mind, and spirit. In the process of becoming followers of Jesus, many Christians have been ostracized from their families. Often, congregations become "surrogate parents" in such ways as helping to arrange marriages or caring for the sick. Many congregations offer literacy training to adults as well as education to the young who cannot afford to go to school. With high unemployment in the country, a number of congregations provide skill training or cottage industry activities. National Churches Fellowship, the umbrella organization that represents the independent churches in Nepal, operates an integrated community development project that includes such programs as preventive disease medicine, literacy classes, village drinking water systems, and resource conservation activities. All people in a community, Christian and non-Christian, benefit from these services.

Prayer and Signs

. . . many wonders and signs were being done . . .
(Acts 2:43)

The "spirit world" is very real to Nepali people. In ministering to individuals who may be suffering, it is often not known whether the problem is mental, physical, or spiritual. Nepali Christians do know, however, that God answers prayer. Often, with prayer comes wholeness. Exorcisms in the name of Jesus do occur; however, this is viewed as the work of God and as all within the scriptural boundaries of ministry. Many Nepalis have become Christians through healing, with prayer for themselves, their families, and also their animals. Healing ministries are central for life in community.

Incarnational Ministry

There was not a needy person among them . . .
(Acts 4:34)

Believers offer mutual ministry in many settings. At the conclusion of a worship service, those desiring ministry remain seated on the floor. The elders, deacons, or fellow believers approach those seated and minister according to their needs, whether spiritual, physical, or economic. Nothing is outside the boundaries of consideration. Committees are not necessary because Christians minister as the need arises.

Perhaps the most personal and effective mutual ministry occurs in the small house fellowship groups. The members of a house fellowship group get to know one another well, are seen as extended family, and minister in informed ways.

Ministry within the fellowship also leads to outreach and care of those outside the body of Christ. Christians are known as caring people. For example, patients know they will receive quality care at the Christian hospital in Kathmandu. The Christian Professional Fellowship of Nepal coordinates blood drives.

Individual Christians live their faith through incarnational ministry. For example, Shanti, a Christian leader, saw that the brothels of Bombay, India, were discarding prostitutes who had contracted AIDS. Many of these prostitutes were Nepalis who had been kidnapped or sold into prostitution at a young age. Some had returned to their villages only to find they were not welcome. Shanti opened her home in Kathmandu and now provides skills training for those who can work and a place to die for those who succumb to the disease.

Leadership and Leadership Training

. . . called together the local leaders . . . (Acts 28:17)

The ordained clergy, the unordained clergy, and the laity serve as leaders in the church. A growing number of the ordained clergy have earned doctorates from institutions outside of Nepal; others have the equivalent of master's or bachelor's degrees in theology. Pastors equip the saints, training congregational leaders, both men and women, for mutual ministry.

The pastor may preach once or twice a month in the larger congregations; otherwise, a roster of laypersons who are literate and well versed in Scripture preach. The pastor, lay or ordained, will most often officiate at baptisms, weddings, and funerals. Servanthood is the key for both ordained and lay leadership roles.

With the rapid expansion of the church in Nepal, there is great need for leadership training in the country. Prior to the democracy movement of 1990, there were only a couple of clandestine seminaries in the country. Presently, there are more than twenty institutions, including short-term discipleship training courses, longer-term Bible colleges, and seminaries offering bachelor's degrees in theology.

Yet leaders of many churches scattered throughout the country remain illiterate. One leader came from a remote village to Kathmandu and pleaded with the Christians there, "Please send someone to our village who can read God's word to us. We heard the good news on the radio. Many of us believe in the God, but we cannot read for ourselves." Leadership training ranges from literacy training, using the Bible as a text, to advanced theological education. Equipping leaders is crucial in a growing church.

Lifestyle

You yourselves know how I lived among you . . .
(Acts 20:18)

Christians are "different," become casteless, and have a thankful spirit.

BEING DIFFERENT. Christians are viewed as "different" in their culture. Determining whether a practice is religious or cultural is not easy because Hinduism and Nepali culture blend together. For example, the weeklong *Dashain* festival is a time when extended families come together and partake in Hindu rituals. Christians find this to be a difficult time; therefore, many of the churches schedule special events during those festivals. Some churches are examining Christian practices as well. For example, they consider the questions, "Why do we celebrate the birth of Jesus in December when the festival of lights, *Tihar*, occurs in November? Since Jesus is the light of the world, could not Jesus' birth be celebrated at *Tihar*?"

LOSS OF CASTE. When one becomes a Christian, caste barriers no longer exist. Food and drink, along with its preparation, can be shared together from the lowest to the highest caste. People with social diseases such as leprosy are welcomed into the fellowship of believers as equals.

Many of the leaders in the church are from the priestly Brahmin caste because they had more opportunities for education and because of their traditional role as religious leaders. However, it is also common to see lower caste leadership, with Brahmins, within the fellowship. A community that crosses caste or class lines gives a clear witness about the nature of Christian community.

THANKFULNESS. Nepali Christians are characterized by their thankfulness. Only in the most recent years has the word *danyabadh* (thank you) come into common usage. Within the Hindu context, receiving a kind deed is not something for which one gives thanks, because it was for the doer's own *dharma* (religious merit) that the kind deed was done. Christians are known as thankful people.

Indigenization

. . . select from among yourselves . . . whom we may appoint . . . (Acts 6:3)

The church of Nepal, by and large, is a self-conceiving, self-supporting, self-governing, and self-propagating church. Although Nepal shares a common border with India, the histories of the church in India and of the church in Nepal are in stark contrast. The church in India grew to a great extent through missionary activity that came in with colonialism. Nepal, by contrast, was never colonized, and the church was never initiated, supported, or governed by nonindigenous mission agencies.[5] The church in Nepal is truly apostolic, a product of the Holy Spirit.

SELF-CONCEIVING. Rather than through Western missionaries, the gospel of Jesus Christ became known in Nepal through Nepali-speaking Indians in West Bengal, through shortwave radio broadcasts and printed literature, and through Nepalis studying or working abroad. Ironically, many villages first heard the gospel through the Gorkhas, the Nepali mercenaries for the British military who had been stationed around the world and then returned to their home villages.

SELF-SUPPORTING. Because of recent relaxation in enforcing the law regarding proselytism, some funding for the church in Nepal is now coming from foreign sources. However, most churches find their own means of support from within the congregation. A more mature, larger congregation helps newer, smaller congregations until they can become self-supporting. Often, the leadership of a congregation is employed outside the church and requires no salary, and worship is held in homes requiring no rent. Larger congregations often do provide salary for a full-time pastoral leader and do pay rent.[6] Tithing is taught, but it is not uncommon for people to give an offering in kind rather than cash.

SELF-GOVERNING. Most local churches are responsible for their own leadership, administration, and funding. Very few churches have written guidelines. Funding from an overseas partner church can lead to erosion of self-governance and the divisiveness of denominationalism. Most Nepali churches recognize the dangers that come from lack of self-governance and are willing to work with less to avoid the loss of independence.

SELF-PROPAGATING. The Nepali church grows through division. These divisions may be planned and positive, or they may be unplanned due to strife and power struggles. Personal evangelism is the key ingredient to the church's growth.

Witness

. . . you will be my witnesses . . . to the ends of the earth.
(Acts 1:8)

Witness takes place through presence, service, dialogue, and evangelism. The church in Nepal is a sending church. Nepali Christians cannot keep silent about their faith! They must share, and this often is on a one-to-one personal basis, whether in a tea shop, with their family or friends, or in the workplace. It's a given, an understood part of their life, that as a friend, they will want to share the gospel with others.

A number of indigenous ministries to minorities have sprung up in recent years within Nepal. For example, Nava Raj became a follower of Christ. He became paralyzed, was healed, and now has a ministry in one of the most remote areas of Nepal. Because Nepal is a labor-exporting country, there are Nepalis many places around the world. Nepali congregations exist even in the Middle East.[7] Nepali Christians engage in global outreach.

Persecution

. . . persecution began against the church . . . (Acts 8:1)

The Nepali church continues to be a persecuted church. In addition to the possibility of prosecution under Nepali law, there is also persecution by fellow Nepalis and family members. Nepal is the headquarters for the World Hindu Federation.

For many weeks, a small house-church in the hills of Nepal secretly had been moving from one home to another for fellowship and worship. One morning, the local police were tipped off to the meeting place; the assembled were taken to the district police station for interrogation and imprisonment.

Nepal in its attempt to promote tourism is very conscious of its image to promote freedom and human rights. Over recent years, persecution has decreased, allowing more cults and sects to enter Nepal. A number of Nepali Christian leaders see the dangers associated with more freedom and have suggested that persecution is good for the church. In reading the New Testament scriptures, many feel that persecution should be expected as a normal part of the Christian life.

Unity

> . . . *those who believed were of one heart and soul . . .*
> (Acts 4:32)

Opposition is not viewed as a barrier to church growth. Rather, it can promote unity within the body of Christ. All Nepali churches use a common hymnbook; the majority of songs are local lyrics and tunes. The production of Christian education materials, for the most part, is a joint effort of the local churches. Annually, thousands of Christians from the churches in the capital city march together on Easter morning. Being one Christian community and living faithfully witness powerfully to the culture.

Conclusion

What are the implications for the "mature" church? Can a mature church in the West learn from an "infant" church in the East? How can a congregation remain vital? How can growth occur?[8] Our contexts are different from the Nepali church, yet the church of Jesus Christ is one, allowing God's people to be united yet different. The Nepali church teaches us to live the Word with our total being in our confession, our witness, and our actions, taking God seriously into holistic ministry in our life together and in the lives of others.

Mission as an Oriental Fan

A Plea for Missionhood of All Believers

H. S. WILSON

Is not evangelism the indispensable ministry of inviting people to participate in the joys and demands of being Christ's disciples? Is not mission the indispensable action of Christians in the world? Global leaders are taking note of the creative influences of religious communities in their societies. How can congregations equip people to be engaged in mission at the personal, communal, and societal levels?

The Christian community, two thousand years old, world over is still vibrant and accounts for about 28 percent of the world's population. This can be considered a success story (Christianity as the world's single largest religion) or a somber achievement of two millennia's missionary effort (Christianity as a minority among all world religions combined). According to World Vision, the Christian population may drop to 27.1 percent in 2010 because of the lower birthrate among Christians as compared to people of other living faiths.[1] Predictions will not diminish the importance of the mission, because it belongs to the very nature of the church; however, this calls for a review of existing mission theologies and practices. Christians, therefore, naturally will try to discern the will of God. In such discernment, it is important that they are both familiar with the historical developments within their community and open to the leading of the Spirit of God. For Christians, in the local congregation, churchwide, and globally, discerning the will of God and participating in it are a mission and evangelism engagement.

Through the centuries, Christians and their churches have formulated many definitions of evangelism and mission. I define evangelism as the indispensable ministry of *inviting* persons to participate in the joys and demands of the discipleship of Jesus Christ and mission as being *active* in the affairs of the world from a Christian perspective and zeal. Mission and evangelism are not coercive activities; rather, they are the gracious invitation to participate in the new humanity that God intends for all of humankind. That invitation demands a commitment to an active discipleship of Jesus Christ, oriented to a relationship with God and simultaneously oriented toward the affairs of the world and God's whole creation.

The mission in which Christians are involved is not their own. Rather, they are called to be involved in the mission of God—*missio Dei*. To engage in such a mission, two things are important. One is the affirmation that the whole of creation belongs to God and that God is still actively involved in the affairs of the world. In spite of a lot of bad news we read in the newspaper or on the Internet or see on television, evil has not entirely taken over the world. God's grace still dominates, even though

> *"Mission and evangelism are not coercive activities; rather, they are the gracious invitation to participate in the new humanity that God intends for all of humankind."*

it is not apparent in all circumstances. In the psalmist's words, "The earth is the Lord's and all that is in it" (Ps. 24:1). Second is the affirmation of the sacredness of human life and the celebration of all life found in creation. Life is a gift from God. In spite of the fallenness of human beings, the image of God in which they are created is not destroyed. Christian faith is about the redemption God offers to the fallen humanity. Without these affirmations, the mission—even a project that is very exciting—ceases to be the mission of God.

What is the goal of the mission of God? It is the establishment of the reign of God. To use the ecumenical formulation: justice, peace, and integrity of creation as God intends for the whole of the created order. Biblical foundations include Isaiah's vision of a new creation ("For I am about to create new heavens and a new earth");[2] the Nazarean manifesto of Jesus ("The Spirit of the Lord is upon me, because he has anointed me to bring the good news to the poor");[3] and the Johannine vision of the future ("Then I saw a new heaven and a new earth").[4] The reign of God is one of the dominant images in the New Testament.[5] Jesus through his life and ministry inaugurated this reign of God and promised its further unfolding through the work of the Holy Spirit to be carried out through the ministry of his disciples. Through individual redemption, salvation, transformation, and societal changes, the reign of God has made inroads into human history. While the New Testament strongly affirms the role of Christians, in the final analysis it is the mission of God in which humans are called to participate.

Mission as an Oriental Fan

To encourage the contribution of every Christian, one has to continuously strive to see the breadth of God's mission in its fullest extent possible. Keeping that as a goal, I have selected the image of an oriental fan. A fan has a possibility of hiding as well as unfolding. When folded, a fan gives a narrower perspective of its nature, but when it is opened completely, it exhibits its fullness and strength. In the same way, one can perceive mission in a narrow way, folded into a bundle of untested biases, preconceived notions, borrowed views, and paternalistic attitudes, or one can be courageous enough to venture into questioning, open to experience, ready to engage in dialogue, to see in fullness.

An oriental fan consists of several blades. The blades are connected to one another, and the fan can be folded into a neat strip by arranging the blades one above another. Folded, one sees a limited view. Even the air it stirs is very limited. But as one opens each blade, one comes to know not merely the breadth of the fan but also the wave of air that is moved. I highlight each blade as a significant mission issue. A few blades will be left open without naming them as, from time to time, new insights emerge in the Christian community, bringing in new missiological challenges that were hitherto not thought out or were not fully acceptable.

Imagine a fan made up of fifteen or more blades; I will dwell on thirteen, grouped into three clusters. The clusters will focus on mission at personal, communal, and societal levels. There will be overlapping levels, because they will all deal with human beings as individuals, community, and social members. All of these are present simultaneously in the local congregation.

PERSONAL LEVEL
1. Mission as a call for personal conversion and personal integrity
2. Mission as a call to become a member of a believing community
3. Mission as a call to provide a nurturing atmosphere
4. Mission as a call to engage in prayer, worship, and devotion
5. Mission as a call to engage personally in evangelism

COMMUNAL LEVEL

6. Mission as a call to usher Christian unity for common witness (to avoid competition and proselytism)
7. Mission as a call to reach the unreached
8. Mission as a call to challenge as well as to preserve traditions and cultures

SOCIETAL LEVEL

9. Mission as a call to build a holistic human community through involvement, presence, and dialogue
10. Mission as a call to break barriers of class, race, caste, and gender
11. Mission as a call to challenge unhealthy economic systems and political practices and institutions
12. Mission as a call to peacemaking (reconciliation, restitution, and reconstruction)
13. Mission as a call to promote an environmentally responsible lifestyle

Conversion and Integrity

Diversities exist among human communities. In a society in which the individual is the central focus, personal conversion is appropriate, but in societies in which individual identity is tied to the community, conversion at the individual level will not be easy and will not be proper. In Christian history, we have examples of both individual and mass conversions. Even in Europe, many conversions were a result of groups embracing Christianity.[6]

In recent years, serious thought has been given to the social formation of a community. Proponents of the "church growth" movement try to identify homogeneous communities and shape their mission enterprise accordingly.[7] I have difficulty theologically in using the homogeneous entity (common characteristics) of a given community—that is, race, language, ethnicity, caste or class, and so forth—as a tool for mission outreach, although historically it has contributed to the growth of the church. Congregations need to be aware of their context but should not limit their outreach to only one type of people.

Whatever may be the form of the community, once the decision is made to be a disciple of Christ, to continue in the path of righteousness and personal integrity is crucial in exercising the missionhood of an individual and the community. St. Paul urges Christians in Philippi to develop their Christian inner qualities.[8] Being mindful of that inner beauty and quality is crucial in exercising one's discipleship according to the model we have in Jesus Christ, regardless of the diversity of opinions about the breadth and scope of mission engagements.

Community and Church

When an individual or a community engages in discipleship in Jesus Christ, the mission call leads that individual or community to be a part of the Christian community at large—the church. There is no room within the Christian faith for lone rangers or for a self-serving, self-sufficient Christian community. Often, overexaggerated pietistic theology focusing on individual sin tends to wrongly communicate that one's personal relationship with God is most important. This is a distorted view of discipleship that will not promote healthy missionhood, either for an individual or for a community.

The vertical relationship with God according to the Spirit of the Scriptures is closely interrelated with the horizontal relationship with the sisters and brothers in faith and beyond, without any option to pick and choose according to one's preferences. There are ample examples of a truncated mentality manifested in segregated living. Interrelatedness needs be to manifested in all aspects of the life of the community: worship, education, charity, and service within and beyond the given community, which itself is a witness to the gospel.

Nurturing Atmosphere

An individual Christian or a community developing its missionhood needs to pay attention to the process of nurturing. In spite of the initial enthusiastic decision, conversion, or induction to Christian faith, it cannot be taken for granted that it will automatically lead to maturation. Discipleship is a calling to lifelong learning. Nurturing atmospheres must be created in home, church, and other institutions. The failure of the church to present a full vision of meaningful life as discipleship of Christ, and a proper nurturing for it, often results in uncommitted Christians. Jesus equipped and nurtured his disciples for future ministry and mission gradually and consistently: "Jesus teaches us, through the progressive method of developing laborers, that the dropout syndrome can be reduced significantly by slowly bringing in our would-be disciples to total commitment in stages."[9]

One contemporary ministerial and missional concern is the Christian confrontation with the societal values in all cultures—individualism and materialism as essential to human happiness. Values that disregard concern for one's neighbors and their needs are contrary to the values of the gospel. While combating them is a major task in itself, the responsibility of providing alternate values, which uphold the vision of the reign of God, is a very demanding task. Providing the required pedagogical tools, methods, and opportunities to have a holistic view of life is a major missiological task. Every disciple in a congregation holds this responsibility for the younger generation.

Prayer, Worship, and Devotion

Missional activism may so overwhelm people that they forget that all sustained work needs power and energy provided by the Spirit of God. Even though the significance of spiritual exercises was recognized and emphasized in the Protestant traditions, the sixteenth-century Protestant impatience toward the prevailing monastic orders and organized spiritual vocations left a deep negative mark regarding this practice. The value of lives dedicated to the vocation of prayer, meditation, and devotion is slowly regaining its place among Protestant communities, due in part to the ecumenical spirit and learnings of the past century.[10] People in one's community who resist membership in a congregation may be very interested in "spirituality."

It is common now even among Protestants to encourage seminary students, pastors, and interested laity to experience the joy of prayer and devotion in Roman Catholic monasteries. A recognition of these spiritual dimensions has created connecting links with spiritual practices of other living faiths. Locally and globally, Christian spiritual centers and centers of other living faiths are becoming open to one another's faith communities, expressing the message that connectedness with the transcendent reality is of vital importance for human life on this planet. Humanity, without the proper balancing of spiritual and material well-being, will create a social environment that is detrimental for creation.[11]

Personal Witness

In the Christian faith community, there can be no inactive members who are quiet about their faith. The good news about Jesus Christ needs to be shared in a world that has ample bad news. One cannot prescribe the exact way in which personal witness should be carried out. Circumstances will dictate how the missionhood is to be exercised by each congregation member in his or her daily life. It has to be carried out with utmost reverence for other people's religious views. In encountering another human being, one is encountering the one who is created in the image of God, in spite of all apparent differences.

The *Mission and Evangelism* statement of the World Council of Churches observes: "Evangelism happens in terms of interpersonal relations when the Holy Spirit quickens to faith. Through sharing the pains and joys of life, identifying with people, the Gospel is understood and communicated."[12] Mission history is full of examples of individuals becoming catalysts in leading their family, kith and kin, tribe, community, and even nations to the Christian faith. Personal witness and evangelism are effective missiological methods, especially where resistance toward organized religion exists.

Christian Unity

Mission cannot be restricted to personal call and merely personal welfare. In Christ, an individual is liberated from bondage to sin, selfishness, and narcissism and thereby empowered to engage in the affairs of the community with the vision of the reign of God. The call to Christian unity is the most important and urgent missiological call. The high priestly prayer of Jesus "that they all may be one" (John 17:21) is a glaringly neglected vision among Christians.

Striving toward Christian unity as a mission of the church might sound strange to some Christians. Christian unity is not an optional matter but, rather, pertains to the very essence of the church. Christian unity is not an afterthought of discipleship; it is willed by Jesus Christ. Therefore, working ecumenically without excuses or undue compromises is the duty of the Christian community. The missionary thrust of John 17:21 is "so that the world may believe that you have sent me." Even if as Christians we can justify the division existing within the community, citing historical and theological reasons, we cannot avoid its being a countergospel witness. Divisions continue because of unreconciled historical memories, ethnic identities, comfort with one's own practices, and fear. Continuing the divisions without serious engagement in overcoming them is a missiological neglect.

Reaching the Unreached

Christianity has spread to all corners of the world, but 70 percent of the world's population still follow their own faith traditions or remain uncommitted to any particular faith tradition. "Re-evangelization" aims at winning back Christians. The church's mission to all these communities is to reach them where they are and bring them into the active fellowship of the church. Even among Christians, a sizable number of nominal Christians or agnostics exists.

Christians use historical methods to reach people of other faiths. They also use new methods that shed some of the glaring classification of others as pagans or heathens, which degrades them by calling them children of the devil and coerces them through offering material benefits or fear of eternal damnation. Some Christian groups continue proselytizing and "sheep stealing" governed by the motivation of promoting their brand of theology and Christianity. When the notion of success becomes a predominant concern in mission outreach, the gospel of Jesus Christ is often experienced as bad news more so than as good news.[13] Even though much progress has been made in eliminating triumphalistic mission practices, Christians are not completely free of these methods.

While churches agree in the proper use of modern mass communication, transportation, and so forth, the division is still apparent as to methods and goals. Some Christian groups prioritize communicating the name of Jesus (that salvation is available only through him) to every individual on earth. This could be done even in an impersonal way, through the distribution of tracts, leaflets, and radio and television programs. Some churches have opted for interfaith dialogue, to relate emphasizing mutual transformation of both Christians and people of other faiths.[14] These differences in approach may also exist among members of a local congregation.

Preservation of Traditions and Cultures

In the history of mission, one can read ample examples of how, knowingly or unknowingly, alien cultures from the West and North were thrust upon new Christian communities along with the Christian faith. The end of colonialism and the search for authentic identities have brought to surface some of the glaring errors carried out in the name and cause of mission. Needed changes to reappropriate traditions and cultures are possible only through the process of self-theologizing, besides the historically upheld three "selfs"—self-support, self-governing, and self-propagation.[15]

Many communities around the world are rereading the Bible in their own contexts and are reviving cultures, traditions, rites, and rituals that are not contradictory to the spirit of the gospel. Sometimes, such attempts are not welcomed because faithful followers have internalized the type of Christianity that was introduced to them. Occasionally, such sincere attempts have been criticized as syncretism. However, these attempts at inculturation and indigenization are crucial if Christianity is to present itself as a global faith and not a religion of only one region of the world.

Christianity has become a global community and will naturally manifest the diversity of the human race. The missiological challenge is preservation of the catholicity of the church in the midst of the plurality of human cultures that need to be reviewed in the light of the gospel. It is not an easy task but is an unavoidable challenge every Christian community in every generation needs to face in order to preserve the integrity of Christianity.[16]

Building Holistic Human Community

Human history is full of tragic atrocities. All major world religions have contributed at one time or another to such atrocities by directly instigating their followers or by failing to guide them with the noble teachings of their faith. Unfortunately, the record of Christianity is deplorable. Jesus, the "peace child" of God, was converted into a gladiator of God as Christians went around the globe imposing Christian civilization and establishing Christian institutions, including the church. Even though organized religions for the most part have ceased such aggression, several political and social institutions continue this role. All of these forces contribute to a broken, compartmentalized world. Some people live with fear for their lives, others are full of hatred of their adversaries, and still others live with phobias of the other. All religions, particularly Christianity with its belief in the incarnation, have a major role to play in rectifying the situation by upholding the dignity and sacredness of all life and the interconnectedness of all human beings.

Today, there is a great need for a better understanding among religious communities, especially as mobility has created regions with multiple religions in many parts of the world. As Hans Küng has alluded, there will not be lasting peace in the world until there is peace among religions. Even though the doctrinal differences and religious practices are hard to reconcile, there could be greater cooperation and collaboration in ethics, paving the way for a holistic life for every individual.[17] Christians, predominantly those living in economically prosperous and militarily strong nations of the world, must shed their self-sufficient and isolationist mentality for the sake of a holistic human community.

Breaking the Barriers of Class, Race, Caste, and Gender

The common elements that govern the barriers of class, race, caste, and gender are division and discrimination among individuals and communities imposed or perpetuated by the power group in a community.[18] Historical circumstances created discriminatory practices and even built institutions to perpetuate them. In some circumstances, churches have been in the forefront of challenging and fighting such discrimination, but historically in many cases the churches have been party to them either actively or passively.

Even though in today's society one may not see a public display of discrimination, such as apartheid or segregation, nevertheless they are often still in place, partly because people have given them up not out of conviction but because of the social and legal changes in the society. Very few Christian communities can boldly declare that their members have shed all discrimination. Full inclusion and integration of women and people of other races, castes, and colors in the ministries of the church is still a struggle. One can say that mission engagement has led to the review of the interpretations of some of the scriptural passages and the rectification of several of the historical theologies, doctrines, and practices that could result in the clearing of barriers; however, unless churches are willing to listen to the gospel afresh and be challenged, especially by those who are victims of discriminatory policies and practices, they will fail to experience unity in diversity and redemption and reconciliation—the message of liberation.

Challenging Unhealthy Economic Systems and Political Institutions

Economic systems in collaboration with political institutions have a greater power today in determining the fate of human communities than ever before. The globalization of trade, commerce, and finance does not allow any part of the human race to be free from its influences, regardless of how far people are from the business and financial centers of the world. The discrepancies between the industrialized north and the developing south are well documented and publicized among nations and churches. All of these imbalances are created by human greed and sin, both individual and collective.

The gospel condemns such forces and proclaims liberation from them. A Christian vision of a just society and economic involvement are a crucial missiological challenge. Several churches and Christian organizations strongly advocating the cancellation of debts of the poorest nations in the world by G7 nations built a global network called Jubilee 2000, basing it on the biblical vision of jubilee found in Leviticus 25.[19] Economic forces today are so interwoven with political forces that prophetic ministry in the political realm is unavoidable. For some Christians and some congregations, any suggestion of political and economic engagement is disturbing, but the gospel's mission imperative demands involvement when forces diminish the holistic life that God intends for everyone. Wherever evil reigns and thrives, the gospel message comes as a redeeming power.

Working for Peace

Mission as peacemaking may sound like an alien agenda for some Christian communities, but it has been an important missiological concern for such churches as the Mennonites and Quakers. A post–Cold War era provides greater scope for a nonpolarized world order, including alternative ways of resolving conflict and demilitarizing international relationships. There may be less fear of major nuclear war but increased localized military clashes of great intensity.[20] Old rivalries have not been overcome completely, be that in Eastern Europe, Northern Ireland, the Middle East, the Horn of Africa, or the Korean peninsula.

In many developing countries, precious resources needed for human development are diverted for mostly nonproductive and destructive military purposes, resulting in a massive number of refugees, destruction of the youth population, atrocities against women and children, and the breaking down of societal infrastructures. Manufacture and sale of military weapons continues. In 1992, while an amount of $815 billion was spent for military machineries and war, the amount spent on UN peacekeeping operations was only $1.9 billion.[21] Military spending will not lessen unless the peace process is given priority in every country and society, including faith communities. The world campaign to ban land mines is one example of such a collaborative effort on the part of various nations, nongovernmental organizations, and churches.

Developing an Environmentally Responsible Lifestyle

The threat to the environment of our planet is well documented. Involvement in environmental issues requires looking at existing theologies and mission practices. Protestant churches often preoccupy themselves with the individual's redemption to the neglect of societal and creational well-being. Until recently, any serious work on the theology of creation or the role and place of land and nature was scant. On the contrary, there are many examples of mission practices imposing the exploitative views of nature on communities that traditionally had a more healthy relationship with the earth and their environment. The role of mission is to learn and adopt worldviews and lifestyles that can contribute to the Christian vision of the wholeness of life.

The old attitude of sheer domination of nature for human gratification needs to be replaced by responsible stewardship. The cooperation of similarly concerned and committed persons of other faiths is of utmost importance and calls for a new ecumenism of global solidarity.[22]

The broad range of possible mission engagements does not mean that any one individual or a congregation can fulfill all of them or is expected to do so. The task is great and the "laborers are few" (Matt. 9:37). However, the broad picture should be kept in mind while engaging in any segment, so that no other aspect of mission is weakened. All issues are interconnected.

Conclusion

The issues under any one of the thirteen blades can be further subdivided and dealt with in greater detail. Human history does not remain constant, and changing situational contexts bring new challenges and opportunities. Christians are called to be alert and to discern the will of God in their missiological engagements.

People of all faiths, be they Jews, Muslims, Buddhists, or followers of primal beliefs, have all suffered persecution of one sort or another. Recent political changes mean that, along with Christians, they will also celebrate the new freedom to be what they are as well as to spread their faith. A multireligious community is here to stay.

World leaders are taking note of the creative influences religious communities can have on their societies. The United Nations Organization's open recognition of the significance of religions in human affairs and the organization of the Millennium Spiritual Summit of the world's religious and spiritual leaders will certainly motivate Christian communities to reexamine their exclusivist attitudes.[23] The participation of churches in such a public event merely as one of the world's religions may be offensive for some Christians. However, that reality cannot be denied. The way forward is a hard look into existing mission theologies and practices. Instead of becoming defensive, one must celebrate these developments, seeing in them a leading of the Spirit in bringing the world religions closer into greater understanding and helping them to shed the unhealthy parochialism that has contributed to many conflicts and destruction in the past. The changing situations do not reduce the significance of Jesus Christ or the missionary calling of Christians. They are indispensable, as a conference on World Mission and Evangelism has stated: "We [Christians] cannot point to any other way of salvation than Jesus Christ; at the same time we cannot set limits to the saving power of God."[24]

15

Youth and Family Ministry
as Congregational and Community Renewal

PAUL G. HILL

Congregations feel the urgent need to share the faith and build the church among their youth. But this mission close to home may seem the most difficult of all. How can one evangelize one's own children? Youth and family ministry is never a solo calling nor a onetime event. Together, how can the congregation engage every age-group in cross-generational ministry that renews the faith community and the world beyond?

"Good God, what wretchedness I behold!" Thus spoke Martin Luther after visiting the homes and parishes in Saxony in 1528. Luther was more than shocked to see the lack of good Christian adult behavior in the churches and, as a result, the shabby state of Christian parenting. Imagine parents attending church in America today and hearing their pastor say, "Good God, what wretchedness I behold."[1] Imagine preachers entering the pulpit and saying this to the congregation. The parents would most likely start searching for a new church home and the pastor would soon be searching for a new call. For Luther, however, when it came to the God-given mandate for all adults and the congregation to nurture children and youth into the faith, creating offense and taking offense was not a major concern.

Luther's critique continued: "Everybody acts as if God gave us children for our pleasure and amusement. . . . We must not think only of amassing money and property for them. But God has given and entrusted children to us with the command that we train and govern them according to His will."[2]

Luther's development of the Small Catechism was his response to this situation, and it addresses our question, "Where are all the Christian adults and how can we help them teach the children?"

161

So as not to think that Luther saw this calling only as responsibility and burden, he actually resisted being the strict taskmaster. In fact, he urged the opposite. He states in the *Book of Concord*: "With childish and playful methods . . . we may bring up our youth in the fear and honor of God . . . then some good may take root, spring up, and bear fruit. . . . This would be the right way to bring up children, so long as they can be trained with kind and pleasant methods, for those who have to be forced by means of rods and blows will come to no good end . . . when we preach to children, we must also speak their language."[3] Luther's vision is one of a playful, supportive, instructive community in which adults and youth grow together in the faith.

Without much of a stretch of the imagination, we recognize that any of Luther's quotes could be spoken and would be true of Christianity in America today.[4] Unfortunately, there is still some "wretchedness to behold."

For example, the Youth and Family Institute of Augsburg College notes that within the Evangelical Lutheran Church in American (ELCA), 70 percent of all junior high youth are engaged in Christian education, the highest level of enrollment of youth among Protestant denominations. This would be a cause for celebration were it not also true that only 32 percent of these youth are involved in Christian education after confirmation, the lowest in respect to other Protestant denominations.

How can we let our life together in Christ deteriorate so rapidly? Sad is the silence that exists in response to this situation. For more than thirty years, we have been losing our youth in this manner. Yet it has been only recently that a renewed commitment to our youth has occurred.[5]

The problem is that the church has too often adopted the age-segregated mentality of the larger culture. A conversation I had with a pastor while working at a summer camp serves as an illustration. Sitting in the dining hall of the camp during a confirmation week, I asked the pastor how it was going. "Fine," she said and then added, "This is my youth week." "Your youth week?" I inquired. "Yes, this is my youth week. I hang with the kids this week, and that's it. I don't do youth the rest of the year," she finished.

> *"Life together lifts up a cross-generational process of conversation, instruction, and care."*

When we only sometimes associate with one another, our life together is an incomplete community in desperate need of cross-generational connections. The business of the body of Christ is to build bridges between the generations, and the wood used for the bridge is the cross of Christ. It is the cross of Jesus that brings us together, and it is the life of the cross that we are called to live.

The Absence of Adults in Age Segregation

Dr. Peter Benson of the Search Institute states: "No culture, in the history of humanity, has ever tried to raise its children in the age-segregated manner in which we are now trying to raise ours."[6] Increasingly, our children and youth are raising themselves. The adults are simply not in the picture. The average teenager spends ten to twelve hours less time *per week* with his or her parents than a teen did in 1960.[7] The consequences are devastating. For example, there is a direct link between boys who are violent and the lack of adults in their lives.[8]

According to psychiatrist Mary Pipher, Native Americans call this cross-generational connection *tioshpa,* meaning community or life together.[9] To be human, to grow up humane, our life together must be a cross-generational life. Children and youth need the presence, love, advice, council, and modeling of adults if they are to grow up healthy. When Abraham Lincoln said, "There is just one way to bring up a child in the way that we should go, and that is to travel that way yourself," he was echoing Prov. 4:1: "Listen children, to a father's instruction, and be attentive that you may gain insight; for I give you good precepts: do not forsake my teaching." Children and youth need adult presence and instruction. It is appropriate to expect adults to play this role. Life together lifts up a cross-generational process of conversation, instruction, and care.

Youth Ministry as Good Gardening

The story goes that a gardener went to the hatchery and bought one hundred baby chicks. Two weeks later, he returned to the hatchery again and bought another one hundred baby chicks. Two weeks passed, and he once again returned and bought one hundred baby chicks. The owner of the hatchery finally had to ask, "Sir, over the past month you have bought three hundred baby chicks. What's going on?" The gardener responded, "Well, I don't know what the problem is with them. I'm either planting them too deep or watering them too much, but they won't grow!" Doing age-segregated ministry is the equivalent of planting baby chicks and expecting them to grow, and it makes about as much sense. So how does real gardening work?

Gardening is the intentional process of creating a healthy ecosystem in which seeds can sprout, grow to maturity, and benefit the rest of the human community. The process of moving from seed to harvest involves a lot of work, tending, cultivating, nurturing, praying (usually about the weather), and not a little pride. And the seed is only one part of the whole process. The quality and quantity of the soil, the lay of the land, the size of the garden, the location of windbreaks, and the seasons all must be considered if the seed is to grow. By themselves, seeds do not grow to be healthy. Filling a silo full of seeds expecting to reap a crop is foolishness.

Yet, in many ways, over the past thirty years that is exactly what we have been doing with our youth. Many congregations have gotten into the unhealthy practice of putting our teens, primarily, in a youth silo and expecting that when they emerge they will be excited, active Christians. In the process of neglecting the ecological nature of faith nurture, we have failed to create a climate and context in which the next generation of youthful seeds can be planted and nurtured into mature, healthy plants.

Segregating (siloing) the youth ministry of the church away from the larger life of the congregation makes it a parachurch. It is considered an appendage of the church but certainly not the primary purpose for being the church. We have fallen into a bad habit within the life of the church of segregating our youth, especially our teens, away from the rest of the Christian community.

We have placed the young in youth room silos, classroom silos, and children's worship silos. We have done this by excessively relying on staff, pastors, and youth ministry professionals. These "gurus" and "professionals" were hired to bring our children into the faith. We now know you cannot hire out faith formation. Essentially, we have tried the impossible task of bringing seed to fruit without proper soil, cultivation, nurture, prayer, engagement, watering, and the protection of weeding. Neither seeds nor Christians can sprout under these conditions.

While visiting a congregation, I was invited to attend the adult Sunday school hour. Coffee, cookies, cake, juice, and tea were set out for everyone. As I walked toward the adult classroom, I was in a rolling conversation with a couple of teenagers. We came to the entrance only to be met by a rather grumpy-looking senior citizen blocking the way of the teens. "This isn't for you," he said to the youth as he let me pass. Now telling a teenager that food sitting out on a table is not to be devoured is tantamount to telling firefighters that they can't use water to put out the fire. It was enormously insulting to them and to me. Yet it was the policy of this church. Teens were not welcome in the adult hour, nor could they enjoy the goodies. Just like Jesus' disciples, this church was pushing the children away from Jesus, or at least away from chocolate chip cookies. Being the honored speaker for the day, I decided to use my position of influence to make a point. I went back to the teens, took one on each arm, and walked into the room, commenting as we entered, "It's OK, they're with me."

Asking the Right Questions

I often hear age-segregated thinking in the questions being asked regarding youth ministry. See figure 1 for several illustrations.

The questions point to an obvious truism: if we want spiritual youth, we need spiritual adults.[10] If we want Christian seeds to grow, then we need Christian gardeners to nurture that seed. The cliché that "faith is caught more than it is taught" is true. And it is caught by youth observing, living, growing, exploring, questioning, and engaging faith with the adults around them.[11] The myth in the church is that youth ministry is about youth. This is true only in part. Primarily, youth ministry is about adults and adult spirituality, which is another way of saying that Youth Ministry is spelled C.O.N.G.R.E.G.A.T.I.O.N.A.L. R.E.N.E.W.A.L.[12]

Adult Identity Formation as Key

Youth ministry begins, then, with adult identity formation. Let me illustrate by sharing an experience I recently had while working with a congregation.

Sitting through our training sessions for more than a day, a baby-boomer mom had a look of love, concern, and stress written on her face. No doubt her minivan or SUV was parked in the church parking lot. Sitting next to the driver's seat would be a car phone or an address book or both. The radio would be set for public broadcasting and the local rock station, and soft drink stains would be dried into the passenger seats. Her minivan was most likely the family living room, kitchen, counseling center, and classroom. She raised few questions during the congregational training session. Taking things to heart, she pondered the words being said about children and youth and about the adults who would raise them. Her presence at the event spoke volumes for the love she had for her own children.

Segregated Thinking	Cross-Generational Thinking
Who can we get to relate to the youth?	How can adults build a relationship with a youth?
How can we create a youth program?	How can we create relationships with youth while doing the ministry of the congregation (service projects, peer missionaries, and so forth)?
How do we get our kids to come to church?	How do we help the home as well as the church building be holy ground?
How many kids showed up at youth group?	How many adults showed up at youth group?
How many kids were in Sunday school?	How many adults were in Christian education classes?
Who can we get to reach out to youth?	How can we help youth reach out to youth?
Who's teaching confirmation?	How many mentors and parents are involved in confirmation ministry?
What adults are leading worship?	What youth are involved in worship leadership?
Can we find a pastor to work with youth?	Can all our pastors commit to connecting with youth?
Can we get a visitation pastor for the shut-ins?	Can a visitation pastor take youth along to visit the shut-ins?
Where is the youth class?	Where is the cross-generational event?

Is this contemporary or traditional worship?	Does this worship include many generations in leadership, and is it relevant to all?
How can we grow a youth group?	How can we grow a healthy church ecosystem?
How do we pull kids away from busy schedules to come to youth group?	How can we connect with youth in the events in which they are engaged all week long?
How can we build a youth group?	How can we build many small group ministries?

Toward the end of the second day, her face lit up. "I've got it," she said. "I'm no longer a taxi driver of my children; I am a spiritual guide to my children." The minivan had taken on a new role—that of chapel. A revolution in self-discovery and self-identity stood before us in the person of this mother.

Within her seemingly simple insight and claim of a new personal identity lies the key to the renewal that must sweep through the church. Every Christian adult—grandparent, aunt, uncle, friend, godparent, and mentor—must come to this realization about himself or herself. Our children need more than a taxi driver who transports them to their next soccer game, movie, shopping trip, or school activity. The family taxi has taken the place of the dinner table in American families. It is the place of conversation, discipline, meals, and relationships. It can also be the place of spiritual conversation, prayer, and inquiry. This is not so much a critique of the lifestyle of the commuter family as it is a protest of the assumption that church is the destination rather than the journey together.

In their new and important book *Passing on the Faith*, Merton Strommen and Richard Hardel reinforce the importance of C.O.N.G.R.E.G.A.-T.I.O.N.A.L. R.E.N.E.W.A.L., especially as it relates to religious practices in the home. Based upon their research study on Effective Christian Education, they note: "Religious practices in the home virtually double the probability of a congregation's youth entering into the life and mission of Christ's church."[13] In related studies and writings, David Anderson and I point out that of the five top religious influences seventh- to-twelfth-grade Protestant youth identify in their lives, the first four are adults. They are, in rank order:

- Mother
- Father
- Pastor
- Grandparent
- Youth group at church.[14]

Christians are called to live life together, in community, nurturing God's human ecosystem. To be a Christian adult, by definition, is to be engaged with youth. Every adult in every congregation is an indispensable youth minister. We do not have a choice on this matter. We can choose only whether we will be any good at it or not. So what kind of choices are we making?

The Sermon on the Mount Revisited

Recently, I had the opportunity to share the telling of the Sermon on the Mount with 650 senior high youth. While I spoke, images capturing various themes from the sermon were projected upon a large screen. Afterward, the youth were invited to write down questions that came to mind while listening to the sermon. I collected all these cards and organized them by topic in anticipation of addressing their musings the following day. To my surprise, the largest group of questions focused on the section in the Sermon on the Mount relating to divorce. The youth wanted to know what this meant for them and how would Jesus look upon their family situations.

The next day, we went through many of their questions, and we spent considerable time on Jesus' teachings regarding divorce. We talked of Jesus' desire for families to be healthy. I noted that Jesus was being particularly critical of the practice of men abandoning women and that the text was about lifting up the egalitarian and mutually respectful nature of marriage as God intends. The teens warmed to this. Yet what really captured the room was talking about this text as an illustration of a larger principle in the sermon. Jesus was calling believers to live their lives with integrity and commitment. Christians are to live walking the talk. Jesus recognizes that hypocrisy is the sin du jour that destroys faith and community for youth.

Teens are not, however, asking for perfect adults. They are asking for integrity. The Sermon on the Mount states it clearly: "Strive first for the kingdom of God" (Matt. 6:33). And it ends with these marvelous words: "Everyone who hears these words of mine and acts on them is like the wise man who built his house on rock" (Matt. 7:24). Integrity in youth ministry is claiming the power of the cross and resurrection for new life— together—on a daily basis. It is the Christian effort not for salvation but to build up the body of Christ. Luther called this the third use of the law, the living, acting work of disciples. Integrity has to do with taking the larger community into account and allowing it to be determinative of our behavior. Integrity is asking the following questions: Does my behavior benefit the body of Christ? Does it enhance our life together? Does it reflect my faith and point to Jesus? Christian integrity is a powerful means for the Holy Spirit to plant seeds of faith in a culture that seriously lacks any sense of depth or integrity.

Strategies for Adults to Connect with Youth

A balanced ecosystem for faith nurture includes Worship, Outreach, Learning, and Fellowship (the four terms in reverse order form the acronym that reminds the community to go with the F.L.O.W.). These four discipleship practices of regular worship, outreach and service to others, learning through Bible study and reflection, and regular communal fellowship come with being in the body of Christ. Christians going with the F.L.O.W. are people of integrity. These faith practices can take many forms. Here are a few examples.

- *Do daily devotions.* Letting Jesus take hold of us through the daily regimen of Bible reading, prayer, and devotions means that baptismal water can run deep and will be a pool in which youth can immerse themselves on their faith journey.
- *Make time for youth.* For youth, time together is both qualitative and quantitative. We cannot separate the two. We need to be there when they want to talk, not only when it is convenient for us.
- *Share your faith journey with youth.* Witnessing in daily life, including the new struggles, doubts, and fears, is a powerful way for youth to learn that God is real and that they are not alone in their searching.
- *Provide structure for youth.* Set boundaries for safety. Explain the reason for such structures and boundaries.
- *Frame your life through religious rituals.* Celebrate baptismal remembrance days, pray with teens when they get a driver's license, or give them reminders they can wear (such as a cross or a watch)

that serve as reference points when they are making decisions. Tell them frequently that you and Jesus love them. Hug them and tell them, "The peace of the Lord be with you always."

- *Burn the baptismal candle for all kinds of passages and marker events.* A pastor I know encourages her families to light the baptismal candle whenever children or youth reach a milestone, such as one's (1) first solid food, (2) first Sunday school class, (3) first day of school, (4) first Bible, (5) first public event in sports, band, choir, dance, and so forth, (6) first date, and (7) first move away to college or job. This short list can be expanded greatly. Use the candle to mark significant life moments with the reminder of God's presence and light in our lives.

- *Do service with youth.* Work side by side furthering the kingdom of God.

- *Organize cross-generational prayer groups.* Most congregations have at least four generations represented. On a regular basis, have small groups representing the various generations pray together about personal concerns, congregational life, the community, and the world.

- *Share cross-generationally in church school.* Many congregations are offering an occasional (once every four or five weeks, for example) cross-generational church school time to engage in Bible study, songs, and discussion together.

- *Help parents be evangelists in their own homes.* Many parents feel unprepared to be spiritual guides for their children. Provide resources for them that are age appropriate so that they can do devotions, prayers, and service and religious rituals in their homes.[15]

Youth ministry is exciting, challenging work of evangelism for every adult in the congregation. It is part of the primary work of the church. It will require a renewal within the whole of the body of Christ in the congregation and in the home.

16

Discovering Hope

Marks of Vitality and Practices That Form Communities for Mission

---

L. SHANNON JUNG

Although frequently disheartened by struggles, the church by God's grace continues not only to survive but to thrive. What can the entire church learn from vital rural congregations? What engenders hope? Congregations need not grab for flashy gimmicks that entertain in order to grow. How can they keep Christ, worship, study, prayer, and care centered in ways that are real and that relate to daily life?

What makes for vital congregations? What evangelism strategies and what discipleship and leadership practices contribute to vitality? I have been blessed by these questions as well as obsessed with answering them. I have been privileged to be part of many collaborative efforts to explore these issues.[1] This chapter summarizes research that focuses on learning from vital rural congregations and presents dynamics and practices that could apply to all congregations, whatever their setting.

The practices that form the stories of such vital congregations tend to cluster around certain characteristics. I first describe those "marks of vitality" and then suggest three theological ingredients or goals that seem integral to generating those marks. The chapter concludes with seven practices that make for renewing town and country congregations. The emphasis throughout falls more on process than on product because, especially in rural churches, if the process is right, then the product will follow.

Marks of Vitality

God has gifted vital rural congregations with ways of acting and being that demonstrate certain distinctive features. Such churches do the following.

Make a clear effort to keep Christ at the center of their life. They work at keeping "the main thing the main thing." By that, they mean remembering that the church should focus on Jesus Christ and on God's mission rather than on their own self-aggrandizement or even primarily on numerical growth. In a very real sense, this is the single most significant mark of vitality, which pervades and colors many—perhaps the majority—of the other marks.

Two quite clear aspects of this focus on Christ are the emphasis vital congregations place on their *corporate worship life* and on *individual and group prayer.* They honor the place of worship and spend a lot of time and attention planning services that worship God. Their services involve the participation of many people. Music has a key role in uplifting and inspiring worshipers. Many of these congregations enjoy a variety of musical styles in their services. Furthermore, these worship services incorporate members of the church into a community focused on God. Worship enables them to become what they already are—the body of Christ. It also reminds them of their common loyalty and just whose disciples they are.

It is as true of prayer as of worship that these believers expect God to act. They pray expecting that God will answer those prayers. The same sense of expectation that pervades their prayer life also leads adults to hold high expectations of themselves and to communicate high expectations for youth. These congregations pray with the full expectancy of God's active presence in all aspects of their life together, including leadership and evangelism. They are open to hearing God's voice.

Attend to local and specific ways of being in the world in mission. They are attentive to particular, distinctive opportunities for mission in their neighborhoods and communities. They have not only a general but also a very specific sense of mission. They pray for specific concerns and for particular people by name; likewise, they praise God's action through events that they experience.[2] They are open to new or traditional calls to mission.

Encourage and practice prayer in the routines of daily life as well as in times of crisis. The people have made a regular habit of praying for God's guidance and support throughout their lives, not only when they are perplexed or worried. The way they pray for one another contributes to the depth of community they enjoy. The practice of collecting prayer concerns also functions as an opportunity for people to share what is going on in their lives.

Take the long view when it comes to discipleship. Vital congregations are persistent in nurturing and challenging themselves and their youth to grow in the life of faith. They do not expect maturity to happen overnight. They are youth–friendly. In many of these churches, youth play significant roles. They see themselves as growing in the life of faith and as disciples rather than as Christians who have already made it to full maturity. The congregation has a strong base of participation and ownership. Newcomers are welcomed with enthusiasm; participation and the use of individual gifts are encouraged. In some congregations, signature ministries have developed as a result of members' sharing distinctive gifts—from automotive repair to beer brewing to cooking to music to playwriting.

Share a spiritual journey. The members share a spirit of tolerance and appreciation of one another, the very opposite of being judgmental and critical. These congregations exude a hospitality, which seems based on a certain humility about their status as disciples. It takes a maturity of faith to recognize one's dependency on God in a way that renders us all equally rich in our journey of discipleship. Many members in these churches feel secure enough in their own deep commitment to be able to appreciate without feeling threatened by other, newer members. They take a pride and a joy in their mission without that developing into arrogance or a lessening of commitment. These are truly servant leaders, joyful in their faith and appreciative of the ways God is in motion in their local setting.

Involve themselves in their communities. Vital congregations are alert to what is going on in their communities and enjoy the lives of the people there. They are aware of and concerned about the environmental health of their communities. Many decorate their churches with reminders of the seasons of nature and exhibit a creation spirituality. They welcome and invite the unchurched and other community groups into their churches.[3]

Practice an informal style that is inviting, warm, and participatory. Clear on their identity as a Christian congregation, they can comfortably live with one another and make decisions appropriate to their particular calling. In regard to worship, rather than adopt a standardized denominational style or simply reject a certain style, they adapt the style to their own circumstances. These churches are intentional communities that are confident that the grace of God is in full operation in their settings.

Engage local mission and practice spirituality in harmony with one another. Believing that God is active and concerned about their lives and that Jesus Christ is at the center of their church frees these Christians to discover a spirituality and mission that fits their situation. God is not a distant or standardized impersonal force; instead, God is active in their congregation and community.

Going Deep with God:
Extending the Life of Discipleship

There is a conglomerate style in these congregations: easy entry and high expectation; informal ethos and deep spirituality; openness to community and deep commitment; a relaxed yet serious stance. These combinations are unusual. The focus is not just on maintaining an orientation toward Jesus Christ and God's purpose but on actually developing a stronger and more profound relationship with God. That is exciting.

Numerous congregations are responding to the desire of parishioners to develop spiritually more satisfying lives. This hunger, which we label "spiritual hunger," is intellectual, emotional, and communal at the least. People hunger for an intimate relationship with God that will guide their lives and both give them a sense of transcendent and lasting connection with worthwhile goals and also enable them to make peace with themselves and their neighbors. The metaphor of spiritual journey seems apt—people yearn to explore God's purposes with other people in a way that makes a difference. In short, they long to be pilgrims and disciples. They want to extend their discipleship and deepen their spirituality.

Three things seem ingredient to this: first, a *community* of people committed to the mind of Christ and, second, a willingness to risk one's own desires in a discipline of *spiritual formation*. Third, a focus on *mission* and being formed by Jesus' mission permeate both of these. Serving others is at the core of Jesus' mission as much as anything except loving God.

All three elements rest on the devotion to be a disciple of Jesus Christ, a member of the kingdom of God. Some might speak of this profound commitment as being born again, having a personal relationship with God, or being filled with the Spirit. However it is expressed, ultimately community, spiritual formation, and mission grow out of the assurance of having been loved by God and vigorously desiring to love God in return.

Discipleship in the church is a response to God, not a result of our enjoying or being comfortable in any particular church. It is not the pastor's manner or preaching, nor is it the congregation's being friendly or likeminded, nor is it our feeling comfortable that produces a loyalty to this or that congregation. Our commitment is first to love and to serve God and only then is it to a particular congregation. The church is the vehicle, the body of Christ, given to us to be the agent of God. This is not a discounting of the church; indeed, in some ways, it is a high estimate of the work of the church. It is important to see, however, that our loyalty transcends being treated in one way or another by other people in the church, or whether there is a nursery or an aerobics class, or how generous the parking is. These people don't feel that the church owes them something or that they are entitled to certain privileges in the church.

Community

A strong commitment to community produces a tolerance of others and flexibility in dealing with them. People can risk getting involved with others. Something far greater than meeting consumer preferences (for example, the choice of hymns, personality preferences, or lifestyle traits) binds these people together. They are disciples of Christ foremost rather than members of a social group of similar people. They share a common desire to serve God. They see one another as being on a journey together and as companions, not as enslaved to one another. They choose to serve others for the greater glory of God. They love one another enough to disagree safely for the greater common good.[4]

Vital congregations develop small groups that share ministries, prayer, Bible studies, or mission projects. People find it difficult to relate to large numbers of people, so it is important to community, if the congregation is large, that each person be in a fairly intimate relationship with some group within the whole. Having a strong and growing set of relationships nurtures commitment to discipleship.

Community itself is built and reinforced by inspiring and energetic worship. Worship celebrates what God has done, is doing, and will do. It reminds us of the reasons for being part of the church community that lie beyond personal preference. It also gives us a glimpse of the kingdom to come in a way that simultaneously brings into being the community of God that already is. Worship and prayer are indispensable to community. The Christian community is God's; the community transcends functions and personalities; worship calls us into relationship for God's sake.

Spiritual Formation

Worship and prayer are spiritually formative events that socialize us into lives of discipleship. They carry us ever deeper into the faith. Corporately, they bind all of the small groups together and enable the body of Christ to continue growing in spiritual maturity and numbers.

Small-group Bible studies that incorporate prayer and discussion of personal faith issues are almost as significant to believers as corporate worship. The practice of reading and examining Scripture with a group in a way that deepens one's prayer life and involves ever-greater faith disclosure has been a historic Christian practice. It remains so. It is one of the disciplines of spiritual formation that enables church members to become disciples. These disciplines involve risky disclosure with others. They enable people to develop stronger communication with God, as well as stronger relationships with others. (There are a plethora of forms for doing this. Among them are the *Kerygma* series, the *Alpha Project, Disciples Bible Study,* and *Renovare.*)

Going onward and deeper with God almost necessitates becoming involved in the disciplines of spiritual formation. This is vital to the growth and adventurousness of a church as well as to individuals. Without the expectation of increasing maturity and experimentation, the possibility of atrophy arises. The element of risk is important.

Spiritual formation happens in families of whatever shape. Parents and children can assist one another in developing faithfulness and raising questions about how their faith relates to their lives. Special relationships within extended families and committed, long-term friendships provide challenge, support, and mutual accountability for spiritual formation.

Mission

Ideally, spiritual formation and community are directed outward as well as inward.[5] It is this outward thrust that we call mission. Particularly in town and country congregations, it is hard to differentiate between evangelism (outreach to the unchurched or nonbelievers) and social ministry (outreach to meet the needs of all others). They are very much entwined. Without this outward thrust, there is a danger that community and spiritual formation can degenerate into practices that meet only our own needs. Jesus' message and example inevitably included reaching out to others as did his whole life. Mission is an essential component in maintaining the transcendent purpose of the church to proclaim the gospel in word and deed throughout the world.

> *"Genuine prayer that expects answers, that worships God, that appreciates the grace incarnate in the world, and that confesses shortcomings is indispensable if the church is to be indispensable in the lives of people and the community."*

The gospel message is that we are to love others as God has loved us. Jesus Christ himself showed us how to call others to discipleship and how to meet the needs of the sick, the hungry, the marginalized, and even the wealthy. The exact shape of the mission that Jesus undertook—and which we are to undertake—depends on the real needs of the people around us. Underlying both evangelism and social ministry is a deep love of God that issues in a desire for the well-being of all people. The notion of salvation that guides our mission is a holistic one concerned with the physical and spiritual well-being of people. Surprisingly, the practices of hospitality, compassion, generosity, and graciousness that develop as a result of mission prove to be deeply satisfying and fulfilling to us. They have the character of mediating Christ's salvation to us.

Practices for Discovering Hope

This three-pronged emphasis on community, spiritual formation, and mission, though theoretical, is quite practical. It promotes a town and country congregation that is continually in the process of renewal.[6] It calls a congregation beyond where it is and urges it to go onward and deeper with God. The emphasis becomes practical in two ways: concrete and specific recommendations and those recommendations taking the form of practices.

1. As we envision the ever-renewing rural—or urban or suburban—congregation with its emphasis on community, spiritual formation, and mission, that congregation has to incorporate a permission-giving or functional structure. It must be open to the emergence of ministries rather than a hierarchical gatekeeper. A pastor or church council that has to control the church's direction and that overfunctions to the detriment of the growth of laity can block the movement of the Spirit. The pastor (or council) has to truly join with the church and be part of the community. The leadership has to be on the path of spiritual formation and has to be missional. Structures count; they are powerfully enabling or powerfully inhibiting of renewal, discovery, and hope. Leadership that empowers others, that recognizes others' gifts, is vital.[7]

2. The daily, regular, specific practice of prayer undergirds everything else in the Christian life. That includes church life. Genuine prayer that expects answers, that worships God, that appreciates the grace incarnate in the world, and that confesses shortcomings is indispensable if the church is to be indispensable in the lives of people and the community. This is heartfelt, passionate, yearning, whole-bodied spirituality.

3. Small groups that incorporate prayer, Bible study, and faith disclosure are very significant. Sharing one's own faith and life issues is not incidental or optional.

4. Worship services anchor the practice of the Christian life. Regular worship is a central practice. Especially important is worship that inspires us to see our lives as being part of a transcendent plan. Worship that expresses the call of God motivates us to respond to God's action through communal and personal mission. Worship calls us to a vision of God's reality; it suggests the way reality is and is intended to be.

5. The church needs to practice caring for others *concretely* (for example, hospital visits, soup kitchens, mission trips, cards, political advocacy, and so forth). Care takes faith out the church doors. This practice of hospitality is supplemented by the practice of being open to receiving hospitality. The abilities to give and to receive reinforce each other. Using one's gifts in outreach to others is encouraged by the recognition that we are enriched by, and indeed we need, others' gifts. Identifying people's gifts and engaging those gifts in ministry build up the body of Christ.

The call to do justice in our relations with all others is an extension of the practice of hospitality. Neither the call to promote justice nor the privilege of hospitality is an add-on to the Christian life. Instead, treating others with kindness and seeking justice for all are symbols of the way that Jesus treated all others; it is what Jesus would do if he were us.

6. The practice of confession and making oneself accountable to others before God cultivates humility. It reminds us that we need God's ongoing sustenance; we need the salvation offered in Jesus Christ. People need this spiritual gift as well as physical care and emotional support. If our salvation is—as we claim—holistic, so too are our evangelism and outreach. We reach out to others because Jesus and the Spirit reach out to us. The practice of confession leads to the practice of evangelism.

7. Finally, one often overlooked vital practice in the church is based on discovering hope. That practice is expectancy, looking forward. In the broadest bandwidth, it means being open to the new, the creative, the inbreaking in whatever town and country setting one's church finds itself. It implies an attitude of expecting that whatever innovation God is calling the congregation to, God will support. Perhaps it involves cooperative programs with other churches of one's denomination or other church bodies.[8] It may mean gathering a whole coalition. It may take the form of welcoming new groups and new ministries. Wherever the Spirit directs the congregation, discovering hope builds community.

PART FOUR

A Church of All People:
The Indispensable Challenge

While we may all agree that mission is indispensable for life in community, it is more difficult to go to the places this may lead us. Part 4 stretches us. By facing our challenges with vision, even when struggling with very difficult issues, Christ builds the church. We engage the challenge of the church's identity in a complex culture and a dangerous world. We face the ongoing issue of race and the deeply divisive issues of sexuality, specifically homosexuality. We see the challenge of a community turned inward, fearful and finally dangerous to itself. We conclude with the church turned outward, taking up its advocacy role in working toward a more just world.

Alongside of but distinct from the faith communities in the United States is American civil religion. Roger Fjeld explores the phenomenon, which is often unnoticed but very formative of the creeds, goals, values, and practices of daily life and in the United States' understanding of the rest of the world. Many people blur the lines between the Christian faith and "American values." More than a question of the relationship between church and state, it is a question of the battle for the "ecclesiology" of the nation. This question is raised anew in the new century as the United States tries to comprehend and respond to terrorist attacks. When people believe that God blesses America in a special way, they find it hard to understand how anyone could hate Americans. How do congregations and religious leaders speak their voice in a pluralistic nation? How does one's faith in a God who loves all peoples shape us to be stewards and servants in the world?

Questions about who is included in the ecclesiology of the nation move us to questions about how much diversity a faith community can handle. We need to face again the deep challenge of race and class and ethnicity. Winston Persaud approaches this difficult subject in a way that moves beyond defensiveness to invitation: "Let us imagine . . ." Congregations may want to welcome diversity, but they resist through protecting their homogeneity. Persaud grounds his vision in the incarnation of Christ, who lived as a particular human being in a particular time and place. In this one Jesus, we now have been given a vast, diverse community.

Gwen Sayler addresses embodiment and carefully asks us to consider the health of the body of Christ. By looking at one church body, she addresses the subject many church bodies struggle with today: the issue of homosexuality. She especially examines the required celibacy of homosexual clergy. She takes a biblical look at 1 Corinthians 7, the issue of sexual abstinence versus appropriate sexual activity. Paul calls for the unity of the one body in, with, and under the diversity of the individual bodies that it comprises. Sayler poses a direct challenge to the churches, asking whether there is room within the body for gay and lesbian bodies.

Elizabeth Leeper raises the question of healthy community from yet another perspective. She begins with a contemporary example of a community "gone haywire," the Heaven's Gate experiment, and step-by-step compares elements of that community with second- and third-century Christian communities. She helps us move beyond shock at reading news accounts of a modern tragedy to being able to discern what makes healthy, sustainable communities. From these diverse examples, congregational leaders can examine the health of their own faith communities.

The book concludes with a chapter that widens the concept of the indispensable church to encompass the globe and all of its people. Beginning with the remarkable effectiveness of the Jubilee coalition, Peter Kjeseth challenges "What happens after the Jubilee?" With careful attention to both the newspaper and Scripture, Kjeseth explores Leviticus and its mandates. He helps the reader see what a difference each individual can make and the necessity of coalitions, even diverse, uneasy coalitions, not to wage wars of vengeance to protect self-interests, but to proclaim good news to the poor, work for the release of the captives, and proclaim the jubilee year of the Lord.

American Civil Religion

A De Facto Church

ROGER W. FJELD

As congregations and church bodies claim their different but indispensable roles in the broader culture, it is important to understand the role of American civil religion. How do Christians take their place in a pluralistic culture without needing to dominate? Living together among people of many faiths is difficult but not impossible. What are the tenets of the formative civil religion, and what is the Christian's calling?

Issues about religion in public life are looming large in America. There are perennial issues about prayer in the public schools and flags in the sanctuaries. There is a resurgence of pressure to teach creationism instead of or alongside of the teaching of evolution. There is a movement to post the Ten Commandments prominently in public schools. And in a more general sense, there is much hand-wringing about the decline in public morals in America, with religious leaders and politicians in the forefront of the debate.

When such issues are discussed or debated, churches and their leaders offer much of the testimony, often giving conflicting testimonials. In those debates, churches often assume that theirs are the only religious voices. However, there is another religious voice in America, one that testifies less obviously but often more persuasively than the voices of the churches. It is the voice of religious conviction that can be described as "civil religion" or "public religion." It is not a church in the formal sense, but it holds a set of core convictions, employs a set of common symbols, and functions in many ways like a church. It is a de facto church. Congregations often experience a strange combination of beliefs and practices of both the Christian faith and American civil religion. This chapter seeks to describe that civil religion—its contemporary shape, its history in

America, its effective ecclesiology, and key doctrinal issues vis-à-vis historic Christianity. As congregations and church bodies claim their different but indispensable roles in the broader culture, it is important to understand the role of American civil religion.

The Contemporary Shape of American Civil Religion

Robert Bellah, sociologist at the University of California, Berkeley, coined the phrase "civil religion in America."[1] His article was the outgrowth of earlier research and an earlier set of lectures he gave at an international gathering of sociologists in Japan in 1963. In that earlier research, he studied the inaugural addresses of all of the American presidents. In them, he was struck by the frequent and consistent religious references, regardless of the religious backgrounds of the various presidents. He recognized a pattern of what he called "civil religion" in those addresses and set out to see whether that pattern reached beyond the political arena into the broader reaches of American life.

He concluded that it did indeed. He argued that American religious analysis has tended too much to be a study of churches, whereas "there actually exists alongside of and rather clearly differentiated from the churches an elaborate and well-institutionalized civil religion in America." He described it as "certain common elements of religious orientation that the great majority of Americans share" and found there a sense of common understanding of the will of God for a nation of believers.[2]

In settings as varied as the Declaration of Independence, presidential inaugural addresses, Memorial Day observances, service club invocations, and informal conversations about the state of affairs in contemporary life, there is a pattern. Bellah calls it "a theme that lies very deep in the American tradition, namely, the obligation, both collective and individual, to carry out God's will on earth. This was the motivating spirit of those who founded America, and it has been present in every generation since."[3]

If one studies the competing religious institutions of the original thirteen colonies—most of them intolerant state churches—it quickly becomes clear that the new nation could not have found common religious ground through the churches. In fact, the vaunted First Amendment safeguards in relation to religion—"Congress shall make no law respecting an establishment of religion or prohibiting the free exercise thereof"—are recognition that when church and state are allies, it is often a dangerous and unholy alliance. Freedom of religion in America is, at least in part, the product of the rear-end collision of colonial state churches.

If there were to be any common religious dimensions to American life, they would have to evolve in the public sector, where people of faith could agree even if their churches could not. To accomplish that, their "civil religion" had to focus on those elements that were and are least controversial. Thus, civil religion in America does not have Christian sacraments or creeds. It does not accord a significant place to Jesus the Christ. It pays little attention to the life to come, preferring to focus on this life. "The God of civil religion is not only rather 'unitarian,' he is also on the austere side, much more related to order, law, and right than to salvation and love."[4] While it deliberately does not identify with any church or group of churches, it carries a powerful Protestant preference and a significant suspicion of Roman Catholics and Jews. It cares little about justice issues relating to women and members of minority groups in America.

But if civil religion in America does not have Christian sacraments or creeds and does not accord a place of high honor to Jesus, it compensates with its own set of sacred symbols and sacred texts:

- Memorial Day, a high holy day, a day to honor all of the dead, combined with special attention to those who have died in defense of the nation and special remembrance of the Founders and the founding of the nation
- Thanksgiving Day, a holiday sufficiently religious so church people have a vehicle for thanking God and sufficiently "public" so that others have a vehicle for expressing religious sentiment of the civic sort
- The Declaration of Independence
- Lincoln's Gettysburg Address and his second inaugural address
- The Bible, especially the portions that teach morality
- The American flag put in church sanctuaries, often placed there during times of national crisis and then balanced by the Christian flag
- The insertion of "under God" into the Pledge of Allegiance (1954) as an assertion over and against "godless communism."

These are the contours of present-day civil religion in America, but this is not how it began.

The Origins of American Civil Religion

Civil religion can originate at either pole:
- As a civil society that deifies its ruler or its values
- As a set of religious institutions that imposes its outlook on the social order.

Ours is of the latter sort. It started as a religious construct and then gradually moved over into the civil order. Sydney Ahlstrom, the late Yale church historian, was fond of saying that we all pay an English and Puritan price for being Americans. The English part is obvious. The Puritan part needs some commentary.

While civil religion in America owes its origin and present shape to a number of sources, the Puritans of New England made the most original and most powerful contributions. They are a most unusual source. They were those members of the Church of England who were the most distressed by the "Elizabethan Compromise" that finally brought peace to England after the turbulent years during and following Henry VIII's reign. The nation and the church had endured Henry's break with Rome; then the attempt of the regents for his son, Edward, to make the Church of England more Protestant; then his daughter Mary's attempt to reestablish the Roman Catholic Church in England; and finally his daughter Elizabeth's forging of a compromise to which all were expected to give allegiance.

These dissenters, who called themselves and were called Puritans, believed the Church of England was a sad caricature of what God intended the church to be, and they set out to purify it. Some of them worked within church and parliament (nonseparatists). Others believed the Church of England was so corrupt that it was no longer the church, so they become "separatists," forming voluntary congregations. When both church and state persecuted them, they sought to leave and find a place to practice their intense religion without interference. While some had to move first to the Low Countries, they ultimately chose a virgin place to construct a new society—the barren shores of New England.

There they established a theocracy, a society in which both church and public life were to draw direction only from Scripture, where all were required to be both church members and responsible citizens, where all of life was to be ruled by their transcendent God. They intended to be "a city set on a hill" to demonstrate, in a new place, that it is possible to be the kind of church and society God intends. So sure were they of their mission—their "Errand into the Wilderness," as Perry Miller put it—that they ascribed everything to God, even the disasters that frequently occurred.[5] Behind every occurrence in colonial and personal life, they saw the hand of God and were committed to being the best Christians God enabled them to be.

The intensity of their beginning did not last. Their children were not always convinced to commit their lives as fully as their parents had. Later settlers came who were only mildly Puritan, more interested in land than in religion. Congregations in frontier settlements became gatherings of the like-minded rather than outposts for Puritan theology and life. But, by then, the original theocratic pattern—state dominated by church—had been replaced by a selected set of Puritan religious beliefs that had moved over into the larger society and operated there without reliance on the churches.

Those religious beliefs are the stuff of American civil religion:

- The idea of a land different from any other; virgin in order to be organized more faithfully.
- The evangelizing zeal for setting an example and persuading the rest of the world to believe and live as they/we do (and a corresponding tendency to want to convert people who are believers in some other set of civic and religious values). The American sense of manifest destiny begins here.
- The determination to have no deliberate conflict between the will of God and the means and goals of our society and nation.[6]

This is a strange beginning in a church of "visible saints" for a set of impulses now principally located in the society, not in the churches.[7] Churches have been strongly influenced by this civil religion, some more than others and some more willingly than others. Some congregation members more than others bring tenets of American civil religion to congregational life and wonder why their church is not more "patriotic" or nationalistic.

The Effective Ecclesiology of American Civil Religion

It may seem strange even to think about ecclesiology in relation to a set of religious impulses that do not claim to be a church. But Sidney E. Mead points us toward a de facto ecclesiology when he borrows a G. K. Chesterton phrase to describe us as "a Nation with the soul of a church."[8] The essence of American civil religion is in a set of beliefs rather than in a set of structures. Or, perhaps it is more accurate to say that the set of beliefs is embedded in the structures of the American nation. The Declaration of Independence begins and ends with an appeal to God, using such deist terms as "Nature and Nature's God" and "Divine Providence." Between those religious bookends is an essentially secular statement of the issues that prompted the Declaration. Presidential inaugurals in America regularly use the same format—appeals to God at the beginning and end, and between them, an extended statement of the matters that need public attention. Presidents and other secular leaders regularly "bless" us as they conclude speeches. They are, or at least some people suppose them to be, the ecclesial leaders in promoting the set of values at the heart of American civil religion. And since that set of values is heavily weighted in the direction of personal morality, we are easily distressed by the misbehavior of our leaders, especially their breaches of public morality.

The basic beliefs identified earlier in this chapter form the doctrinal basis for American civil religion. No matter what one's particular religious affiliation or nonaffiliation, the formative effect of American civil religion pervades our culture. We see ourselves as a chosen people who have formed what the Preamble of the U.S. Constitution calls "a more perfect union" in order to carry out the will of God for a nation of believers. Not only are we called to believe and behave, but we are also called to share this vision with an unregenerate world. It is our manifest destiny to be that city set on a hill, to persuade the rest of the world to understand and respond to the will of God the creator. If American civil religion is a church, these beliefs constitute the mission commitments of that church.

> ✿ *"The United States has always been a nation of people with many and varied religious beliefs."*

Toward that end, Americans embrace a conception of their own history that liberally mixes fact and enabling myth. Frances Fitzgerald did a fascinating study of what has been taught at different times in the twentieth century as "American history." She described "what history textbooks have taught our children about their country, and how and why those textbooks have changed in different decades."[9] The triumphs have gradually been exaggerated, and the brokenness has been muted. The sense of a special people in a special nation with a special mission is highlighted, even where there is no reference to God or religion. History is always evidence, not just fact. In the teaching of American history, the evidence has been stacked toward relative innocence and manifest destiny.

Although the United States has always been a nation of people with many and varied religious beliefs, the assumption of American civil religion is a general Christianity with a strong emphasis on American superiority. It ignores the religion of native peoples, treating them as heathens to be conquered by God's chosen people on their mission in the wilderness. It is threatened by non-European immigration. Although it may promise to "unify" a nation, it negates the diversity of a healthy pluralism.[10] With the resurgence in interest in religion playing a more visible role in public life, the issue is not only that of the proper role of church and state but the underlying assumption that that role should be a civil religion.[11] American civil religion traditionally has offered an ecclesiology that excludes the faith of many, including many Christians.

The Doctrinal Denials in American Civil Religion

Civil religion is consensus religion—broad areas of general agreement and an agreement to ignore those things about which there is not general (or at least a perceived majority) agreement. American civil religion does not mention sacraments or creeds, and although it assumes a Christian base, it neglects the significance of Jesus. For example, the *Reader's Digest* understands itself as a teaching journal, teaching an American way of life that is superior to that of any other human community on earth. While it is not a religious journal, it wants to undergird the moral agenda of American civil religion, especially the part about a nation of believers doing the will of God. The *Digest* has a vested interest in ignoring Jesus, churches, sacraments, and creeds and in attacking the world and national councils of churches. Jesus is a "good man," a "moral influence," or a "spiritual guide." There is nothing about his suffering and crucifixion; his divinity, salvation, and resurrection; or the call to discipleship that works for justice.[12] The denial of what Lutherans and many other Christians consider to be central doctrine does not end with the almost total silence about Jesus. American civil religion has a very different understanding of both law and gospel than does the Bible or do the Lutheran Confessions. Underlying that denial is a rejection of what Christians have learned to call original sin. Instead, Americans are encouraged to hold a sense of relative innocence about ourselves and about what is normative in our culture and nation:

- In American civil religion, nature is—like "nature's God"—good. Civilization and sophistication are problematic, so we are a good bit short of perfect, but we are not "by nature sinful and unclean," no matter what our liturgies lead us to say about ourselves.
- There are "better people" and better nations in the world; we as Americans, however, see ourselves as the best.
- In this good world of our own construction, Americans prefer to believe "equal opportunity" exists unless laziness or "acts of God" interfere.
- Predestinarian and determinist outlooks are rejected because such beliefs stifle individual initiative.
- American civil religion needs to find evil outside ourselves, in such things as "the evil empire" and internal moral decay, caused by those who do not discipline their lives and make their expected contributions to the common good. In fact, this culture is most at home when it can identify a common external enemy as well as the perennial internal enemy of moral decay.

Law, in such a mind-set, is synonymous with the will of God, with the added conviction that God has a special task for America. Law relates to "order" of a sort that is minimally constricting for the good people but constrains those without self-discipline. Our attitudes toward welfare and graduated income tax are driven by this sense that everyone has the capacity to care for the self and for the self's significant others. In the civil religious frame of reference, law does not universally confront or condemn everyone. There is no recognition of Paul's assertion:

> Now we know that whatever the law says it speaks to those who are under the law, so that every mouth may be stopped, and the whole world may be held accountable to God. For no human being will be justified in his sight by works of the law since through the law comes knowledge of sin.[13]

That sense of relative innocence is documented in an interesting study by historian David Noble.[14] He studied the pattern of references to Adam and Eve in American literature and public discourse and proposes that Americans think of themselves as Adam and Eve before the fall and of their land as "the new world garden." That suggests that they may sometimes be gullible but seldom culpable.

"Gospel" also takes on distorted meaning in civil religious contexts. Mostly, gospel is not a subject of much interest to those who practice the civil form of religion. But if they do talk about gospel, it is laced with self-help:

- There is relatively little attention to saving grace, and if there is, it tends to quote with approval Ben Franklin's "God helps him who helps himself."
- There is some recognition of sin, but it is construed as offense against piety or self-discipline, not as describing a universal human condition.
- There is the "gospel of wealth" popularized by Andrew Carnegie.
- There is the "gospel of self-help."
- There is the good news of self-approval à la positive thinking.
- Grace is understood as God helping people to complete what the natural being is able to start, which translates into belief in a "gracious God" rather than a God of grace. For Lutheran Christians, these are especially serious denials of doctrine. Luther has persuaded us to approach the whole of Scripture through the lens of law and gospel.

The Evangelical Lutheran Church in America constitutional "Confession of Faith" says: "The proclamation of God's message to us as both Law and Gospel is the Word of God, revealing judgment and mercy through word and deed, beginning with the Word in creation, continuing in the history of Israel, and centering in all its fullness in the person and work of Jesus Christ."[15] The denial of key biblical understandings of human brokenness and of the real power of God's law and God's grace are terrible betrayals of what the transcendent God has revealed.[16]

The Recovery of Transcendence

American civil religion is a pattern of belief that competes for our allegiance. It diverges from biblical Christianity in significant enough ways that it needs to be challenged at several points:

- It is near enough to the Christian faith that it can both substitute for and distort what people need to understand about themselves and about God.
- It is enough the embodiment of the American ethos to grant false divine sanction for nationalistic means and goals.

At the same time, it must be said that civil religion is probably inevitable, or at least a better alternative than no religious commitments at all. This is especially true in a nation as diverse in origins as ours. Civil religion provides much of the glue that binds us together and does that a lot more efficiently than the churches have managed to do. The prospects for us as a nation would be grim if there were no concern for the will of God and no attempts to restrain self-interest.

So there are some choices about whether and how to invest ourselves in relation to American civil religion:

- We can seek to merge denominational Christianity with civil religion in a "Christian nation" framework.
- We can seek to stand in opposition to civil religion—and risk being marginalized when it comes to pressing issues in nation and culture.
- We can seek to invest in enriching civil religion so that it more nearly serves as a genuine vehicle for the will of God. We can be both critical and supportive, especially by offering our best theology to enrich the theological foundations of civil religion.

Toward the latter end, the place to begin is the reassertion of the transcendent nature of God. If the culture has ears to hear what God is really saying to us as individuals and as a nation, there is hope. Once in a while, that note is sounded. Listen to Lincoln in his second inaugural address:

> It may seem strange that any men should dare to ask a just God's assistance in wringing their bread from the sweat of other men's faces; but let us judge not that we be not judged. The prayers of both (sides) could not be

answered; that of neither has been answered fully. The Almighty has His own purposes. "Woe unto the world because of offences! For it must needs be that offences come; but woe to that man by whom the offence cometh!" If we shall suppose that American Slavery is one of those offences which, in the providence of God, must needs come, but which, having continued through His appointed time, He now wills to remove, and that He gives to both North and South, this terrible war, as the woe due to those by whom the offence came, shall we discern therein any departure from those divine attributes which the believers in a Living God always ascribe to Him. . . . Yet, if God wills that it continue, until all the wealth piled by the bondmen's two hundred and fifty years of unrequited toil shall be sunk, and until every drop of blood drawn with the lash, shall be paid by another drawn with the sword . . . so still it must be said, "the judgments of the Lord, are true and righteous altogether."

It takes an extraordinary amount of candor to recognize and admit, even to ourselves, how far short we fall of what God expects of us. The natural instinct is to move to the shallow end of the pool, there to admit a little sin and seek a little forgiveness, before plunging back into the lusts of life. That works as long as one's own life seems to be under control and our national security and prosperity seem to be assured. But those who operate with a sense of relative innocence and confidence are at risk of being plunged into deep despair when these supports collapse. Are we not wiser to recognize our utter dependence on a transcendent God? Are we not called to meet a much higher standard in our life together as American citizens in a global community?

What then becomes of our sense of being a special nation? That idea is not as wrong as it first appears. But the biblical text that governs us on that score is not the one about being "a city set on a hill" but rather the one that says, "Every one to whom much is given, of him or her (them) will much be required" (Luke 12:48).[17] So much has been given to us by God, who is both righteous and merciful; so much is expected of us as stewards of those gifts. Our allegiance must be to the transcendent God, whose righteousness and mercy are both beyond our understanding. Our calling is to serve both that righteousness and that mercy in our dealings with one another and in our commitment to the one world in which we are called to live as servants.

Imagining the New Community in Christ and the Challenges of Race and Class

---

WINSTON D. PERSAUD

The ongoing and indispensable challenge of the church is how to respond to racism, classism, and sexism. In this postmodern and postcolonial era, unresolved divisions reemerge. How can the church view race and ethnicity as gifts, not difficulties? How do people learn to share power? And how can the church of Jesus Christ be a church risen from the dead, able to fully utilize all members of the body of Christ?

John Lennon's song "Imagine"—both the lyrics and the tune—has an arresting quality. For a long time now, I have been thinking about writing a theological response to Lennon's song. More specifically, I have been thinking about writing a theological critique of the eschatological vision he proffers. Invariably, whenever I hear "Imagine," I pause and listen, and I ponder its imaginative eschatological longing for a world that does not exist. Lennon longs for a world different from and better than the world we have and know. He wants "the world to be as one . . . [To] live as one."

Lennon is not the only one imagining a different kind of world from the one we know and in which we live. I, too, imagine a different world. I try to imagine it is true that Christians believe that in Christ there is a new creation[1] in which old distinctions and barriers that militate against equality and unity in the Christian community are not allowed to dominate the life of the community. What would this mean for congregations if it were true, however fleetingly and fragmentarily?

We are keenly aware that the world of the twenty-first century is a world of the Internet. It is also postmodern and postcolonial. In this milieu, there is much truth to the saying "perception is reality." We know and we perceive that, on both the global and the local fronts, new "unities" as well as old antagonisms and unresolved divisions continue to emerge and reappear with surprising speed and power. Increasingly, we are being linked together in faster and more decisive ways than we might have ever imagined just ten years ago![2] With this incredibly fast-paced interlinking of peoples and cultures come heightened expectations that there will be both the welcome of diversity in our communities and the subtle and even blatant protection of the homogeneity of our communities. At the root of the protectionism is the fear of losing power and control over oneself and one's family. We have not found a way around the pervasive belief in and the need to have power over others in order to gain self-worth and increased value among our peers and in the wider community.

> *"I try to imagine it is true that Christians believe that in Christ there is a new creation in which old barriers are not allowed to dominate the life of the community."*

This state of affairs is not confined to the so-called secular world or to the world of the "other" religions. It is inevitably part and parcel of the Christian church. It is, therefore, to the "world" of the church—specifically, how the church concretely expresses itself as the new creation in Christ—that I will attend. With the theme of the new creation in Christ in mind, I will try to imagine what the church in its contemporary global, national, denominational, and local expressions might look like. Each is a religious, socioeconomic, and political reality. As a teacher of the church and a member in the pew in a local congregation, I will "imagine" the world of the new creation in Christ. We begin with some of the *givens*.

Race and Ethnicity as Gifts

Race and ethnicity are part of the givens of God's creation. Every human being belongs to (or should we say comes from?) a specific ethnic community. Racial and ethnic differences do not reflect a mistake by God. They are intrinsic to being particular human beings, living in particular communities. When we say with Luther that before God we stand *coram Deo* as sinners in need of God's undeserved mercy and forgiveness in Jesus Christ, it is particular human beings marked by gender, race, ethnicity, and class who stand in the presence of God. When we say that such "standing" before God places us on common ground or, as we are more apt to say, on a level playing field, we are saying that God sees our specificities and does not regard them as problems or as denoting levels of righteousness among us. If this is true, and we all confess this to be true to the Scriptures, the Creeds, and the Confessions, then there are radical, surprising, and disturbing implications for the way we teach, order our lives, and imagine and "fashion" the church.

Another of the givens of the Christian understanding of reality and of God's gift of undeserved salvation in Jesus Christ is that the incarnation of the eternal Word happened in a particular human being, a Jew, Jesus of Nazareth, who lived in first-century Palestine. It is this Jesus, who walked among us and who was crucified and raised from the dead, who is declared and confessed as the cosmic Christ. There is a human concreteness to his reality. The cosmic Christ is the crucified and risen Jesus who was known as a carpenter's son. His family was known.[3]

The gospel, the good news of salvation in and through Jesus Christ, comes through the particularities of gender, culture, race, and ethnicity, and the gospel transcends those necessary factors. As St. Athanasius declared in the fourth century of the Common Era, the gospel is about the divine taking on humanity that we might take on divinity. In Jesus Christ, God entered into the very fabric of human reality; the Word became flesh and dwelt among us (John 1:14). Thus, being human is not strange to God, the source of life and wholeness. There is no getting around the historical "conditionedness" of the message of the gospel. It always comes in human language, and it participates in human culture. This is a given in this postmodern world in which we live.

The Exercise of Power and Authority

Who, then, is truly fit to pronounce this good news? Who, then, is fit to proclaim the Word and administer the sacraments? Responding in a sacramental vein, we say, "Anyone who is called and ordained." Nevertheless, we recognize the indelible character of our baptism through which we all are called to witness to the Word. All Christians are commissioned to tell the good news of Jesus Christ to a world longing for forgiveness and personal and social healing.[4] The Holy Spirit, who empowers such witnessing in word and deed, does not favor anyone on account of gender, ethnicity, race, or class. The Holy Spirit, who gives life, calls all to life in Jesus Christ and sends forth all who believe, both ordained and lay, to bear witness to the transforming power of Jesus Christ. Vivified by and participating in God's power, we are to point to God alone as the source of life and wholeness. No one is exempt from this way of being.

But let us be clear and honest, to be duly authorized to proclaim the Word and administer the sacraments is to be in a position of power. The ways in which we view and value structures and systems necessarily lead us to assume that those who "handle" things of power, including and especially "holy" things, are vested with extraordinary power. They are not only set apart, but also set above. I used to think that this view was prevalent only among people, both ordained and lay, in the "colonies." But that is just not true. Christians, whether they are in the "first," "second," or "third" world, are not immune to thinking in these ways and structuring life accordingly.[5]

Let us imagine that in his coming in the givenness of his particularities Jesus broke down the walls of division. A consequence would be that those who exercise authority and power, including those who proclaim the Word and administer the sacraments, are to be a "mixed" lot. Also, those among whom such exercise of authority and power occurs are to be a mixed lot. What might this mean?

One unmistakable implication is that our congregations would have to seek to be mixed. This would mean that we would then be with people with whom we would not normally spend time. Here, we would be spending time around what is most precious in all the world, the good news of Jesus Christ.

Mixed congregations are necessary to the proclamation of the gospel. Mixed congregations historically played a decisive role in preserving and proclaiming the gospel. In the first century, the church in a radical change moved from being overwhelmingly Jewish to being increasingly non-Jewish and mixed. "Paul's theology . . . made it possible for those mixed congregations of the second generation to rescue that which was of intrinsic value from the shambles of Palestinian Christianity and to survive an age of transition."[6] The non-Jewish believers in Christ were also equally fit to be preservers and bearers of the most decisive news God has given: the gospel of God's justifying grace through the death and resurrection of Jesus Christ.

What would happen to our congregations if the dominant and non-negotiable vision of the Christian community was of people from the four corners of the earth (Acts 10) meeting around the Word and sacraments? Imagine that it were true that what constitutes our identity as Christians is that we share one baptism into Christ. Imagine that before God we are to live as who we are, a new people created through faith in Jesus Christ in the power of the Holy Spirit.

What would happen if those who find themselves in positions of power and dominance merely on account of their race, ethnic identity, or class resolve that such criteria will not be primary in the exercise of their offices? Instead, they would use criteria that stand in stark contrast to the criterion of prejudice, rooted in stereotypes of race, ethnicity, and class.

Here, the chief criterion of who can be trusted to seek "my good" would be eschewed. What would we have to gain and what would we have to lose in pursuing this presumptuous scenario?

Critical to embracing this scenario would be the eschewing of our own proclivity to view positions of power and authority as ontologically constitutive of our being.[7] The history of the Christian church is replete with examples of this form of idolatry. Before God, we are not constituted by the power we have over others. Neither ethnicity nor gender nor class makes us more worthy of God's grace in Jesus Christ. The pivotal Reformation insight—justification by grace alone, through faith alone, on account of Christ alone—is still the good news!

Being Communities of Diversity

Are ethnically homogeneous churches the only way forward? We continue to persist in using mission strategies that guarantee that our congregational memberships are overwhelmingly homogeneous in terms of ethnicity, race, and class. But that violates the truth that God has created diversity and invites people from the four corners of the earth to hear and believe the good news of Jesus the Christ. De jure or de facto, preserving and promoting only "our own kind" has had tragic consequences. We know this only too well. No Christian can rest easy in the face of the persistent reminder of the sin and evil of the Holocaust. Among the lessons we are being pressed to learn from the tragedy of the ethnic genocide in Burundi and Rwanda is that the demonic is inherent in a closed "ethnic" Christianity. Let me hasten to add that the demonic is also inherent in any other Christianity.

The worship life of a congregation indicates how open we are to diversity. There is no one way to worship, but some ways are more faithful to the gospel than are others.[8] Some ways are so class based that there is no place for the "outsider" to be at home fully and to belong.[9] We need forms of worship that facilitate the gathered community to be diverse in terms of such factors as educational attainment, social class, ethnicity, and age. We have to work at ensuring that the forms in which the gospel message is presented in worship do not militate against people hearing and experiencing the gospel. For some cultures and ethnic groups, to follow individually and quietly the printed order of worship without any instruction and guidance from the worship leader or assistant is not as highly valued as it is in and among other cultures and ethnic groups. Having a printed text is not really the issue; how the worship leaders use it is.

For example, giving clear and nonintrusive instructions as the worship proceeds might be most helpful and convey a welcome that would otherwise not be felt by many. What level of education does one need in order to worship without embarrassment in our congregations?

The matter of who might be "at home" in a typical congregation is more complex than might first meet the eye. A friend of mine from Guyana, who had grown up Lutheran and was also a college graduate, was once asked in a Lutheran congregation in the United States whether she does not miss worshiping with her "own people." The obvious assumption was that her ethnicity determined the form of worship with which she would be at home. In my friend's case, it was the *form* of worship, not the kind of people, that was determinative of the community with which she would be at home. Sadly and tragically, people are deeply conscious of what "kind" of people should belong to "their" church. In the popular media and in mainstream culture, we see and hear that only the majority or our "kind" really counts. But that is not the way of Jesus Christ, who cares no less about the lost sheep than about the ninety-nine.

I wonder why we keep thinking in closed ways of "my people" and "their people" (I recognize that such thinking is inevitable and, at times, necessary). Perhaps there is a deep fear in us that if the church were more diverse we would lose our opportunities to be somebody, somebody with power and authority. Imagine what would happen if we were to look close to home and wonder if God is grieved by the way we draw the boundaries around those who hear the Word of life, leaving so many outside. Would we stand condemned just as white South Africans (among others) on a global scale were publicly condemned for their racism and the implementation of apartheid? Imagine that it was not just blue-collar Afrikaaners, for example, who were so grasping at power over the blacks as if that were constitutive of their ultimate value and worth!

Hearing the Word is fundamentally a communal experience. We need one another to hear the Word of life in Jesus Christ. Some are chosen to exercise the ministry of leadership for the sake of the gospel and for good order. Imagine that there are qualified people who would provide a diversified leadership. Would that make a difference in the way we witness to the gospel? Servant leadership and the proclamation of the gospel in word and deed belong together. Servant leadership means not the absence of power but the presence and exercise of a different kind of power, the kenotic power of Jesus.[10]

One of the greatest challenges to being this kind of mixed community is the question of how power and authority will be exercised. Imagine that we actually recognize that those who are different from us in terms of race, ethnicity, and class are our equals in Christ. Imagine that this were true, whether they were far from us or in our communities. Imagine that we all exercised this equality in our life together. What would it look like?

Imagining Shared Power in Community

Gender, race, ethnicity, skin color, and class are moral, political, and economic categories. Locally, nationally, and globally, we see and hear that ethnic/racial, class, and cultural differences engender and elicit negative feelings of distrust, superiority, insecurity, and even outright hatred that are often not founded on reality. In our congregations and church bodies, to whom do we easily ascribe truthfulness, honesty, ethical fairness, economic viability, superior education, and power? We carry stereotypical expectations about who will look after "our good." Some of us readily advocate that once the playing field is level, leadership in the church at all levels should be diverse. But we would not want people different from ourselves or our kind to exercise authority over us. Among other factors, our own sense of self would be threatened.

Let us imagine that we eschewed the "quarterback" approach to leadership, whereby only one ethnic group stereotypically is considered capable to lead. In this highly "commodified" world, there may be the tendency to look upon the "professional" experience of members of one ethnic group or class as being of a higher value than that of members of another ethnic group or class. We may call this the "currency exchange" rate of ethnic/racial and classbound professional experience. In the Christian community, there is no place for this approach. It is anathema. Imagine that this stereotype were replaced by an approach that reflects the new creation in Jesus Christ. When Paul lists many of the gifts of the Spirit, he does not say that only Jews or Greeks are capable of possessing any of those gifts.[11] To have suggested that would have undercut the radical message that in Christ there is a new creation and that old distinctions and divisions are no longer in force.[12] Imagine that in sending Jesus, God expects that those who believe in him would not be guided primarily by ethnic, racial, and class identity but by the gospel of Jesus Christ.

I sometimes try to imagine what our congregations will look like in the year 2050, when there is expected to be a major demographic change in the United States. Analysts project that by 2010 the ethnic/racial composition of the population of the United States of America will be 71 percent white, 13 percent Hispanic, 12 percent African American, and 4 percent Asian. More striking are the projections for the year 2050: 53 percent white, 25 percent Hispanic, 14 percent African American, and 8 percent Asian.[13] Already, the religious landscape in the United States and Canada is notable for its increasingly obvious plurality and diversity. "Almost unnoticed, the United States has become the most religiously diverse place on the planet."[14] How should we respond theologically and missiologically in this new "georeligious" and demographic context?

When the community in Christ gathers around the Word and sacraments, imagine that those who proclaim the Word and who preside at the table are a mixed group! That would be shared authority that handles power, God's power! We eagerly look for signs that this is already happening, for God has not left us without hope, hope that we glimpse and experience in concrete ways. We wonder whether what we imagine is mere wishful thinking, a sham. We know that in the face of so many signs to the contrary, God, who raised Jesus from the dead, is the God of life. We do not live for today as if there is no future that shapes our present. Rather, empowered by the Holy Spirit, we fix our gaze upon the Risen One, who had been crucified. Thereby, already, the new community in Christ from all four corners of the earth shows, however partially and with humility, the reign of God that has come and is coming.

The Body of Christ
and the Issue of Required Celibacy

GWEN B. SAYLER

How does the contemporary church deal with the difficult struggle around the issue of homosexuality? A body of Christ theology challenges the church to understand that no member of the body is dispensable. The health of the whole body depends on healthy relationships among individual bodies within it. Does the gift of sexuality include sexual orientation? Are chastity and celibacy synonymous? How much difference is permissible?

Since New Testament times, the presence of different kinds of individual bodies within the larger body has posed ecclesiastical challenges for Christian communities. One need look no further than the Pauline corpus to witness the struggle of the church to discern how to be the one body of Christ in, with, and under the diversity of bodies that comprise it.

In Western churches today, the struggle tends to focus on a category of difference unknown in biblical times—that of sexual orientation.[1] Christian communities today agonize over whether to include persons self-identified as homosexual within the body of Christ. How much bodily difference is permissible? Is there room within the body for gay and lesbian bodies?

In this chapter, I will examine and critique the practice of mandated celibacy as an avenue for the inclusion of homosexual bodies within the body. The official discourse of the Evangelical Lutheran Church in America (ELCA) regarding its expectations for homosexual clergy and rostered lay leaders will serve as an example of this practice.[2] This discourse will be examined as will Paul's discourse on marriage and celibacy in 1 Corinthians 7. Then, I will use the logic and assumptions underlying Paul's discourse to critique the ELCA discourse. Based on this critique, I will propose a reconfiguration of the conversation about homosexuality as a resource for congregations and judicatory bodies.

Discourse of the
Evangelical Lutheran Church in America

The ELCA was formed in 1988 by the merger of three predecessor bodies. Like many denominations, it struggles with the issue of homosexuality. Official conversations focus primarily on interpretation of the few biblical texts that refer to same-sex sexual intercourse. Insofar as the texts are ambiguous and their contexts far different from the contemporary context, the ELCA has been unable to reach a consensus regarding "what the Bible says" about homosexuality.[3]

Despite this lack of consensus, the ELCA was compelled early in its existence to take a public position regarding the presence of homosexual clergy in ministry. Although there had been homosexual clergy in the predecessor churches, the matter of their inclusion within the body had been handled quietly, without public ado.[4] Almost simultaneously with the merger, this approach was challenged by the public announcement by three seminary students from Pacific Lutheran Theological Seminary in Berkeley, California, that they were homosexuals seeking ordination.

Primarily in order to deal with this challenge, the ELCA quickly produced the document *Vision and Expectations* to express "both the vision for ordained ministry in the life of this church and the high expectations its members have of those who serve in this ministry."[5] Adopted as official policy in 1990, this small document (sixteen pages) is divided into four sections: (1) The Call to Ordained Ministry; (2) Faithfulness to the Church's Confession; (3) The Ordained Minister as Person and Example; and (4) Faithful Witness.

Sexual relationships are discussed in the third section. After stating that the ordained minister is to be an example of holy living, the document lists qualities of holy life under three subheadings: *Responsibility to family; Separation, Divorce, and Remarriage;* and *Sexual conduct.*[6] Homosexuality is addressed specifically only in the final sentence of the final paragraph of the section:

> Sexual conduct. The expectations of this church regarding the sexual conduct of its ordained ministers are grounded in the understanding that human sexuality is a gift from God and that ordained ministers are expected to reject sexual promiscuity, the manipulation of others for purposes of sexual gratification, and all attempts of sexual seduction and

sexual harassment, including taking physical or emotional advantage of others. Single ordained ministers are expected to live a chaste life. Married ordained ministers are expected to live in fidelity to their spouses, giving expression to sexual intimacy within a marriage relationship that is mutual, chaste, and faithful. Ordained ministers who are homosexual in their self-understanding are expected to abstain from homosexual sexual relationships.[7]

On the surface, the meaning of the paragraph seems straightforward. Sexuality is a gift from God, and all forms of sexual exploitation are to be rejected.[8] Because the definition of "sexuality" is assumed rather than given, however, implications for homosexual bodies remain unclear. Does the gift of sexuality include sexual orientation? If so, is homosexual orientation a gift, or is the gift limited to heterosexual orientation? Given that homosexual clergy are expected to abstain from all homosexual sexual relationships, it appears that the latter is the case.

The contrast between expectations for single pastors (chastity) and homosexual pastors (permanent abstinence) supports this conclusion. Chastity and celibacy are not necessarily synonymous. In living chaste lives, single heterosexual pastors are free to discern whether they are called to remain single or to enter into marriage. This freedom of discernment is not granted to homosexual pastors. Interestingly, only homosexual sexual relationships are prohibited for homosexual clergy. Either the document assumes that it is not harmful for them to enter into heterosexual marriage, or the possibility that homosexual clergy would choose this route was not entertained.

The ambiguity in the paragraph reflects the deep ambivalence of the ELCA regarding the inclusion of homosexual bodies within the larger body. On the one hand, the official discourse does offer homosexual clergy an avenue to serve within the body. On the other hand, there is a deep hesitancy to affirm these clergy as embodied homosexual individuals with all the sensations, feelings, and needs for intimacy that their heterosexual sisters and brothers experience. This ambivalence is understandable in light of the ELCA's ongoing struggle to determine its stance on homosexuality in general. Nonetheless, the church in the third millennium needs to reflect on implications of this position for the health of individual homosexual bodies and of the body as a whole. Does mandated celibacy for homosexual clergy further the mission of the church, or does it impede it? How does the witness of Scripture contribute to this particular conversation?

Few biblical texts talk about celibacy. First Corinthians 7 does so within the context of Paul's concern for the health of the larger body. Because the concept of sexual orientation was unknown in the ancient world, it is impossible to detect a direct correlation between Paul's argument in 1 Corinthians and the ELCA's policy of mandated celibacy for homosexual clergy. Nonetheless, the rationale Paul offers for marriage and celibacy within the context of his concern for the health of the larger body opens interesting possibilities for the shape that contemporary conversations about homosexuality might take.

Paul's Discourse in 1 Corinthians 7

Most scholars concur that Paul wrote 1 Corinthians to exhort a divided Corinthian church to become reunified. The persuasive force of 1 Corinthians is its call for the unity of the one body in, with, and under the diversity of individual bodies that it comprises.[9] Throughout the letter, Paul grounds the identity of individual believers in their baptismal identity within the one body of Christ (for example, 1:2; 6:11; 12:12-13). Individual bodies are temples of the Holy Spirit and are called to live as such (3:16-17; 6:19). Diversity abounds among the many bodies that make up the Corinthian church, particularly in terms of gifts. Honoring all members in their diversity is essential for the integrity of the body (12:1-27).

Paul believes that the one body is dangerously permeable, open to the threat of pollution from the outside world. Because of the danger of pollution, the health of the whole body depends on healthy relationships among the individual bodies within it.[10]

This theme becomes particularly clear in Paul's lengthy discussion of sexual relationships in chapters 5 through 7. Consistently, Paul presents the sexual desire of individuals as a dangerous force that must be properly channeled to protect the body from pollution. His concern about the power of sexual desire permeates his discussion of celibacy and marriage in chapter 7.

The introductory phrase "Concerning those things of which you wrote" (7:1) indicates that Paul is responding to questions or statements addressed to him by members of the Corinthian community. The meaning of the quotation "It is good for a man not to touch a woman" (7:1) is ambiguous. It may be the answer to a question, or simply a repetition of an assertion of some members of the community. In any case, the quotation raises the issue of sexual abstinence versus appropriate sexual activity as a primary concern of the chapter.

The basis of Paul's advocacy for appropriate sexual activity within marriage becomes clear immediately. Individuals need to enter into marriage as a protection against the threat of wrongful sexual activity (*porneia*, 7:2). Within this relationship, each partner has sexual responsibilities toward the other (7:3-4). Mutually agreed upon abstinence is appropriate as a temporary measure entered into for the sake of prayer. Resumption of appropriate sexual activity is necessary as a protection lest Satan tempt the individuals through lack of self-control (7:5).

After establishing his rationale for appropriate sexual activity within marriage, Paul states his personal preference for sexual abstinence. Then he qualifies it by adding "but each of us has a particular gift [*charisma*] from God, one this, the other that" (7:7). Traditional interpretations often assume that the "gift" highlighted is celibacy. Another possibility is that the "gift" is Paul's prophetic calling, with celibacy as simply one aspect of that calling.[11] In any event, Paul makes the point that sexual abstinence is preferable but appropriate for only some within the community.

Paul's awareness of the limitations of his endorsement of abstinence is clear in his advice to the unmarried and to widows (7:8-9). If the desires aroused by sexual passion cannot be controlled, they need to be channeled into appropriate sexual activity within marriage—"it is better to marry than to burn" (7:9). After exhorting those who are married not to divorce but also making allowance for its possibility (7:10-16), Paul encourages believers to remain in whatever condition they were when called (that is, circumcised or uncircumcised, slave or free, 7:17-24). Then he returns to the issue of sexual abstinence versus sexual activity for the unmarried. At this point, the apocalyptic context of Paul's thought becomes explicit. Convinced that this world will end soon ("the impending crisis," 7:26), Paul urges the married to remain married and the unmarried to remain unmarried. What counts is the most expeditious use of what little time is left to further the mission of the body (7:25-35, 39-40). Yet, as is clear in Paul's words to men about their virgins (probably women to whom they are engaged), the power of sexual desire is such that marriage remains preferable to loss of control due to sexual passion (7:36-38).

Thus, throughout 1 Corinthians 7, Paul's affirmation of celibacy for some is situated within the context of his concern for the health of the broader body and its imperative for mission. Paul assumes that sexual desire is integral to embodiment and is a powerful force in the life of the individual. If that desire can be controlled, then sexual abstinence offers the individual an opportunity for undistracted dedication to the mission of the body. If that desire cannot be controlled, however, it needs to be channeled into appropriate sexual activity within marriage for the sake of the health of the entire body.

Paul's preference for celibacy is interconnected with his own sense of prophetic calling and with the urgent need to focus totally on the work of the Lord in the brief time left before the final judgment. Despite his preference that believers remain celibate, Paul is clear that few persons possess the self-control necessary for permanent abstinence. The power of sexual desire simply is too strong to make celibacy viable for most individual believers. From Paul's perspective, sexual relationships never are a matter simply of individual choice. The unity and health of the entire body are at stake in the ordering of sexual desire among its individual bodies.

Reading the ELCA Discourse in Light of Paul's Discourse

The witness of Scripture in 1 Corinthians 7 suggests that the practice of mandating celibacy for a selected group of bodies within the body is fraught with consequences that the drafters of the ELCA document *Vision and Expectations* may not have envisioned. Requiring a group of the baptized to maintain a self-control that Paul believes most individuals do not possess places pressures on individuals and on the body that are almost inevitably detrimental to the health of both.

The variety of lived experiences of homosexual ELCA clergy illustrates this point.[12] In accord with the church's official discourse, many homosexual clergy remain celibate. Some regard their ability to abstain from sexual relationships as a gift. For others, celibacy is not a gift. It is a discipline requiring enormous expenditures of energy. These pastors have to learn to cut themselves off from the possibility of intimacy, to live a solitary life to which they believe they have not been called. Usually, celibate homosexual pastors are expected to pretend that they are unmarried heterosexuals. In terms of personal health and energy to do ministry fully and freely, the cost to these individual bodies is great. By implication, the cost to the health and mission of the entire body is also great.

Like the majority of believers addressed in 1 Corinthians 7, many homosexual clergy discover that they are not able to abstain permanently from sexual relationships. As a result, some resign from the ministries to which they have been called. Others attempt to dull the force of their sexual desire by overindulging in food or alcohol. Some enter into heterosexual marriages, hoping against hope that they can learn to become someone they are not. Others enter into secretive temporary sexual relationships with all sorts of unhealthy consequences for themselves and their ministries. Still others choose to enter clandestinely into a permanent committed relationship with a partner. These pastors live in fear that their committed relationship will be discovered and that they will be removed from the public ministries to which the church has called them. Disciplinary records of the ELCA and other denominations illustrate the incredible pain caused for the individuals, their congregations or institutions, and the entire body as the removal process unfolds.

Despite the ELCA's well-intended attempt to provide an avenue for the inclusion of homosexual bodies within the body, its policy of mandated celibacy for homosexual clergy has had detrimental effects on many clergy and on the mission of the body as a whole. The logic and assumptions underlying Paul's discourse in 1 Corinthians 7 elucidate why the policy has failed. Sexual desire is integral to embodiment. It is such a powerful force that the health of the whole body depends on how effectively it is channeled into appropriate sexual relationships. A few believers have the self-control necessary for permanent sexual abstinence; most do not. The ELCA's attempt to require of all homosexual pastors a self-control that Paul claims cannot be required has polluted the body, not purified and united it.

Reconfiguring the Conversation

The practice of mandated celibacy for homosexual clergy is one small part of the much larger conversation about the church's response to homosexuality. As is true for many denominations, eventually the ELCA will have to come to a decision regarding whether there is room within the body for gay and lesbian bodies. In the case of the ELCA, this decision will be based on biblical and theological studies in dialogue with the history of Lutheran tradition. Until that decision is reached, however, it behooves the ELCA to reconfigure the conversation to address how present practices may be detrimental to the health of individual homosexual Christians and to the mission of the body as a whole.[13] This reconfigured conversation needs to take place on congregational as well as judicatory levels, and it needs to respond to the realities of homosexual laypeople as well as of homosexual clergy. Although silent about their sexuality because they fear rejection or exclusion from the body, many homosexual laypeople have stories to share about the suffering present policies have inflicted upon them.

Two terminological clarifications will facilitate reconfiguring the conversation. First, the word "sexuality" refers to a person's entire sense of embodiment. This includes, but is not limited to, a person's specific sexual behavior.[14] Heterosexuals are heterosexual whether they engage in sexual intercourse or not. The same is true for homosexuals. Any practice that implies that homosexuals are welcome as long as they do not "act" on their sexuality ignores this basic reality.

Second, in our time and place, the definition of marriage is limited to a permanent sexual relationship between two heterosexual partners. Because this language automatically excludes them, homosexuals have developed the terminology of "committed relationship" to define the permanent sexual relationship of two homosexual partners. Functionally, the terms *marriage* and *committed relationship* serve the same basic purpose but for different constituencies.

With these terminological clarifications in place, Paul's focus on baptismal identity provides a helpful starting point for reconfiguring the conversation. For Paul, the baptismal identity of each believer is the sine qua non for any discussion of the unity of the body. Because they all have been baptized into one body, Christians in all their incredible diversity can take courage to move beyond their fear of those different from themselves to genuine dialogue. The conversation about homosexuality, like the conflict-laden conversations in the church at Corinth, is not about a group "out there," far removed from and different from the community undertaking the discussion. Rather, it is an intracommunity conversation of the baptized seeking to discern how most faithfully to live as the body of Christ in a particular time and place.

> ✺ *"Because they all have been baptized into one body, Christians in all their incredible diversity can take courage to move beyond their fear of those different from themselves."*

In this conversation of the baptized, Paul's conviction that sexual desire is integral to embodiment can provide a springboard to a discussion on how sexual relationships between any two people need to be ordered to maintain the health and empower the mission of the whole body. What qualities, attitudes, and actions contribute to the well-being of the partners and of the whole community? Such qualities as faithfulness, mutuality, and commitment come to mind immediately. Many more can be added.

Within this reconfigured conversation, the ELCA needs to address directly two pressing interrelated issues: (1) its present practice of requiring homosexual clergy to control rather than channel their sexual desires, and (2) its silence regarding how homosexual members of the body are called to deal with their sexual desires. Given the shortcomings of the present practice, and the dangers inherent in privileging silence over dialogue, it seems appropriate to raise the question as to whether the practice of mandated celibacy should be lifted and the silence surrounding homosexual bodies within the body broken.

Again, at some point, the ELCA and other denominations struggling with the issue will have to come to a decision regarding whether there is room in the body for homosexual bodies. In the interim, what would happen if those persons who are homosexual in their self-understanding were held to the same standards of healthy sexual relationships (for example, mutuality, commitment, faithfulness) as their heterosexual brothers and sisters? Until it is determined whether the body's purity and unity necessitate excluding homosexuals from it, what would happen if their sexuality were acknowledged and guidance in living as sexual beings was offered to them as well as to their heterosexual sisters and brothers?

Certainly, this interim change in practice would free homosexual clergy to engage more freely and fully in the ministries to which they have been called. The mission of the church would be served well by this infusion of energy and freedom from fear. At the same time, homosexual members of congregations no longer would be left adrift regarding what healthy sexual relationships for them might look like. In particular, young gays and lesbians, often plagued by shame and fear of exclusion from the community, no longer would be left to navigate their sexual desires with little or no guidance from their congregations. This also would serve the mission of the church well.

Perhaps the objection might be raised that changing the practice during the interim time of study and conversation is tantamount to endorsing homosexual relationships. There is some merit in this objection, as there is merit in the objection that the present practice is tantamount to condemning homosexual relationships. The risks in this proposal are real. Yet the risk to homosexual bodies and to the health of the whole body in maintaining the status quo is great, too.

The witness of Scripture in Acts 5:17-39 can be a helpful resource to the ELCA and to other denominations struggling to discern how to be the body of Christ in, with, and under the sexual diversity of bodies comprising their membership. The book of Acts testifies to the struggles of early Jewish Christians to discern whether there was room within the body of Christ for gentile bodies. Those struggles were waged with all the passion and vehemence invested in today's discussions about homosexuality.[15] In the story recorded in Acts 5, the early apostles are persecuted for their commitment to inclusivity in the name of Jesus and are brought before the Jewish council. As the council debates their fate, the great leader Gamaliel counsels letting them go on the grounds that "if this plan or this undertaking is of human origin, it will fail; but if it is of God, you will not be able to overthrow them—in that case you may even be found fighting against God!" (Acts 5:38-39).

When all is said and done, the decision whether there is room in the body for homosexual clergy and laypeople belongs to God, not to us. God's will will be done, and God's kingdom will come in, with, and despite us. If changing the present practice is contrary to God's intention, it will fail. If not, it may open new doors to new possibilities for mission in our ever-changing world. How we as congregations and denominations choose to be the body in, with, and under the diversity of our bodies has far-reaching consequences. Lives are at stake in our conversation.

Can This Community Live?

A Historical and Contemporary Perspective

ELIZABETH A. LEEPER

The indispensable challenge in each era revolves around the question of how distinct a religious community needs to be within its society. What is the balance between openness to new ideas and holding fast to traditions? What can the church learn from the tragedy of a religious community gone haywire? What can congregations today learn from the early church? What factors determine whether a religious community thrives or dies?

During the past two millennia, many different Christian communities have come into existence. Some thrive, providing a firm foundation for future communities. Others go awry, occasionally with devastating results. Jonestown and Waco, the Solar Temple, and Heaven's Gate—these stand as tragic reminders of what can happen when a religious community goes terribly wrong. What factors play into whether a religious community thrives? Its organization? Beliefs? Practices? How distinct should the new community be from society? How accepting of society's norms and values? What implications do these questions raise for the local congregation? By focusing on two Christian communities—the twentieth-century Heaven's Gate and the second-century church in Rome—we shall explore what makes a new religious community viable.

Heaven's Gate Community

The Heaven's Gate community burst upon public consciousness in March 1997 with the gruesome discovery of mass suicide. The thirty-nine casualties—twenty-one women and eighteen men from ages twenty-six to seventy-two—were members of an obscure cult who were renting a hilltop mansion in an upscale California neighborhood. Carefully orchestrated over several days, their suicides followed a "recipe" found on some of the victims. It read: "Take the little package of pudding or applesauce, and eat a couple of teaspoons to make room to put the medicine in and stir it. Eat it quickly, drink this vodka mixture . . . then lay back and rest quietly." In addition to the lethal mixture of barbiturates and alcohol, they had placed plastic bags over their heads to hurry the process via suffocation, just in case too few drugs had been ingested. They killed themselves in three groups, each group cleaning up after the preceding one—removing the plastic bags and placing a purple shroud over each body. The last two members still had the plastic bags over their heads; there was no one left to tidy up after them.[1]

This tragedy marked the end of an attempt in Christian community. The group known as Heaven's Gate had their start twenty-three years earlier when Marshall Herff Applewhite, former seminarian and son of a Presbyterian minister, was fired from his job as music teacher at a Catholic college, reportedly for having a sexual relationship with a male student.[2] Divorced, depressed, and lonely, Applewhite checked himself into a psychiatric hospital in Houston in search of a cure for his homosexuality; there he met his future spiritual partner, nurse Bonnie Lu Trousdale Nettles. Together they set out on a spiritual journey of self-discovery that they described as "a time of wandering in the wilderness."[3] The result was a new message synthesized from popular UFO beliefs, space aliens, and the fulfillment of Christian prophecy.

Nettles and Applewhite recruited members during town hall meetings held across the United States. The group was initially diffuse, with few guidelines and no clear organization; turnover was high; and the group came close to disintegrating. At this juncture, the leaders changed tactics: Nettles and Applewhite stopped recruiting and led their followers into seclusion, separated from society, for seventeen years. Forming tight bonds with their charismatic leaders, the community cultivated a strong sense of purpose and mission. They became students in a classroom, taking on new names in accord with their new identities. Nettles became known as Ti and Applewhite as Do, from the ends of the musical scale.

Ti and Do taught that the kingdom of God was a physical place known as the "Next Level" or the "Evolutionary Level Above Human" located in "deep space." Human beings would enter the Next Level by overcoming all human desires and addictions, separating from everything and everyone that kept them tied to the human level of existence. To help in this transformation, representatives were sent from the Kingdom Level to assist humans in the overcoming process. The group saw Jesus as such a representative. Just as Jesus was the incarnation of a member of the kingdom of heaven, so too were Ti and Do—the latest and last of the kingdom's emissaries, offering a final chance for salvation.

The Process of Transformation

Jesus' task, Do taught, was to offer the way to the kingdom of heaven to those who recognized him and chose to follow. According to Do, when Jesus said, "The kingdom of heaven is at hand," he meant: "Since I am here, and I am from that kingdom, if you leave everything of this world and follow me, I can take you into my Father's kingdom."[4] Because Jesus had been through the process of metamorphosis himself, having made the successful transition from the human level to the Evolutionary Level Above Human, he was qualified to take others through that same transformation.

At the same time, however, Ti and Do taught that Jesus was not God. Members of the Evolutionary Level Above Human, or kingdom of heaven, related to one another as Older or Younger Members, as "Father" and "Son." The Mind of God flowed through Jesus by coming down the pipeline, through Jesus' Father, Jesus' Father's Father, and so on, through a powerful "chain of minds."[5] One was saved by Jesus—not through faith but by doing as he instructed. According to Do, Satan distorted Jesus' message, giving out misinformation that all one need do is believe and accept Jesus as savior. This prevented people from doing as Jesus did and overcoming the world.[6]

In the beliefs of Heaven's Gate, following Jesus and overcoming the world entailed giving up all "human-mammalian behavior." The body, said Do, was merely a vehicle, like a suit of clothes; it was not a part of the person. Just as human bodies could not enter the Next Level, neither could human emotions and behaviors.[7] Thus, all attachments had to be given up, all addictions overcome, not for moral reasons but simply because there was no place for them in that heavenly realm.

Members of the Evolutionary Level Above Human were genderless. Population in the kingdom increased through metamorphosis, not reproduction. Emphasizing Jesus' saying about those who make themselves eunuchs for the sake of the kingdom of heaven, Heaven's Gate members tried to attain a genderless state in this life. While buzz haircuts and unisex clothing sufficed for most, some men went further, literally making themselves eunuchs for the sake of the kingdom of heaven.[8]

Following Jesus also meant abandoning family, friends, and possessions. They quoted Luke 14:26 ("If any man comes to me and hates not his father, and mother, and wife, and children, and brethren, and sisters, yea and his own life also, he cannot be my disciple")[9] to justify separating married couples. Children were not considered capable of making such a decision and so were not allowed in the community. Members with children left them behind with friends and relatives before joining.

Members of the Heaven's Gate movement were encouraged to have no thoughts of their own nor undertake any activities on their own volition. All opinions were to be prefaced with "I could be wrong, but . . . ," which meant, Do explained, that they should lose their self-confidence, no longer trusting their own judgment.[10] They were instructed to be like putty in the Father's hands.

A set of behavioral guidelines called the 17 Steps was issued. Couched in the form of a set of questions intended for self-examination, they included such items as "Can you follow instructions without adding your own interpretation?"[11] As the need for instruction and supervision increased, additional guidelines "for learning control and restraint" followed. Three forms of misconduct—deceit, sensuality, and knowingly breaking instructions or procedures—were considered major offenses. In addition, the list included thirty-one lesser offenses, such as "Trusting my own judgment—or using my own mind."[12]

Do and the group enjoyed playing with the term *brainwashing,* saying that what they sought was to have their brains washed of human mind and filled with the Father's Mind. Members were not to get "hooked" on any one "right" habit, practice, or procedure. Various diets—water fasts, juice fasts, vegetable diets, fruit diets—were tried in order to master different lessons in overcoming; the issue was not that there were certain correct foods but to learn to follow instructions. Members sought the goal of becoming a "cog in the wheel," accepting whatever instructions were given, never striving to be unique.[13] Applewhite and Nettles reinforced their teaching by physically and mentally isolating the community from society. The Heaven's Gate movement lived in a state of high tension with society, deviating considerably from society's most cherished norms.

Tension with the environment enhances the likelihood of a movement's success or failure: if the tension and conflict between the movement and society are too intense or the group appears too deviant, then the costs of membership become too high, leading to many defections. At the same time, however, a new movement needs some sense of difference and tension with society in order to be attractive to potential converts.[14] Heaven's Gate attracted young women and men, educated yet still unattached to careers or families, who sought spiritual experiences outside the norm.[15]

After many years of isolation, however, the community seemed to reach a stagnation point. Announcing that the end was near, they launched one last recruitment drive over the Internet. A few new converts joined the community to await the spaceship that would carry them to their final destination as metamorphized members of the kingdom of God. Soon thereafter, a new, extraordinarily bright comet approached the earth. Comet Hale-Bopp was the sign for which Heaven's Gate had been waiting. A message on the Internet notified the world of the group's intent: "Red Alert—Hale-Bopp brings closure to: Heaven's Gate."

Former members speculate that Do had reached a dead end with the Heaven's Gate community. Despite years of stringent exercises in overcoming, the members were not metamorphizing into new heavenly beings. The final transformation was postponed from happening here on earth to occurring on board the spaceship back to heaven. The Heaven's Gate community struggled for years with the goal of overcoming human existence. With its rejection of all that it means to be a human being and a member of human society, the Heaven's Gate community left themselves with no earthly options; the only way they could succeed as a community was to cease to exist as a community—through the death of all its members.

Early Christian Communities

During the second and third centuries, early Christian communities were also working at establishing their identity over and against the dominant (and sometimes hostile) culture. On issues from sexuality to family, from civic responsibility to occupation, Christians found themselves at variance with their pagan neighbors. In Rome, Christian teachers sought to present Christianity in a positive light, attractive to potential converts, while at the same time instilling a deep-rooted sense of Christian distinctiveness among the church's members.

Christianity arrived in the city of Rome around the middle of the first century. By the middle of the second century, the Christian community had grown large enough to have several worshiping centers, informal schools, and a diversity of teachers. Christian leaders debated theology, sparred over the person of Jesus and his mission, and taught different meanings of salvation. For Christianity, the second century was a time of controversy and fierce give-and-take, as Christians tried to reach a consensus for practice and belief. Despite the conflicts, however, the Christian community in Rome thrived, though sometimes at the cost of some of its members. How did a heterogeneous community, such as that at Rome, live when much more closely bound and homogeneous communities, such as Heaven's Gate, died? We can gain some insights by focusing on the mainstream Christian community in Rome, which emerged from the fray as the community in continuity with other Christian communities around the Roman Empire and the progenitor of the church in Rome in the coming millennia.

Community in Rome

All communities must deal with the issues surrounding human sexuality. This is as true for our churches today, as we struggle with the place of lesbian and gay Christians, as it was for Heaven's Gate over the matter of celibacy.[16] For the community in Rome, the issue centered on how to understand Jesus and Paul on sexuality and marriage. Christians in Rome struggled with basic questions regarding sexuality: does entry into the Christian community necessitate the end of sexual behavior, or should Christians continue to marry, enjoy sexual activity, and bear children? Marriage and family implied continuity with society, giving people a stake in the world, yet Christians claimed no longer to be of this world but citizens of the heavenly kingdom. Did separating from the world mean separating as well from human biological imperatives? Or did God create humans as sexual beings who remained thus even upon conversion?

Around the middle of the second century, the Roman Christian teacher Justin wrote an open letter to emperors Antoninus Pius and Lucius Verus in which he highlighted Christian virtue with regard to sexuality. Christians, Justin argued, "do not marry except in order to bring up children, or else, renouncing marriage, we live in perfect continence."[17] To reinforce his point, Justin related the story of a young man who sought to be castrated. Because of Roman law, he had to submit his request to the local prefect before a doctor could carry out the procedure. Prefect Felix of Alexandria refused. Obedient to the law, the young man accepted this decision; nevertheless, undaunted, he continued to live his life in celibacy, as if the operation had been performed.

Christian teachers taught that sexuality and its accompanying passions should be conquered. Justin told his story as an example of how Christians overcame the natural inclinations of the flesh, as opposed to the pagans who indulged their every whim. Debate raged within Christian communities across the empire as to the appropriate place (if any) for sex and marriage. Like Heaven's Gate many centuries later, some members believed that sexuality of any kind had no place in Christian community. Tatian, a pupil of Justin, broke with his teacher on this matter. Leaving the community in Rome, he traveled to Syria, where he preached a Christianity of sexual continence. Christians should live now as they would in heaven—celibate, as eunuchs. For a couple of centuries, the Christian communities in Syria followed this teaching, insisting upon vows of celibacy prior to baptism.[18]

In Rome, however, the community was able to accommodate human sexuality within the bonds of marriage. Here, early Christians welcomed children and found a place for sexuality in their begetting. Thus, the church maintained a state both of cultural continuity and of medium tension with Roman society, two of the criteria essential for new religious movements to succeed.[19] In contrast, by banning marriage, all sexual behavior, and children, the Heaven's Gate community took a much starker position relative to society, demanding more of its members than many were able to give.[20] The tension between Heaven's Gate's demands and normal social and biological imperatives proved too extreme; where the community in Rome remained lively and viable, finding room and theological justification for both celibate and sexually active members, that of Heaven's Gate stagnated.

While finding accommodation with society in matters of marriage and children, the community in Rome emphasized its distinctiveness by regulating who could become a member. A period of testing and teaching preceded initiation into the community. Certain occupations—pimp and prostitute, actor and gladiator, pagan priest and astrologer, even military governor and magistrate—were unacceptable professions for Christians. Such converts had to find new lines of work or be dismissed from the community. Restrictions were placed on other vocations: soldiers could not take the military oath, sculptors were forbidden to create cult objects, and even teachers were advised to find other careers.[21] Baptism marked the beginning of a new life with a new Christian identity, so that one was no longer part of the old order.

The rituals associated with the baptismal liturgy dramatized this newness of being. Those being baptized would face the west, the place of darkness, and renounce Satan as the symbol of their old life and of the pagan world. Then they would turn around to face the east, the direction of the rising sun, and profess faith in Christ. Eventually, a number of new names—Christian names—became popular, completing the break with pagan society and marking Christians with a new identity.

The Christian community in Rome thus made clear demands upon its members, carefully detaching them from paganism's cultural dominance. Following baptism, members had to abide by certain guidelines or risk rejection. The community set standards of behavior and expected compliance. Christians were not to behave as the pagans did. Thus, rigid boundaries were established between the church and the world. Studies have shown that such "boundary definition" is vital for solidifying group identity, cohesion, and motivation.[22] Members need to be clear on the distinction between "us" and "them" and to know that they have been called for a higher purpose. All communities, whether secular or religious, past or present, need a reason for existing that distinguishes them from all others and makes them attractive to newcomers. To thrive, however, this boundary cannot be absolute. Within these social boundaries, Christians in Rome had considerable freedom. They did not isolate themselves completely from society but continued to live in their neighborhoods, shop at the markets, talk to their neighbors, and do their jobs. Christian cultic practices—the Mysteries—were hidden, but Christians themselves remained visible, actively witnessing to the world around them, inviting others to join them in their community.

> "All communities, whether secular or religious, need a reason for existing that distinguishes them from all others."

Important too was Christian intellectual life. Justin became a Christian after a lifetime of searching for truth. Calling himself a Christian philosopher, he continued to wear the philosopher's cloak after his conversion. He taught that both Christians and wise pagans who existed before Christ lived according to reason.[23] This meant that the life of the mind was important, something not to be washed clean ("brainwashed") but to be used under appropriate Christian guidance. The communities of Heaven's Gate and Rome differed in their understanding as to the source of such appropriate guidance. While Christians in Rome had many teachers, debating vigorously about the nature of truth, the members of Heaven's Gate looked only to Ti and Do (and after Nettles's death, to Applewhite alone) for knowledge of the mind of God. There was a single pipeline for truth; thus, the Heaven's Gate community attached themselves firmly to Do, the final (and sole) link to that pipeline, or "chain of minds," extending from the kingdom of God to earth.

Eventually, Christians in Rome and elsewhere did narrow the debate and set bounds as to what was and was not acceptable Christian belief and practice. Some beliefs were labeled heresy, and their practitioners were no longer considered part of the community. Over the centuries, the degree of intellectual freedom would wax and wane as Christians broke out of these boundaries to explore new areas of thought and to debate new issues. Even today, Christian communities struggle with the balance between openness to new ideas and holding fast to traditions and teachings of the past. But the very fact that such struggle is possible is itself a sign of a community's vigor and vitality.

Clear Boundaries and Openness to the World

With a strong combination of clear boundaries yet openness to the world, the church in Rome grew steadily. Its outreach ministry expanded to assist the needy of the community. Although numbers are uncertain, we know that in the mid–second century, the wealthier members of the community contributed for the care of "orphans and widows, and those who are in want on account of sickness or any other cause, and those who are in bonds, and the strangers who are sojourners among [us], . . . and all those in need."[24] A century later, in 251 c.e., Cornelius, bishop of Rome, wrote to Fabian, bishop of Antioch, describing the church at Rome as caring for "above 1500 widows and persons in distress."[25] Heaven's Gate had no such outreach of service to the world.

The mid–third century was a time of great persecution and suffering for the church. Christian communities were torn asunder through death and defection. When the persecution ended and Christians regrouped, a real struggle for the survival of the community ensued. Those who believed in strict discipline, including expulsion of all who had denied their faith during the persecution, split from the community in Rome to form their own church. It was the remnant, however, those advocating mercy and forgiveness, who remained in fellowship with the larger Christian body and who survived, growing dramatically by the next century. The schismatic church, like so many groups following, discovered that when the bar is set too high, when the tension within the community and between the community and society is too great, that community falters and fails.

So it was and so it is today, as some of the most recent attempts at community have revealed. Each church body and every local congregation needs to assess the difficulties and "indispensabilities" of being a faith community in its particular culture. Together, we need to examine our identity, boundary definitions, restrictions, mission, and ministry in the world.[26] Without the openness to the world and the family, without the freedom of discussion and thought, without the social network that proved so favorable in second- and third-century Rome, the Heaven's Gate community of the twentieth century reached a dead end. Living in too high a tension with society to attract large numbers of converts, closed to recruitment after their initial invitation, and unwilling to allow natural propagation through childbirth, the group remained isolated and closed in upon itself. Rejecting the world completely, the movement had neither room nor reason to grow. Instead its members suffocated, metaphorically and, in the end, literally. The plastic bags on the heads of the last two members mutely tell the story of the death of an experiment in Christian community.

After the Jubilee

The Church's Advocacy Role

PETER L. KJESETH

If the church of Jesus Christ is to thrive in the world, it must take seriously its mission of advocacy for justice. This calling leads the church into the difficult challenges of an economically unjust global society. Where will the church find power in the biblical mandate? How has the Jubilee 2000 coalition opened doors for sustained, persistent liberating activity? What are the new urgent issues arising in the current governmental administration?

The rich get richer and the poor get poorer. This is where global capitalism has brought us. But who would have foreseen the remarkable effectiveness of the Jubilee 2000 coalition? Who would have anticipated the public power that the biblical tradition of the jubilee would exercise in the complex, multistreamed movement struggling for fundamental change in the structuring of the world economy? And who can predict how far this battle for change will go or how it might change the church, including local congregations, in the way we interpret our own biblical tradition?

It is beyond dispute that the neoliberal economic world order, global capitalism, has produced cruel disparities. Under this "Washington Consensus," two-thirds of the world's population live in poverty, one-third on the brink of malnutrition and starvation.[1] Things at the turn of the millennium had never been better for the dominant, rich nations, the G8/G7 (the United States, the United Kingdom, Canada, France, Germany, Italy, Japan, and sometimes Russia). They exercised control of the world markets. Their agencies—the so-called Bretton Woods institutions, the World Bank, the International Monetary Fund (IMF), and their related regional development banks—regulated international loans and the flow of capital, to the advantage of the rich nations.

But for the fifty or so poorest nations of the world, globalization had meant crushing debt service, virtual exclusion from the benefits of technology and truly free trade, lack of development worthy of the name, economic slavery for the workforce, and dehumanizing poverty for the general population. Research published in June 2000 indicated that the African continent had actually seen a rise in poverty in the five years since the United Nations had committed itself at a meeting in Copenhagen to reduce extreme poverty by half and reach universal primary education by the year 2015.

Jubilee 2000—A Good Beginning

Jubilee 2000 activists in sub-Saharan Africa saw the demonstrations at the meeting of the World Trade Organization (WTO) in Seattle, in November 1999, as a major victory for the Jubilee coalition and, even more significantly, as a watershed event in contemporary economic history. Observers were impressed by the depth and breadth of the coalition: representatives of international labor, environmental groups, aid organizations and non-governmental organizations (NGOs), performing artists, feminists, academics of various stripes, and especially the churches. Some called the anti-WTO demonstration the most significant U.S. protest since the waning days of the Vietnam War, at base an attack on contemporary conventional wisdom. Young Americans were asserting that there is more to life than money.[2]

Confrontation in Seattle was the climax of one phase of the Jubilee 2000 movement. There had been massive street demonstrations, international crowds numbering in the tens of thousands linking arms and chanting "Break the chains of debt" at G8 meetings in Birmingham (1998) and Cologne (1999). Not surprisingly, the G8 leaders decided to hold their July 2000 meeting on the remote Japanese island of Okinawa, where the tumultuous street crowds could not influence them. Ever alert, Jubilee 2000 UK called this move an example of "island mentality."[3] Clearly, the Okinawa meeting of the G8 was a setback for the Jubilee 2000 movement, but only a temporary one.[4] The 1990s had seen a formidable growth in the depth and breadth of the movement, a momentum that could not be stopped.

Although many U.S. church leaders, including many local congregations, were committed to hunger appeals, it was music stars and other celebrities who had taken up the cause of debt cancellation and given it hot issue status in the media. The February 21, 2000, issue of *Newsweek* devoted a major story to the involvement of rock star Bono in Jubilee

2000.[5] Critical questioning of neoliberal global capitalism, never absent, increased significantly in the late 1990s.[6]

There were significant developments in governmental circles. The March 8, 2000, publication of the Meltzer Commission Report had blockbuster significance for insiders in the world economic scene. Conservative Republican senator Jesse Helms had insisted on the establishment of this commission as a condition for continuing U.S. support of the IMF. The blue ribbon, bipartisan commission recommended unanimously that bilateral and multilateral creditors should write off all the debts owed by the forty-one Heavily Indebted Poor Countries (HIPC) to all financial institutions. It also publicly chastised the World Bank and the IMF for their failures and recommended curtailment and clarification of their powers.[7]

Then, on May 22, 2000, the World Bank published its own mea culpa, admitting that much of its development activity in the past decades had been counterproductive.[8]

The Role of the Churches

In Africa, as well as worldwide, it was the churches that spearheaded the establishment of national Jubilee 2000 movements.[9] Some leaders in Jubilee 2000 were involved with the South African Kairos Document of 1986 or took inspiration from that movement. A number of U.S. activists moved without question from involvement in Kairos USA during the quincentenary to committed action in the Jubilee 2000 world coalition.[10] The religious community became the engine driving the movement. The reception held in Washington, D.C., to celebrate President Bill Clinton's commitment to debt reduction in his state of the union address was sponsored by members of the steering committee of Jubilee 2000/USA: Bread for the World, Catholic Relief Services, Church World Service, the Episcopal Church, the Evangelical Lutheran Church in America, Lutheran World Relief, the National Council of Churches, Oxfam, the Presbyterian Church USA, the United Church of Christ, the United Methodist Church, the U.S. Catholic Conference, and World Vision. The Christian community exercises intentional coalition power.[11]

More important but less easy to document is the effect of grassroots participation on the part of members of the various churches, faith communities, and local congregations. Elected representatives attest again and again to the importance of a constituent's informed letter or facsimile. Web sites such as Jubilee 2000 UK and Jubilee 2000 USA keep congregation members informed on the world scene. Lutheran congregations and individuals who seek guidance regarding the next concrete step to take in effective advocacy can turn to the Lutheran Office of Governmental Affairs (LOGA) and state Lutheran Offices of Governmental Ministry.[12]

The Jubilee 2000 experience has taught us again to trust the depth of Christian conviction in our churches and the effectiveness of individual faith witness. The Reverend David Duncombe, retired pastor in the United Church of Christ, in the summer of 2000 began a second forty-five-day fast to pressure Congress to vote total funding for the debt cancellation President Clinton had promised. He visited one legislator's office each day to urge his cause and to dramatize with his increasingly emaciated body the intense human suffering that the debt burden causes in the poorest countries of the world.[13]

Several legislators joined Rev. Duncombe in fasting for shorter, symbolic periods. One of them was Congressman Spencer Baucus, Republican of Alabama, long known as a staunch conservative, who made a sudden switch to become the most active congressional supporter of third world debt cancellation when a friend, active in Bread for the World, explained to him in detail the suffering of those countries enchained by debt. This touched him at the point of his deeply held Christian faith, and the rest of his actions flowed naturally from there.[14]

The Public Power of the Biblical Traditions

The Jubilee 2000 movement dramatically demonstrated the power inherent in the biblical traditions that shaped it, the jubilee tradition of the Hebrew scriptures in Leviticus 25, and Jesus' inaugural sermon in his hometown of Nazareth as recorded in Luke 4:16-30. These texts have spawned countless new studies, symposia, consultations, and discussion guides related to the issue of third world debt.[15] They also furnished the effective symbols for mass public liturgies and for what might be called street exegesis.[16]

The ram's horn, the shofar, blasts out the jubilee call not only in synagogues but also in cathedrals, in small country churches, and at mass meetings and marches around the world. The sound carries passionate contemporary meaning for huge crowds, who likely know little about the details of the jubilee tradition of Leviticus 25.

The chants of the street liturgies—"Break the chains of debt! Let the captives go free!"—are shouted by tens of thousands, many of whom have only the vaguest sense of Jesus the liberator. Videotapes—quickly copied and cheaply available—show crowds from heavily indebted countries, scores of people from different religious traditions lifting high the Jubilee

2000 logo, chanting the slogans, even carrying crosses. And these human chains of shouting, singing humanity have attracted thousands of youth. For many of them, this was their first experience of the interpretation of Leviticus 25 or Luke 4—or of any biblical text. And it happened in the open, in public, tied to corporate action on behalf of economic justice for the poorest of the world. This was exegesis in the streets, evangelism in the streets.

In hindsight, it is surprising to recall how mystified at the turn of the millennium even many Jubilee 2000 activists were by the power of the World Bank and the IMF. After the Meltzer Commission Report and the World Bank's admission of failures, we can affirm that the persistent public recall and recital of the jubilee tradition of cancellation of debt played a key role in demystifying the power of the economic establishment. The battle is not over, of course, but we have been taught to trust the intrinsic power of our own traditions.

> "*This was exegesis in the streets, evangelism in the streets.*"

Beyond Jubilee 2000—The Path Ahead

However heady and surprising the success of Jubilee 2000, the early years of the new millennium saw one-third to two-thirds of the human family still mired in poverty. It was not only that they were chained down by unpayable debt but that their economies were locked into unfavorable trade arrangements. Aid practices were often self-defeating, and the power of global capitalism was virtually unregulated.

The strongest third world voices, including those from Africa, insisted that the goal in the decades ahead must be the *eradication* of global poverty. Charity, emergency measures, and Band-Aiding had, time after time, proven disastrously inadequate. A total approach was needed. The pillars of the relationships between rich and poor countries—aid, trade, and debt—needed reexamination and restructuring.

No one has argued that the eradication of global poverty will come about quickly. Realistic hope of cutting world poverty by half will involve decades of struggle and commitment. Christian communities will need to play a role in tandem with other religions and with various key entities in civil society, in academia, and in government. Churchwide and regional judicatories, agencies, committees, and task forces will need to work in creative coalitions. Local committees will need the efforts of congregations of many faiths working together with all kinds of local organizations to change unjust systems. This will not happen unless at least one congregation becomes a catalyst for hope.

Certain contours of this long-term commitment are clear. Jubilee 2000 and its successor manifestations have earned the right to ask for continued involvement. Jubilee has set the style: advocacy is driven by the great, overarching vision and by small concrete step after small concrete step. As in the antiapartheid battle, we will want to take our cues from the third world, especially from sub-Saharan Africa, where poverty is most pernicious. We will be challenged to dig ever more deeply into our own traditions. And we will want to make intentional connection between microeconomics and macroeconomics in the battle for a new economic world order.

In Solidarity with Sub-Saharan Africa

Framed by representatives of civil society from thirteen African countries, the Lusaka Declaration is aimed at an "African Consensus" in opposition to the "Washington Consensus" on sustainable solutions to the world economic dilemma—beginning with the debt crisis.[17] The declaration endorsed the demand for total debt cancellation. Moreover, setting conditions for the cancellation of debt should be removed from the total control of the G8 surrogates, the World Bank, and the IMF. New, more representative structures are needed.[18] The only condition for debt cancellation should be that moneys saved from debt service should be used for poverty reduction.[19]

The declaration called for the creation of new international structures related to the United Nations that, with representation from third world countries, would mediate in economic disputes and oversee future loans and grants. These structures could change the way the aid game is played. The declaration also insisted upon transparency and democratic procedures in the World Bank, the IMF, and the WTO. Their decision making had traditionally been conducted in secret and without representation from the poor countries for whom crucial decisions were being made.

The framers of the declaration also looked critically at their own Africa scene. They pledged themselves to work against "localized symptoms of our debt burden," war, corruption, and "other evils." Here, they pointed to corrupt leaders who betray their own people and to the technocratic, political, or commercial elites who continue to promote the "Washington Consensus."

Not rhetoric but careful research is needed on specific situations in specific countries with the goal of building legal claims for reparations. The genocidal decimation of the Herero people by the German colonizers in Namibia in the early 1900s is a specific case in point.

In May 2000, Archbishop Ndungane of Cape Town, successor to Desmond Tutu, launched the Debt and Reparations Fund in Switzerland. At the time, it was not clear how legal claims for reparations would be pressed or how money from German and Swiss banks would be transferred to the fund, but it was dramatically clear that reparations was a lead item on the sub-Saharan agenda.

Digging More Deeply into Our Traditions

Individual Christians and congregations have only begun to reclaim dimensions of the biblical tradition that can empower people for long-term struggle in solidarity with the poorest nations of the world. Though scholars have questioned whether the jubilee tradition of Leviticus was ever actually or fully practiced in Israel's history, it was part of the sabbath tradition that stood at the heart of Judaism and was included in the Leviticus text for good reason. When the leaders in exile thought of return to the promised land, they wanted to avoid the injustices that had occurred before the exile.[20]

There are profound theological and sociological impulses in the Leviticus text that explain the immense power that it has exercised in recent experience. These impulses will need deeper exploration as the world debate about economics continues. "The land shall not be sold in perpetuity, for the land is mine" (Lev. 25:23). This raises old questions in new forms in relation to the present situation in the third world, especially in relation to sub-Saharan Africa. How can the Western tradition of private ownership of land be maintained as absolute and sacred when it roots in colonial land acquisition at gunpoint and eventuates all over the world in wildly profitable real estate speculation that leaves millions of poor people deprived of land to live on? Traditional African systems of land tenure were not built on the principle of private ownership. The land belonged to the people, for the common good. This is not far from the view of the Leviticus passage. The people are tenants on the land, not owners.

The Leviticus passage intends to be legislation, not just theological rhetoric. In the fine print, it distinguishes between land in a walled city and land in a village or open country. The emphasis is on land cultivated by people for *food*. The jubilee year redistribution was intended to ensure

the basic necessities of life, a place to live and to grow food, for as many
as possible. Equity, social balance, was the goal.

The Leviticus legislation presupposes that sufficient food is the right of
each. "You shall not lend your brother your money at interest, nor give
him your food for profit" (Lev. 25:37). Though in the original context of
the legislation, the "brother" was clearly the fellow Jew, contemporary understanding of the global human family opens this passage for wider application and calls into question any notion that food can be used for
profit and speculation or as a weapon in foreign affairs.[21]

A careful encounter with the dynamic of Leviticus 25 invites us to re-
visit a number of old debates in the history of Jewish and Christian
thought. Do we need to reexamine the debates about usury? Why did Au-
gustine and Jerome urge upon all Christians the duty of lending without
interest? And could Luther's sermons on usury (1519, 1524, and 1540) say
anything to us today? If by usury we mean the exploitation of another's
need for the sake of disproportionate gain, then the universally available
statistics on third world debt cry to high heaven.[22]

Equally profound, painful, and ultimately creative questions continue
to arise in revisiting Luke 4:16-30. The interlocking traditions in Luke-
Acts touch on the issues of rich and poor, on communalism, and on the
necessary tension between the Christian community as alternative community and the powers of culture, finance, and government.[23]

Luke initiates the ministry of Jesus with the imagery of the sabbatical
year, the jubilee: "The Spirit of the Lord is upon me . . . has anointed me
to preach good news to the poor . . . to let the oppressed go free" (Luke
4:18-19). Third world exegetes call this text the "manifesto of Nazareth."
In Luke's telling of it, Jesus' words are countercultural enough to provoke
the first attempt to assassinate him. The leaders of Nazareth take Jesus
outside the city to hurl him into an abyss. His words and deeds must not
contaminate the community (Luke 4:29).[24]

Luke depicts the early Christian community as sharing all property
(Acts 4:32-35 and 5:1-11) in a way that fulfills Deut. 15:4: "And there will
be no poor among you." It also reflects the great prophetic visions of the
Isaiah tradition. These texts forcefully press the vision of a community of
common good, where the basic needs of all are met.[25] They compel the
Christian community of the world to keep searching and struggling for an
economic structure that will establish equity and balance—no small task.
How do we together find a way to affirm minimum economic rights for
all and yet avoid the ideological and practical pitfalls that undermined
communist regimes in the last half century?

The plight of two-thirds of the world will continue to send us back to
our biblical roots for guidance and inspiration. From this tradition, we

will get no new ready-made economic world order that we can call the kingdom of God on earth, but step by concrete step we can take guidance as we move forward.

In light of the Lusaka Declaration's call for reparations, it will be instructive, for example, to look again at the story of Zacchaeus. It is a text unique to Luke. He must have felt it was essential for his community to remember this story, to think about it and to act upon it. Zacchaeus, the rich man, deeply involved in the taxation system of the ruling power, committed himself to the Jesus movement (saw *salvation!*) by paying back the people he had cheated on his way to affluence (Luke 19:1-10).[26]

It is not just the Lukan tradition that is being mined for impulses that will empower the struggle for economic justice. The Gospel of Matthew is another world, with essentially the same economic message as Luke, but employing a different set of images and stories. Matthew's account of the last judgment in chapter 25 has always carried an unmistakable message. The sheep will be separated from the goats on the basis of how they have treated the hungry, thirsty, sick, and imprisoned. Matthew's form of the Lord's Prayer (Matt. 6:9-13) refers explicitly to the forgiving of debt: "as we have forgiven our debtors" (v. 12). In the essay "Debt and Jubilee: Systems of Enslavement and Strategies for Liberation," Gerald West, professor of Old Testament at the University of Natal, Pietermaritzburg, carefully places this petition in the history of Israel's struggle for economic justice. He concludes the essay by affirming: "By praying this prayer we participate proformatively in proclaiming and preparing the way for a more just socio-economic system."[27]

Other New Testament texts reveal new meanings in light of the present situation. Jonathan Draper, professor of New Testament at the University of Natal, goes to the heart of the matter in Mark 12:13-17: "Give to Caesar the things that belong to Caesar and give to God the things which belong to God." Draper argues that the saying about God and Caesar must be interpreted in light of the text that precedes it, the story of the tenants in the vineyard (Mark 12:1-12), which is a parable of eschatological reversal. Verse 9—"he will come and put the tenants to death and give the vineyard to others"—yields up its meaning only when read in terms of land-tenure practices in first-century Palestine, where the rich and powerful could one way or another seize land from the poor. The point of the parable is that the land belongs to God. God will return the land and its fruit to the poor. Read in this context when Jesus, in the following text, asks the question "What belongs to Caesar in Palestine?" the first readers of Mark's account would answer, "Nothing belongs to Caesar in Palestine."[28]

The Open Future

We have no way of analyzing exactly where we stand in the historical process. We have seen that the World Trade Center and the Pentagon walls are not invulnerable. Although many nations expressed their sympathy, the "Washington Consensus" cannot be taken for granted as serenely hegemonic in the globe as the Soviet Union once was in the Eastern bloc. The United States will no doubt continue as a global power politically and militarily, but the elites who control global economic power are a small minority. The vast majority of our world community—those living in poverty—will not disappear from our TV and computer screens, nor from our consciences. The sheer numbers and the depth of their misery may challenge us to new commitments toward justice.

Although severely tested by the catastrophe of terrorist attacks, the catastrophe of global poverty is already galvanizing the religions of the world into common action. We will want to deepen our cooperation with them.[29] There are new beginnings in grassroots movements all over the world that explore the connection between microeconomics and macroeconomics. They affirm a "trickle up" theory of economic development in opposition to the discredited "trickle down" theory. We will want to strengthen our ties with them.[30] In local communities, the formerly disenfranchised are speaking up and voting. Members of congregations who for years "fed the poor" and collected used clothing and household goods for "the homeless" now ask, What else can we do? We will want to listen to the voices of the recipients of charity. Congregational and church-body level social ministry must include social justice.

We do not know how far the battle for change in the world economic order will go. But in any case, our role is clear. We gratefully stand with the Jubilee 2000 coalition in all its diversity, with the environmentalists, the world labor organizers, the feminists, the NGOs and aid organizations, and the celebrities and experts, each playing their role. The mandate and power of the tradition are unambiguous. We are called to declare good news to the poor, to work for release of the captive, and to proclaim the jubilee year of the Lord. The challenge is difficult. God's word, God's people, the church, is indispensable.

Afterword

Why is life together in the church so difficult? Each faith community will need to answer that question for itself. In the mercy of God, we live in the forgiveness of sins in Jesus Christ, which frees us for our communal vocation of public ministry.

We have seen the difficulty of living together with our differences, even—perhaps especially—at worship, where sharing the sign of peace contrasts the fractured peace of the world and resonates with the world's deep longing for peace. We have experienced people's individual control issues spilling over into the congregation, and yet trust in God can build healthy communities of diversity. We come together with our different readings of the Bible. We have not attained a community of difference in which everyone's gifts are used and all people's leadership is welcome. And yet we believe that through faith, there is no longer Jew or Greek, there is no longer slave or free, there is no longer male or female, for all are one in Christ Jesus.

The church will grow and wane through the centuries. By God's grace, we are called to participate in God's mission, which includes the church; thereby God creates and re-creates the church in each generation. The Trinity, ground of diversity in unity, empowers congregations to enthusiastically adopt a vision for outreach. Our confessional foundations compel us to call people to faith. Mission means being active in the affairs of the world from a particular Christian perspective and discerning faith tenets distinct from American civil religion, which too often views the world only through a U.S. lens. When that window on the world is shattered, faith communities are challenged to more clearly discern their mission in a pluralistic culture, in a world of many faiths still crying for justice and peace. Mission is an indispensable result of healthy life together as the body of Christ, for we cannot help but speak of the things we have seen and heard.

The church is the body of Christ, and we are individually members of it. Life in community is not equal to sameness. The challenge of living as the differently abled body of Christ is great, but we can trust God's lovingly holding us together. We have seen and heard of the beliefs and practices of the early church's life together in Christ. This Christ empowers Christians to hope on behalf of those who are without hope, to believe in God on behalf of those who are without faith, and to love on behalf of those who live without love. The *communio* of Christ becomes an embodied sign of the interdependence of all life and an ecclesial grounding for moral deliberation.

As the church faces difficult issues, the members and member churches of Christ's body need one another's gifts. We need to respect one another so that we can trust one another. Long-established and newly configured church bodies and congregations can learn from vital, young global faith communities. What are the essentials to being the church in contemporary society? How can churches face challenging issues? Is there room within the body for gay and lesbian bodies? From the early Christian churches to ever-arising new groups, faith communities struggle with difficult issues and with their very identities so that they can be open to the world.

When congregations face difficult issues, we have the resources of Scripture, including the psalms, which help us to lament so that we can again experience God's transforming power. We need to use the Word and to proclaim it wisely and boldly in our specific context. We need to study it intergenerationally and center our life together in worship and prayer, which deepens resources for the routine of daily life as well as for times of crisis. Then we shall be equipped to do exegesis in the streets, to engage vigorously, freely, in working for justice in God's interdependent world.

The challenge is great. The difficulties remain, but nothing can separate us from the love of God in Christ Jesus.

Notes

Introduction

1. Dietrich Bonhoeffer, *The Communion of Saints* (New York: Harper and Row, 1960), 106–20.

Chapter 1
Seeking Peace in the Assembly

1. See Ted Peters, "Worship Wars," *Dialog* 33 (1994): 163–73; and Carol Doran and Thomas H. Troeger, *Trouble at the Table: Gathering the Tribes for Worship* (Nashville: Abingdon, 1992).

2. See Gregor Goethals, *The Electronic Golden Calf: Images, Religion, and the Making of Meaning* (Cambridge, Mass.: Cowley Publications, 1990), esp. 107–57.

3. See, for example, Juan Mateos, *Beyond Conventional Christianity,* trans. Kathleen England (Manila: East Asian Pastoral Institute, 1974).

4. Alexander Schmemann, *For the Life of the World: Sacraments and Orthodoxy* (Crestwood, N.Y.: St. Vladimir's Seminary Press, 1973), 151.

5. See Gordon Lathrop, *What Are the Essentials of Christian Worship?* Open Questions in Worship 1 (Minneapolis: Augsburg Fortress, 1994), 8–10; for an extended exploration of the organization of the Christian assembly, see his *Holy Things: A Liturgical Theology* (Minneapolis: Fortress Press, 1993), and for a wide-ranging discussion of the meaning of liturgical assembly, see his *Holy People: A Liturgical Ecclesiology* (Minneapolis: Fortress Press, 1999).

6. See chapter 10, by James R. Nieman, "Practice *Where* You Preach: Conditions for Good Preachers."

7. Dietrich Bonhoeffer, *Sanctorum Communio: A Theological Study of the Sociology of the Church,* trans. Reinhard Krauss and Nancy Lukens, Dietrich Bonhoeffer Works 1 (Minneapolis: Fortress Press, 1998), 211.

8. Laurence Hull Stookey, *Eucharist: Christ's Feast with the Church* (Nashville: Abingdon, 1993), 65.

9. Hence the long-standing preference for natural over synthetic materials in church building and decor.

10. See chapter 3, by Ann L. Fritschel, "The Psalms: Individual Laments as Communal Hymns."

11. See Thomas H. Schattauer, "Liturgical Assembly as Locus of Mission," in *Inside Out: Worship in an Age of Mission,* ed. Thomas H. Schattauer (Minneapolis: Fortress Press, 1999), 1–21.

12. Schmemann, *For the Life of the World,* 151.

Chapter 2
Life Together Is Only in God

1. The pastor of whom I write is Wilhelm Loehe, a great missional pastor who lived and worked most of his career in Neuendettelsau, Germany. He was responsible for lay renewal and missionary work to North America, was a founder of the deaconess movement, and was active in many social welfare causes.

2. Thomas L. Friedman, *The Lexus and the Olive Tree* (New York: Anchor, 2000).

3. Many contemporary writers in science and theology recognize that the physical characteristics of the universe reveal a fundamental unity between all things. Many of these writers conclude that a diversity in unity is designed into the creation. See, for example, the writings of John Polkinghorne or Ian Barbour.

4. I am thinking particularly of Adolf von Harnack and Albrecht Ritschl.

5. See, for example, Wolfhart Pannenberg, *Systematic Theology,* vol. 1, trans. Geoffrey Bromiley (Grand Rapids, Mich.: Eerdmans, 1997); and Robert Jenson, *Systematic Theology,* vol. 1 (Oxford: Oxford University Press, 1998).

6. The term *communitarian* is not one usually used in contemporary theology. I prefer to use it, though, on the American scene, with indebtedness to the work of Amitai Etzioni. There is already an impressive body of literature of communitarian ethics that captures the sense of wholism that I am attempting to communicate by the term. "Communitarian" does not "prefer" a group over the individual or vice versa. Rather, it recognizes that healthy social life in a "community"—whatever the particular kind or circumstance— contributes to individuals and receives from them and that this give-and-take cannot be divided. A communitarian community is one in which the whole is more than the sum of the parts and in which the parts are celebrated as parts, though they cannot be divided from one another without loss both to the community and to the individual as a person.

7. Colin Gunton, *The One, the Three and the Many* (Cambridge: Cambridge University Press, 1993).

8. See chapter 19, by Gwen B. Sayler, "The Body of Christ and the Issue of Required Celibacy."

9. See chapter 5, by Norma Cook Everist, "Re-membering the Body of Christ: Creating Trustworthy Places to Be Different Together."

Chapter 3
The Psalms

1. For the possible results of losing the liturgical use of the lament psalms, see Walter Brueggemann, *The Psalms and the Life of Faith,* ed. by Patrick D. Miller (Minneapolis: Fortress Press, 1995), esp. chapter 5, "The Costly Loss of Lament," 98–111.

2. This exploration is based on the exegesis of several laments. Unfortunately, space limitations prevent demonstration of the exegesis of Psalm 22.

3. Thorkild Jacobsen discusses the nature of the relationship between the believer and the personal God in *The Treasures of Darkness: A History of Mesopotamian Religion* (New Haven, Conn.: Yale University Press, 1976), 161ff. For a discussion of laments as psalms of disorientation, see Walter Brueggemann, "Psalms and the Life of Faith: A Suggested Typology of Function" in *Psalms and the Life of Faith,* 3–32.

4. For a discussion, see Steven J. L. Croft, *The Identity of the Individual in the Psalms,* JSOT SupSer 44 (Sheffield: JSOT Press, 1987).

5. Psalm 88 is the one lament psalm in which this move is not made; rather, it ends on a note of despair. This is useful in situations where movement too quickly toward confidence would not be accepted by the listener as having one's pain truly understood.

6. Gerstenberger has shown there may be family or community locations for many of the psalms. This suggests that liturgical ritual could take place outside of the temple and that the pronouncement of good news, that God has heard and will answer the psalmist, was not limited to the professional clergy. E. S. Gerstenberger, "The Lyrical Literature," in *The Hebrew Bible and Its Modern Interpreters*, ed. Douglas A. Knight and Gene M. Tucker (Philadelphia: Fortress Press, 1985), 429–30.

7. Kathleen Norris, *The Cloister Walk* (New York: Riverhead, 1996), 96.

8. The Hebrew of verse 29 is uncertain in meaning: "All the fat ones of the earth will eat and worship, all they that go down to the dust shall kneel before God (him), even he that cannot keep his soul alive." The NRSV follows the Greek: "To him, indeed, shall all who sleep in the earth bow down; before him shall bow all who go down to the dust, and I shall live for him."

9. See chapter 18, by Winston D. Persaud, "Imagining the New Community in Christ and the Challenges of Race and Class."

10. See chapter 10, by Karen L. Bloomquist, "*Communio* as a Basis for Moral Formation, Deliberation, and Action."

11. Marvin L. Anderson, "The Desecration of the Land: Lament as a Liberative Act," presented at the World Congress of the International Association for Religious Freedom, August 3, 1999, Vancouver, B.C.

Chapter 4
The Well-Being of Individuals and the Health of the Community

1. E. A. Skinner, "A Guide to the Constants of Control," *Journal of Personal and Social Psychology* 71 (1996): 549–70.

2. Judith Viorst, *Imperfect Control: Our Lifelong Struggles with Power and Surrender* (New York: Simon and Schuster, 1998).

3. Ellen Langer, *Mindfulness* (Reading, Mass.: Addison-Wesley, 1989). Many people believe that the most important contributions of the twentieth century to the emotional well-being of elderly people came from the research of social psychologist Ellen Langer.

4. Shelley E. Taylor, *Positive Illusions: Creative Self-Deception and the Healthy Mind* (New York: Basic Books, 1989).

5. See chapter 3, by Ann L. Fritschel, "The Psalms: Individual Laments as Communal Hymns."

6. Jutta Heckhausen and Richard Schulz, "A Life-Span Theory of Control," *Psychological Review* 102 (1995): 284–304.

7. Depression has reached epidemic proportions, not only in the United States but worldwide. The World Health Organization in 2001 predicted that depression will become the second leading cause of disability and death worldwide by the year 2020.

8. The United Nations study points out that the ten nations in the world with the highest rates of depression today are all nations that made up the former Soviet Union.

9. Robert Putnam, *Bowling Alone: The Collapse and Revival of American Community* (New York: Simon and Schuster, 2000). Robert Putnam illustrates and statistically documents a remarkable decline in involvement in civic engagement and commitment.

10. See chapter 20, by Elizabeth A. Leeper, "Can This Community Live? A Historical and Contemporary Perspective."

Chapter 5
Re-Membering the Body of Christ

1. See Ephesians 2:11ff., which describes the Christ event as reconciling disparate, even alienated people, in this case Jews—the near—and Gentiles—those far off—making them "one new humanity." "For he is our peace; in his flesh he has made both groups into one and has broken down the dividing wall, that is the hostility between us" (v. 14).

2. See chapter 12, by Craig L. Nessan, "We Are the Body of Christ: Ecclesiology for a Church in Mission."

3. See James M. Gustafson's classic work *Treasure in Earthen Vessels* (New York: Harper, 1961).

4. Barbara Brown Zikmund, *Discovering the Church* (Philadelphia: Westminster, 1983), 19.

5. I define pluralism as the state in which people, diverse in religion, race, ethnicity, sex, age, and ability, maintain that diversity and yet autonomously participate in the common society. Although the term describes people of different religions, people within a church may differ from one another in many of those respects, sometimes more than people who belong to different religious groups.

6. See Hans Küng, *The Church* (New York: Sheed and Ward, 1967).

7. H. Richard Niebuhr, *The Purpose of the Church and Its Ministry* (New York: Harper, 1956), 24.

8. The epistle writers, especially Paul, were extremely concerned about factionalism and disunity in the community of believers in both intra- and intercongregational issues (cf. 1 Corinthians 1 and Philippians 2).

9. Jürgen Moltmann, *The Church in the Power of the Spirit* (New York: Harper and Row, 1977), 22.

10. See Christian Grumm, "In Search of a Round Table," in *In Search of a Round Table: Gender, Theology and Church Leadership,* ed. Musimbi R. A. Kanyoro (Geneva: World Council of Churches, 1997), 28–39.

11. Paul Minear, *Images of the Church in the New Testament* (Philadelphia: Westminster, 1960), 11–27. Although Minear gives little attention to the contextual use of each image, he shows that there are more than one hundred if the Greek words are counted separately.

12. Absent is a popular contemporary image, "family," a description of a congregation that presents any number of problems, one being the promise of intimacy at the expense of inclusivity. For Christians to be called "brothers" and "sisters" is a sign of a radical new relationship in Christ, which is not insular but countercultural. See chapter 6, by James L. Bailey, "The Pauline Letters as Models for Christian Practice: 1 Thessalonians as a Case Study."

13. See Dale B. Martin, *The Corinthian Body* (New Haven, Conn.: Yale University Press, 1995).

14. See Parker Palmer's classic work *The Company of Strangers* (New York: Crossroad, 1981).

15. Members of the Lutheran Deaconess Community include in their Deaconess Litany, which they have prayed weekly for one another for over forty years, the phrase "that we not think more highly of ourselves than we ought to think nor deprecate ourselves in unbelief, calling common what God has called clean." *The Deaconess Litany,* The Lutheran Deaconess Conference, Valparaiso, Indiana, 1959, revised 1997.

16. Moltmann, *The Church in the Power of the Spirit,* wrote that it is not the church that has a mission of salvation; it is the mission of God that includes the church, creating a church as it goes (64).

17. See Suzanne de Dietrich, *The Witnessing Community* (Philadelphia: Westminster, 1958), 16–17. The church's vocation is as a witnessing community, taken out of the world, set apart from God to be sent again into the world. Two temptations are to consider the separate life as an end in itself or to succumb to a slow process of assimilation by which God's people loses its identity.

18. For a full discussion of how this concept can be developed in the congregation, see Norma Cook Everist, *The Church as Learning Community* (Nashville: Abingdon, 2002).

Chapter 6
The Pauline Letters as Models for Christian Practice

1. The primary inspiration for thinking about Pauline *practice* comes from Abraham J. Malherbe, *Paul and the Thessalonians: The Philosophic Tradition of Pastoral Care* (Philadelphia: Fortress Press, 1987), with its focus on how the apostle "founded, shaped, and nurtured a community" in the city of Thessalonica (1).

2. Some scholars suggest that the newly formed community probably met in an apartment complex (*insula*), the place where Thessalonians of modest means both worked and lived. Malherbe, *Paul and the Thessalonians*, 17, provides this description: "A typical *insula* would contain a row of shops on the ground floor, facing the street, and provide living accommodations for the owners and their families over the shop or in the rear." Malherbe follows Ronald F. Hock, *The Social Context of Paul's Ministry: Tentmaking and Apostleship* (Philadelphia: Fortress Press, 1980), 26–49, in concluding that Paul's occupation as a leather worker provided the place and opportunity for his evangelism among other workers.

3. See Rainer Riesner, *Paul's Early Period* (Grand Rapids, Mich.: Eerdmans, English trans., 1998), 337–41, who describes the strategic location, economic and political importance, size, and population (likely 65,000) of Thessalonica in Paul's day.

4. Malherbe, *Paul and the Thessalonians*, 47. On page 51, Malherbe writes: "Their conversion resulted in distress and dejection which threatened their adherence to the faith. Their feeling of isolation, heightened by opposition or suspicion from non-Christians, was exacerbated by Paul's abrupt departure." Riesner, *Paul's Early Period*, 371, agrees that the situation of the new converts is one of "social isolation." He notes further: "Another typical problem of recent converts is the cooling of their initial enthusiasm; having initially seemed transported into a completely new world, they soon discover the concerns of daily life catching up with them."

5. Here Paul uses the dative plural of the Greek word *thlipsis*, translated "by these persecutions" in the NRSV. *Thlipsis* can refer to overt hostile actions or more subtle social pressure as well as to external affliction or internal distress.

See Heinrich Schlier, *Theological Dictionary of the New Testament*, vol. 3, ed. Gerhard Kittel, trans. Geoffrey W. Bromiley (Grand Rapids, Mich.: Eerdmans, 1965), 139–48, for the multiple meanings of this word.

6. Wayne A. Meeks, *The First Urban Christians* (New Haven, Conn.: Yale University Press, 1983), 85, employs this phrase to characterize Paul's use of affectionate and familial terms for participants in his newly established communities.

7. Paul employs *adelphoi* for the Thessalonians in 1:4, 2:1, 2:9, 2:14, 2:17, 3:1, 4:1, 4:10, 4:13, 5:1, 5:4, 5:12, 5:14, 5:25, 5:26, and 5:27. The NRSV translates the term inclusively as "brothers and sisters."

8. Prior to this point in the letter, Paul has spoken of their "labor of love" (1:3) and Timothy's testimony to their "faith and love" (3:6). Beverly Roberts Gaventa, *First and Second Thessalonians*, Interpretation (Louisville: Westminster John Knox, 1998), 58, is undoubtedly correct in emphasizing that "love" implies concrete actions, such as "intercessory prayer, financial support, and hospitality," rather than "a sentimental attachment or personal affection."

9. The image of a nurse was used by some philosophers in the ancient world to signal their gentleness and understanding of human nature. See Abraham J. Malherbe, "'Gentle as a Nurse': The Cynic Background to 1 Thessalonians 2," in Malherbe, *Paul and the Popular Philosophers* (Minneapolis: Fortress Press, 1989), 35–48.

10. See Abraham J. Malherbe, "Exhortation in 1 Thessalonians," in Malherbe, *Paul and the Popular Philosophers*, 53–55, 59.

11. See later in this chapter for Paul's emphasis on the practice of praying.

12. Paul also encourages this greeting among Corinthian and Roman Christians (see 1 Cor. 16:20, 2 Cor. 13:12, and Rom. 16:16). See William Klassen, "Kiss (NT)," in *The Anchor Bible Dictionary*, vol. 4, ed. by David Noel Freedman (New York: Doubleday, 1992), 89–92.

13. See chapter 16, by L. Shannon Jung, "Discovering Hope: Marks of Vitality and Practices That Form Communities for Mission."

14. See 1:5, 2:1, 2:2, 2:5, 2:11, 3:3, 3:4, 4:2, and 5:2; see also 2:9.

15. These two texts read as follows: "For we know, brothers and sisters beloved by God, that [God] has chosen you, because our message of the gospel came to you not in word only, but also in power and in the Holy Spirit and with full conviction; *just as you know* what kind of persons we proved to be among you for your sake" (1:4-5; emphasis added), and "*You yourselves know*, brothers and sisters, that our coming to you was not in vain, but though we had already suffered and been shamefully mistreated at Philippi, *as you know*, we had courage in our God to declare to you the gospel of God in spite of great opposition" (2:1-2; emphasis added).

16. Hock, *The Social Context of Paul's Ministry*, 48, makes this point.

17. For 3:4, I have altered the NRSV translation by rendering *proelegomen* as "we were repeatedly telling you beforehand" about the probability of suffering to be faced by the Thessalonians, because the imperfect tense can describe

continuing or repeated action in the past. Rendering the imperfect as "repeated past action" rather than "attempted past action" seems appropriate to the context since Paul has already drawn attention to their willingness to suffer (see 2:14).

18. Seneca, a first-century philosopher, declares the living voice and example more important than the written word: "Of course, however, the living voice and the intimacy of a common life will help you more than the written word. You must go to the scene of action, first, because men put more faith in their eyes than in their ears, and second, because the way is long if one follows precepts, but short and helpful, if one follows patterns" (quoted by Elizabeth A. Castelli, *Imitating Paul: A Discourse on Power* [Louisville: Westminster John Knox, 1991], 52).

19. Paul's additional words in 2:15-16 regarding "the Jews who killed the Lord Jesus and the prophets and drove us out," prompting God's wrath, present interpreters with serious problems. See Gaventa, *First and Second Thessalonians*, 35–39.

20. See Robert C. Tannehill, *Dying and Rising with Christ* (Berlin: Verlag Alfred Töpelmann, 1966), 100–104.

21. Ibid., 103.

22. The Greek word *kopiaō* suggests strenuous work.

23. The Greek word is *proistēmi*.

24. For the use of *noutheteō*, see J. Behm, *Theological Dictionary of the New Testament*, vol. 4, trans. and ed. G. W. Bromiley (Grand Rapids, Mich.: Eerdmans, 1967), 1019–22.

25. See Robert Jewett, *The Thessalonian Correspondence: Pauline Rhetoric and Millenarian Piety* (Philadelphia: Fortress Press, 1986), 104–5, and Gaventa, *First and Second Thessalonians*, 81–82.

26. This phrase is derived from the Greek word *eucharisteō*, which means "to give thanks" and is not meant to be a direct reference to the chief liturgical prayer that begins the Lord's Supper rite.

27. Paul's words in Phil. 4:4-7 are similar in import.

28. The salutation in 1:1 ends with the words "grace to you and peace," and the letter's conclusion in 5:28 reads, "The grace of our Lord Jesus Christ be with you."

29. See chapter 14, by H. S. Wilson, "Mission as an Oriental Fan: A Plea for Missionhood of All Believers."

Chapter 7
Believing in God through Others; Believing in God for Others

1. Augsburg Confession, Article VII, *The Book of Concord: The Confessions of the Evangelical Lutheran Church*, trans. and ed. Theodore H. Tappert (Philadelphia: Fortress Press, 1959), 32.

2. See chapter 18, by Winston D. Persaud, "Imagining the New Community in Christ and the Challenges of Race and Class."

3. Surprise is, of course, an essential element of this parable. Its point is not to give us an opportunity to use other people and their need as a way to serve Jesus, that is, merely as means to an end. Rather, it is in addressing their need for their own sakes that Jesus is also served in a hidden way.

4. Dietrich Bonhoeffer, *The Cost of Discipleship*, trans. R. H. Fuller (New York: Macmillan, 1963), 202–9.

5. See chapter 14, by H. S. Wilson, "Mission as an Oriental Fan: A Plea for Missionhood of All Believers."

6. Eta Linnemann, *Jesus of the Parables: Introduction and Exposition*, trans. John Sturdy (New York: Harper and Row, 1966), 58–64.

7. See the thanksgiving hymns from Qumran, esp. 1QHa xii, 29–40, 1QHa xv, 17–19, 30–31, 1QHa xvii, 12–15. See G. Vermes, *The Dead Sea Scrolls in English* (Baltimore: Penguin, 1968), esp. 163f., 174f., 180; Theodore H. Gaster, *The Dead Sea Scriptures: In English Translation* (Garden City, N.Y.: Doubleday Anchor Books, 1957), 145–47, 161–63, 170.

8. *Luther's Works*, vol. 27, ed. Jaroslav Pelikan and Walter A. Hansen, trans. Richard Jungkuntz (St. Louis: Concordia Publishing House, 1964), 388.

9. Ibid., 393.

10. Wolfhart Pannenberg, *Jesus—God and Man*, trans. Lewis Wilkens and Duane A. Priebe (Philadelphia: Westminster, 1968), 334–49.

Chapter 8
The Community of Faith as a Confessional Norm

1. See James A. Scherer, *Mission and Unity in Lutheranism* (Philadelphia: Fortress Press, 1969), 1–29; and *Lutheranism and Pietism: Essays and Reports*, 1990 (St. Louis: Lutheran Historical Conference, 1992), vol. 14.

2. The work of Philip Jacob Spener began a renewal in church and society through prayer and Bible study in what we would call today "small-group" ministries. This pietism spread throughout German and Scandinavian Lutheranism and interacted with Reformed Protestantism, including Puritanism. Lutherans from the University of Halle participated in the beginnings of the modern missionary movement. Mission societies supporting the worldwide mission of the church soon sprang up throughout Europe.

3. See chapter 7, by Duane A. Priebe, "Believing in God through Others; Believing in God for Others."

4. *Luther's Works* [LW], vol. 40, 146–49.

5. *The Book of Concord* [BC], ed. Theodore E. Tappert (Philadelphia: Fortress Press, 1959), 416, paragraph 45. See also *The Book of Concord*, ed. Robert Kolb and Timothy J. Wengert (Minneapolis: Fortress Press, 2000), 436.45; and LW 23:284–88.

6. Cf. Large Catechism, BC 368.30—371.48 and 406.309—407.312, where the law's bad news is also discussed.

7. Augsburg Confession [AC], Article II.

8. Ralph W. Quere, "Extra Ecclesiam Non Est Salus: God's Efficacious Presence in Baptism in the Gathering of the Elect," unpublished seminar paper, 9th International Congress for Lecture Studies, Heidelberg, August 1997.

9. See chapter 15, by Paul G. Hill, "Youth and Family Ministry as Congregational and Community Renewal."

10. *Melanchthon: Selected Writings*, ed. E. E. Flack and L. J. Satre, trans. C. L. Hill (Minneapolis: Augsburg, 1962), 113 (translation altered).

11. George Williams, *The Radical Reformation* (Philadelphia: Westminster, 1962), 155–59, 252.

12. See The Epitome of the Formula of Concord [FC] with its longer Solid Declaration [SD]: FC SD XI (BC 624.45–50).

13. Williams, *The Radical Reformation*, 839–43.

14. See William Hordern, *Evangelism, Luther and the Augsburg Confession* (Winnipeg, Canada: Evangelical Lutheran Church in Canada, Division for Congregational Life, 1983), 13-22. See also "Joint Declaration on the Doctrine of Justification," trans. and ed. by a staff team of the Institute for Ecumenical Research, Strasbourg (Hong Kong: Clear-Cut, 1997), hereafter JD with paragraph numbers.

15. See *Versoehnung* in 1 John 2:2 and *Gnadenstuhl* in Rom. 3:25 in the Luther German Bible.

16. See Gustav Aulen, *Christus Victor* (London: S.P.C.K., 1975), 101–22. A response correcting Aulen's narrowing of Luther's Christology is given in Paul Althaus, *Theology of Martin Luther* (Philadelphia: Fortress Press, 1966), 292ff., esp. 218–23.

17. *Luther and Erasmus: Free Will and Salvation*, trans. and ed. E. Gordon Rupp and Phillip S. Watson et al. (Philadelphia: Westminster, 1969), 138, 200, 206f., 244, 331f.

18. Herman Sasse, *This Is My Body* (Minneapolis: Augsburg, 1959), 269–72 (emphasis added).

19. Michael Reu, *The Augsburg Confession: A Collection of Sources with an Historical Introduction* (Chicago: Wartburg, 1930), 348ff.

20. Annex to the "Joint Declaration on the Doctrine of Justification" written by a team of Lutherans and Roman Catholics and published in November 1998 to clarify and supersede the June 1988 "Response of the Catholic Church" with Declaration and Clarifications. See note 13 above.

21. *The Myth of God Incarnate*, ed. John Hick (Philadelphia: Westminster, 1977), 167–85; and John Hick, *The Metaphor of God Incarnate* (Louisville: Westminster John Knox, 1993), passim, esp. chapters 4, 9–11, 15.

22. H. Richard Niebuhr, *The Kingdom of God in America* (New York: Harper, 1959), 193.

Chapter 9
Living Together Faithfully with Our Different Readings of the Bible

1. United Methodist participants in a two-year "dialogue" on this issue concluded that what divides them in this debate are different notions of "the authority of the Bible" and "the nature of God's revelation." Positions included a wide range of views. At the end of that two-year dialogue, the United Methodist Church General Commission on Christian Unity and Interreligious Concerns and the General Board of Discipleship sponsored a "Consultation on the Authority of Scripture and the Nature of God's Revelation" (December 7–9, 1999, Nashville, Tenn.), at which I presented an earlier and longer version of this essay.

2. An excellent resource for congregations wanting to study and discuss these issues in depth is Phyllis A. Bird, "The Authority of the Bible," in *The New Interpreter's Bible*, ed. Leander E. Keck (Nashville: Abingdon, 1994), 1.33–64. See also the articles on "Scriptural Authority" in *The Anchor Bible Dictionary*, ed. David N. Freedman (New York: Doubleday, 1992), 5.1017–56.

3. See the excellent Web site http://gbgm-umc.org/umw/bible/, which can be used with Maxine Clarke Beach, *The Bible: The Book That Bridges the Millennia*, pt. 1, *Origins and Formation*, with a study guide by Toby Gould (New York: Women's Division, General Board of Global Ministries, United Methodist Church, 1998), a congregational study resource.

4. Excellent resources for congregations wanting to learn more about the formation of the various canons are R. H. Pfeiffer, "Canon of the OT," and F. W. Beare, "Canon of the NT," in *The Interpreter's Dictionary of the Bible*, ed. George A. Buttrick (Nashville: Abingdon, 1962), 1.498–520 and 520–32, respectively; David N. Freedman, "Canon of the OT," and A. C. Sundberg Jr., "Canon of the NT," in *The Interpreter's Dictionary of the Bible, Supplementary Volume*, ed. Keith Crim (Nashville: Abingdon, 1976), 130–36 and 136–40, respectively; James A. Sanders and Harry Y. Gamble, "Canon," *Anchor Bible Dictionary*, 1.837–52 and 852–61, respectively; "Names and Order of Books of the Bible in Several Traditions," in *HarperCollins Study Bible: NRSV with the Apocryphal/Deuterocanonical Books*, ed. Wayne A. Meeks (San Francisco: HarperCollins, 1993), xxxvii–xl; Daniel J. Harrington, "Introduction to the Canon," *New Interpreter's Bible*, 1.7–21; and Pheme Perkins with Marc Z. Brettler, "The Canons of the Bible," in *New Oxford Annotated Bible: New Revised Standard Version with the Apocryphal/Deuterocanonical Books*, 3d ed., ed. Michael D. Coogan (New York: Oxford University Press, 2001), Essays, 453–60.

5. The Jewish canon "closed" around the end of the first century of the Common Era (c.e.) to the first quarter of the second. A traditional name of the Jewish Bible is "Tanakh," formed from the initial letters of the Hebrew names of the sections of the Jewish Bible (Torah, Prophets, and Writings). Achieving a stabilized canon, however, did not prevent the order of the

twenty-four books from remaining somewhat fluid up to the present (see Sanders, "Canon," *Anchor Bible Dictionary*, 1.840–41).

6. The Samaritan canon consists solely of a Samaritan version of the first five books of the Hebrew Bible, called the Pentateuch (see Bruce K. Waltke, "Samaritan Pentateuch," *Anchor Bible Dictionary*, 5.933–40).

7. The Septuagint itself exists in multiple forms, represented by different manuscript traditions. In short, the Greek Jewish Bible was not one but many. Due to its Christian use, it lost out to the Hebrew Bible, which became the Bible of emerging "normative Judaism" at the end of the first century C.E. (see Melvin K. H. Peters, "Septuagint," *Anchor Bible Dictionary*, 5.1093–1104).

8. See D. C. Parker, "Vulgate," *Anchor Bible Dictionary*, 6.860–62. From about the middle of the sixth century C.E. to the sixteenth century, the Latin Bible called the Vulgate was functionally the only "authorized" Bible for Western Christianity, and even today it is normative for Roman Catholic Bible translations. Its Old Testament reflects the order of the Septuagint and is based on both the Greek texts and the Latin translations that began to appear in the second century C.E. (called the "Old Latin" Bible, which contained both Testaments and existed in several variations); it also incorporates some of Jerome's translations of Hebrew texts (ca. 342–420 C.E.), which were "much criticized in his own time" (Pierre-Maurice Bogaert, "Versions, Ancient [Latin]," *Anchor Bible Dictionary*, 6.800). In Roman Catholic Bibles, therefore, the Old Testament consists of Hebrew scriptures integrated with the Apocryphal/Deuterocanonical books, found only in the Septuagint, in the order in which they occur in the Septuagint.

9. Some Protestant Bibles collect the Apocryphal/Deuterocanonical books in a section between the two Testaments; others omit them altogether.

10. See Hans Peter Rüger, "The Extent of the Old Testament Canon," *Bible Translator* 40 (1989): 301–3; and Bruce M. Metzger, "Bible," *Oxford Companion to the Bible* (New York: Oxford University Press, 1993), 79, cited at http://gbgm-umc.org/umw/bible/canon.html (The Women's Division, General Board of Global Ministries, The United Methodist Church).

11. See J. Neville Birdsall et al., "Versions, Ancient," *Anchor Bible Dictionary*, 6.787–813. Examples of ancient versions include Aramaic, Armenian, Georgian, Latin, and Syriac.

12. "Other vernacular translations" refers to translations into "common languages." The word "vulgate" in Latin means "common" and is the basis for the English word "vulgar." The Bible today is translated into over eighty "common" languages.

13. See Emanuel Tov and Eldon Jay Epp, "Textual Criticism [OT and NT]," *Anchor Bible Dictionary*, 6.393–412 and 412–35, respectively; and Pheme Perkins with Michael D. Coogan, "Textual Criticism," *New Oxford Annotated Bible*, Essays, 460–66.

14. See, for example, the Revised Standard Version (RSV), New Revised Standard Version (NRSV), New International Version (NIV), or New American Bible (NAB).

15. Bart D. Ehrman, *The Orthodox Corruption of Scripture: The Effect of Early Christological Controversies on the Text of the New Testament* (New York: Oxford University Press, 1993).

16. The well-known story about "the woman caught in adultery," for example, is lacking in "most ancient authorities" (see the NRSV note at John 7:53-8:11; also see the NAB and NIV). Manuscripts that include it agree neither on its content nor on its placement in the Gospels. Some manuscripts place it, in one form or another, after 7:36 or at the end of John, or after Luke 21:38 or at the end of Luke (see the footnotes in the NRSV and NAB). In view of this manuscript evidence, this story is more part of *tradition* than Scripture—unless we identify "Scripture" with Old Latin translations and versions of the Bible dependent on it, like the Vulgate and KJV.

17. See Eugene A. Nida, "Theories of Translation," Raymond F. Collins, "Versions, Catholic," Jack P. Lewis and Ernest S. Frerichs, "Versions, English," Harry M. Orlinsky, "Versions, Jewish," and Herbert G. Grether, "Versions, Modern Era," *Anchor Bible Dictionary*, 6.512–15, 813–16, 816–38, 838–42, and 842–51, respectively; Pheme Perkins, "Translations of the Bible into English," *New Oxford Annotated Bible*, Essays, 466–71; and Keith R. Crim, "Modern Versions of the Bible," *New Interpreter's Bible*, 1.22–32.

18. This was the consensus of a consultation on "Next Steps in Translation," November 19–20, 1999 (sponsored by the Bible Translation and Utilization Program, National Council of Churches of Christ in the U.S.A.), which involved Jewish, Eastern Orthodox, Roman Catholic, and Protestant Bible translators.

19. See David J. Lull (creative consultant), "The Bible under Fire: The Making of the *RSV* Translations," Odyssey Productions, commissioned by the Bible Translation and Utilization Program, National Council of Churches. This TV documentary film premiered on the Odyssey Channel, November 21 and 29, 1999. Through the Interfaith Broadcasting Commission, it aired on NBC affiliates March and September 2000. "The Bible under Fire" includes the story of how, in the midst of Senator Joe McCarthy's hunt for Communists in every sector of American society, some critics of the RSV, published in 1952, charged that the RSV translators were part of a Communist plot to undermine American churches. In that political climate, critics dubbed the RSV "Lenin's Bible" and the "Red Bible," a tag helped by its red cover. A military manual in the early 1960s included a warning against "fellow travelers" and included the National Council of Churches among the places where they might be found; having made that association, the manual includes a warning against using the RSV.

20. An rsv footnote offers "a virgin" as an alternate reading.

21. Those who wish to find the basis for the "virgin birth" in Matt.1:23 in the rsv can still do so, although it is inappropriate to talk about a "virgin *birth*" in Matt.1:23, which at most speaks of a "virginal *conception*." The idea of a "virgin *birth*" comes from the noncanonical *Infancy Gospel of James*, which is the source of much of Marian piety. It is also worth noting that the bishops of the Catholic Conference of the United States found no doctrinal deficiency in the rsv and granted it their *imprimatur!*

22. The Hebrew word is *'almah.*

23. This Hebrew word is *bethulah.* The Greek word *parthenos,* which Matthew uses, has a double meaning: "virgin" or "young, unmarried or recently married woman."

24. Isaiah gave his sons names that would remind Ahaz, Judah's king, of Isaiah's prophetic critique of the king's foreign policy: "A remnant shall return" (7:3 nrsv note), "God is with us" (7:14 nrsv note), and "The spoil speeds, the prey hastens" (8:3 nrsv note). We cannot exclude the possibility that Isaiah has Ahaz's wife or another unnamed woman in mind in 7:14; it is also possible that the "prophetess" of 8:3, who bore Isaiah's third son, is a different woman from the mother(s) of the sons named in 7:3 and 14. For an interpretation that both takes account of the historical context of Isa. 7:14 and upholds Christian doctrine, see the note on this text in the Roman Catholic nab.

25. See Peter J. Thuesen, *In Discordance with the Scriptures: American Protestant Battles over Translating the Bible* (New York: Oxford University Press, 1999), 109–11.

26. Congregations might discuss what influences their thinking about "inclusive language" translations and about the translation of "the Jews" (*hoi Ioudaioi* and related terms) in the New Testament, especially in Acts and the Gospel of John (also see Matt. 27:25), which are other examples of how the norms of confessional communities in the translation process define what views "Scripture" authorizes. For the latter issue, see, for example, *Removing the Anti-Judaism from the New Testament,* ed. Howard Clark Kee and Irvin J. Borowsky (Philadelphia: American Interfaith Institute/World Alliance, 1998). Some modern translations try to make it more difficult for readers to use the Bible for Christian anti-Jewish propaganda. The most "progressive" translations on this point are translations that are among the most "dynamic" or the freest, to the point of being paraphrases (see the Living Bible and its successor the New Living Translation; the Good News Bible, also called Today's English Version; and the Contemporary English Version). The translations most susceptible to Christian anti-Jewish propaganda are those that seek to be the most "formal" and the most "literal" (see the kjv, American Standard Version, rsv, nrsv, New American Standard Bible, niv, and nab). The "authority" of the whole witness of the Bible, which is to God's love for the whole world, especially for Israel and the people called "Jews" (see especially Romans 9–11),

does not "authorize" anti-Jewish attitudes and behavior. This issue illustrates how translations are at the heart of the "authority of Scripture," that both are intertwined with tradition, reason, and experience, and that both shape and are expressions of the identities of the communities that produce their Bibles and construe their "authority."

27. See, for example, Lev. 21:7, 14; Ezek. 44:22; Matt. 5:31-32; 19:3-9; Mark 10:2-12; Luke 16:18; and 1 Cor. 7:10-16. See also the requirement that bishops be "married only once" (1 Tim. 3:2).

28. Such passages occur throughout the Old Testament but see also 1 Cor. 7:21, a notoriously difficult passage to translate, and Philemon, which has resisted every attempt to read Paul's letter in only one way.

29. See, for example, 1 Cor. 11:1-16; 14:33b-36; and 1 Tim. 2:8-15.

30. See Col. 3:18; Eph. 5:22; Titus 2:5; and 1 Peter 3:1.

31. Victor Paul Furnish argues that the church needs to apply two tests to moral teachings in the Bible generally and, in this instance, to moral teachings about sexuality: (1) Do they belong to the "kerygmatic core"? (2) Do they pass the test of the best knowledge about human nature in general and human sexuality and gender in particular? The church has applied similar tests to biblical statements on slavery, divorce, capital punishment, and the role and status of women in the church. When it found them wanting, it based its opposition to such statements on the kerygmatic core of the Bible. The biblical texts about same-sex sex also fail both tests and, therefore, are not binding on Christians or the church. See the videotape "Dialogue on the Bible, Theology, and Homosexuality," featuring presentations by Victory Paul Furnish and Richard B. Hays, 2000 Perkins Ministers Week, Perkins School of Theology, Southern Methodist University, Dallas, Tex. Also see Victor Paul Furnish, *The Moral Teaching of Paul: Selected Issues*, rev. ed. (Nashville: Abingdon, 1985), chap. 3.

32. Neither of these agreements would be true to Scripture or be healthy for the church.

33. Even if that were possible, would it be desirable, true to Scripture, or true to God's Spirit, which blows where it wills, so that we do not know where it comes from and where it goes (see John 3:8)?

34. We do not have space to ask the same questions of Rom. 1:26-27. The other texts commonly cited in this debate are Genesis 19 (and the parallel story in Judges 19) and Lev. 18:22 and 20:13. When the current debate begins with these texts, as it does, the focus of the debate will necessarily be on same-sex *sexual activity* and, in particular, specific acts of *genital* sex—namely, anal intercourse—because that is what these biblical texts talk about. One of the limitations and missed opportunities of this debate, therefore, is that when these biblical texts set the agenda, same-sex *love* gets reduced not only to *sex* but to a particular act of *genital sex*. A tragic consequence of that agenda is that the Bible has a lot more to say about love than about sex, let alone about male same-sex anal intercourse, so that the debate never gets around to talk

246 *Notes*

about same-sex *love.* That agenda also degrades same-sex *relationships* by implying that they are nothing but arrangements for engaging in specific acts of
genital sex. Excellent resources for congregations who want to study and discuss these issues are collections of essays that cover a wide spectrum of views:
for example, Robert L. Brawley, ed., *Biblical Ethics and Homosexuality: Listening to Scripture* (Louisville: Westminster John Knox, 1996); David L. Balch,
ed., *Homosexuality, Science, and the "Plain Sense" of Scripture* (Grand Rapids,
Mich.: Eerdmans, 2000); Sally B. Geis and Donald E. Messer, eds., *Caught in
the Crossfire: Helping Christians Debate Homosexuality* (Nashville: Abingdon,
1994); Tex Sample and Amy Smith Delong, eds., *The Loyal Opposition: Struggling with the Church on Homosexuality* (Nashville: Abingdon, 2000);
Choon-Leong Seow, ed., *Homosexuality and Christian Community* (Louisville:
Westminster John Knox, 1996); Jeffrey S. Siker, ed., *Homosexuality in the
Church: Both Sides of the Debate* (Louisville: Westminster John Knox, 1994);
and Walter Wink, ed., *Homosexuality and Christian Faith: Questions of Conscience for Churches* (Minneapolis: Fortress Press, 1999).

35. See the excellent discussion of this issue in Dale B. Martin, *"Arsenokoitês* and *Malakos*: Meanings and Consequences," in Brawley, *Biblical
Ethics and Homosexuality,* 124–29.

36. See the JB and Frederick W. Danker, Walter Bauer, William Arndt, and
F. Wilbur Gingrich, *A Greek-English Lexicon of the New Testament and Other
Early Christian Literature,* 3d ed. (Chicago: University of Chicago Press,
2000), 613 (hereafter BDAG). The classic statement of this view is Robin
Scroggs, *The New Testament and Homosexuality: Contextual Background for
Contemporary Debate* (Philadelphia: Fortress Press, 1983/84), 62–65. Gordon
D. Fee, *The First Epistle to the Corinthians,* New International Commentary on
the New Testament (Grand Rapids, Mich.: Eerdmans, 1987), 244, agrees with
Scroggs on this point, though he disagrees with his contention that the bibli-
cal world only knew the pederastic form of homosexuality.

37. See the NRSV and NIV. BDAG (613) says that this translation is "too narrow." Richard B. Hays, *First Corinthians,* Interpretation (Louisville: Westminster John Knox, 1997), 97, rejects both proposals.

38. See the KJV, ASV, NAS, and NASU. Hays, *First Corinthians,* 97, proposes
"sissies" or "dandies." For a discussion of this translation of the Greek word,
see Martin, *"Arsenokoitês* and *Malakos,"* 124–28.

39. Examples of excess include enjoying luxurious food, drink, and clothing, and giving too much attention to one's appearance. Examples of certain
sexual acts include being sexually penetrated like a woman. See, for example,
Hans Conzelmann, *1 Corinthians,* Hermeneia (Philadelphia: Fortress Press,
1975), 106, who translates this Greek term "pervert [effeminate]" and identifies the two Greek terms with "passive" and "active" males in homosexual intercourse. Other examples are "enjoying sex with women too much" and
masturbating (see Martin, *"Arsenokoitês* and *Malakos,"* 128).

40. The Septuagint uses this Greek word for a gentle but effective tongue in Prov. 25:15 and 26:22 (compare the adverb in Job 40:27). Matthew 11:8 and Luke 7:25 use it for garments worn in royal houses. The Septuagint uses this Greek word in the sense of weakness in Gen. 42:4; 44:29; Exod. 23:25; Deut. 7:15; 28:61; 2 Chron. 6:29; 16:12; 21:15, 18, 19; 24:25; Job 33:19; and Isa. 38:9; 53:3 (see also the verb in Gen. 42:38; 2 Sam. 13:5; 4 Macc. 6:17; and Job 24:23).

41. See Aristotle, *Nicomachean Ethics*, VII.iv.1, 1147b, iv.4, 1148a, and vii.1, 1150a; cf. VII.i.4, 1145a-b (where the Greek word for "softness, delicacy, effeminacy, weakness" is paired with the terms for "luxuriousness," "wantonness," "daintiness," "insolence," "fastidiousness" and "the lack of restraint"). For the use of the word "effeminate" for the "seduced" male who plays "the woman's role" in same-sex sex, compare Plato, *Laws*, VIII, 836E and Plutarch, *Dialogue on Love*, 751D (where this word is parallel to another Greek word for "womanishness, delicacy, effeminacy").

42. Martin, "*Arsenokoitês* and *Malakos*," 128-29.

43. See, for example, BDAG, 135, and Fee, *The First Epistle to the Corinthians*, 244, who finds compelling support in the pairing of the two Greek words.

44. The Greek words *to arsen* ("the male sex") and *hē koitē* (a euphemism for "intercourse"), which combine to form the second Greek word in 1 Cor. 6:9 (*arsenokoitai*), occur in Lev. 18:22 ("You shall not have intercourse [*koimēthēsē koitēn*] with a male [*meta arsenos*] as with a woman") and 20:13 ("whoever has intercourse [*koimēthē . . . koitēn*] with a male [*meta arsenos*] as with a woman"). The question, however, is whether the first part, *arsen-*, is the subject or object of the second part, *-koitai*: "a male who has intercourse" or "intercourse with a male," respectively (see Fee, *The First Epistle to the Corinthians*, 244).

45. L. William Countryman, *Dirt, Greed, and Sex: Sexual Ethics in the New Testament and Their Implications for Today* (Philadelphia: Fortress Press, 1988), 118. Consider two examples (see Martin, "*Arsenokoitês* and *Malakos*," 119): The meaning of the word "understand" has nothing to do with the meanings of its component parts, "under" and "stand"; on the other hand, though the word "chairman" once referred to a "man" who sat on a particular piece of furniture reserved for the "man" who applied rules of order to a meeting, it no longer *necessarily* refers either to a male or to a chair. The latter word illustrates the difference between a word's history (its "etymology") and its meaning, derived from usage; both words illustrate the error of deriving a word's meaning from its component parts.

46. Martin, "*Arsenokoitês* and *Malakos*," 123.

47. Ibid.

48. Ibid., 119, 123.

49. These comments also apply to 1 Tim. 1:10.

50. Instead of interpreting these verses in isolation from their literary context, we really need to relate them to ever-widening contextual circles within

Paul's Letter to the Romans, beginning with 1:18-32, then moving out to 1:18-
3:20, 1:18-8:39, and finally to the argument of the whole letter, whose theme
is "the righteousness of God" (1:16-17). For different views of this passage, see
Richard B. Hays, "Relations Natural and Unnatural: A Response to John
Boswell's Exegesis of Romans 1," *Journal of Religious Ethics* 14:1 (1986):
184–215; Richard B. Hays, *The Moral Vision of the New Testament: A Contemporary Introduction to New Testament Ethics* (San Francisco: HarperSanFran-
cisco, 1996), chap. 16; Dale B. Martin, "Heterosexism and the Interpretation
of Roman 1:18-32," *Biblical Interpretation* 3:3 (1995): 332–55; Bernadette J.
Brooten, "Patristic Interpretations of Romans 1.26," in *Studia Biblica* 18, ed.
E. A. Livingston (Kalamazoo, Mich.: Cistercian Publications, 1985), 287–88;
Bernadette J. Brooten, *Love between Women: Early Christian Responses to Female Homoeroticism,* Chicago Series on Sexuality, History, and Society
(Chicago: University of Chicago Press, 1996); and David E. Fredrickson, "Natural and Unnatural Use in Romans 1:24-27: Paul and the Philosophic Cri-
tique of Eros," in Balch, *Homosexuality,* 197–222.

51. In 1 Corinthians (NRSV), see 6:13 ("The body is meant . . . for the Lord,
and the Lord for the body"), 6:15 ("Do you not know that your bodies are
members of Christ?"), and 6:19 ("Your body is a temple of the Holy Spirit
within you").

52. See William A. Beardslee, *First Corinthians: A Commentary for Today*
(St. Louis: Chalice Press, 1994), 56–62.

53. For an argument that the lawsuits dealt with sexual matters, see Antoinette Clark Wire, *The Corinthian Women Prophets: A Reconstruction
through Paul's Rhetoric* (Minneapolis: Fortress Press, 1990), 75. Regarding sex
with prostitutes, see Beardslee, *First Corinthians,* 56–62.

54. First Timothy 1:9-11 lacks a reference to this Christian understanding
of the community; here the reference is to "the sound teaching that conforms
to the glorious gospel of the blessed God" (NRSV) and that God "entrusted" to
"Paul" (1:10-11), which is a reference to "the law" (1:9). See chapter 21, by
Peter L. Kjeseth, "After the Jubilee: The Church's Advocacy Role."

55. See, for example, Hays, *Moral Vision,* 388–89.

56. Although scholars do not agree whether the notion of "sexual orienta-
tion" was known prior to the nineteenth century (see the literature cited by
Martin, "Heterosexism," 332–55, and "*Arsenokoitês* and *Malakos,*" 132 n. 5;
William R. Schoedel, "Same-Sex Eros: Paul and Greco-Roman Tradition," in
Balch, *Homosexuality,* 46–47; and Brooten, *Love between Women,* 241–44; for
a treatment of this thesis in Jewish literature, see Daniel Boyarin, "Are There
Any Jews in 'The History of Sexuality'?" *Journal of the History of Sexuality* 5
(1995): 333–55), the Bible nowhere discusses sexual *orientations;* it only dis-
cusses sexual *activity.*

57. The only possible reference in the Bible to female same-sex sexual activity could be Rom. 1:26, but scholars disagree about that (see Brooten, *Love
between Women,* 244–53).

58. For Ruth and Naomi, see Ruth 1:16-17. For Jonathan and David, see 1 Sam. 18:1-4; 20:1-42; and 2 Sam. 1:26. For Jesus and the "beloved disciple," see John 13:23; 19:26; 20:2; and 21:7, 20.

59. Naomi kissed her daughters-in-law (Ruth 1:10), David and Jonathan kissed (1 Sam. 20:41), and the disciple "whom Jesus loved" reclined "on Jesus' breast" (John 13:23), which is an expression for "the place of honor" and may not be meant literally.

60. First Corinthians 13:12 (NRSV).

61. Compare Hays, *First Corinthians,* 97, 99.

Chapter 10
Practice *Where* You Preach

1. D. *Martin Luthers Werke: Kritische Gesamtausgabe, Tischreden* [hereafter *WA Tr*], vol. 5 (Weimar: Hermann Böhlaus Nachfolger, 1912–21), no. 5388.

2. *WA Tr* 2.2580.

3. See chapter 17, by Roger W. Fjeld, "American Civil Religion: A De Facto Church."

4. See chapter 2, by Duane H. Larson, "Life Together Is Only in God: The Achievement of Personhood in Community."

5. Stephen L. Carter, *Integrity* (New York: HarperCollins, 1996), 3–12.

6. Ernst Käsemann, *Jesus Means Freedom*, trans. Frank Clarke (Philadelphia: Fortress Press, 1969), 16.

7. Johann Baptist Metz, *Faith in History and Society: Toward a Practical Fundamental Theology*, trans. David Smith (New York: Seabury, 1980), 100ff.

8. Lucy Atkinson Rose, *Sharing the Word: Preaching in the Roundtable Church* (Louisville: Westminster John Knox, 1997), 89ff.

9. Justo L. González and Catherine G. González, *The Liberating Pulpit* (Nashville: Abingdon, 1994), 47ff.

10. Matthew 7:16.

Chapter 11
Communio as a Basis for Moral Formation, Deliberation, and Action

1. See, for example, Martha Ellen Stortz, "Practicing Christians: Prayer as Formation," in *The Promise of Lutheran Ethics,* ed. Karen L. Bloomquist and John R. Stumme (Minneapolis: Fortress Press, 1998), as well as other articles in this collection, which tend to approach Lutheran ethics as a way of life.

2. See chapter 1, by Thomas H. Schattauer, "Seeking Peace in the Assembly: God's Mission, Our Worship, and the World's Hope."

3. Rufus Black, "Towards an Ecumenical Ethic," Oxford: British Library Thesis Service D193907 (1996), 304.

4. Wolfgang Greive, ed. *Communion, Community, Society* (Geneva: Lutheran World Federation, 1998), esp. Israel-Peter Mwakyolile's chapter, 187.

5. Dorothy Bass, ed., *Practicing Our Faith* (San Francisco: Jossey-Bass, 1997), 5ff. The topics listed are among those addressed by different authors of the chapters.

6. Lewis S. Mudge, *The Church as Moral Community* (New York: Continuum, 1998), 125.

7. Thomas F. Best and Martin Robra, eds. *Ecclesiology and Ethics* (Geneva: Lutheran World Federation, 1997), 67.

8. Ibid., 68–69.

9. *Ecclesiology and Ethics,* ed. Best and Robra.

10. Constitution of the Lutheran World Federation (1990), Article III.

11. See chapter 2, by Duane H. Larson, "Life Together Is Only in God: The Achievement of Personhood in Community."

12. Joachim Track, "Gleanings . . .," in *The Church as Communion,* ed. Heinrich Holtze (Geneva: Lutheran World Federation, 1997), 54.

13. *The Church as Communion,* ed. Holtze, 13ff.

14. "The Blessed Sacrament of the Holy and True Body of Christ, and the Brotherhoods," 1519, in *Luther's Works,* vol. 35, ed. Theodore Bachmann (Philadelphia: Muhlenberg, 1960), 58.

15. Evangelical Lutheran Church in America, "The Church in Society: A Lutheran Perspective" (Chicago: ELCA Division for Church in Society, 1991).

16. Gloria Albrecht, *The Character of Our Communities: Toward an Ethic of Liberation for the Church* (Nashville: Abingdon, 1995).

17. David Hoekema and Bobby Fong, eds. *Christianity and Culture in the Crossfire* (Grand Rapids, Mich.: Eerdmans, 1997), 102.

18. In many ways, Wartburg Seminary has long been involved in making these kinds of local-global connections, most prominently in the key role it played in the struggle for Namibian independence.

19. The Lutheran World Federation is pursuing these possibilities further through a study-action program on economic globalization. For further information, contact kbl@lutheranworld.org.

20. In his article "Toward a Hermeneutic of the Household," *Ecumenical Review* 51:3 (July 1999): 243–55, Lewis Mudge refers in this sense to how ecclesiology and ethics came together at the last WCC assembly.

Chapter 12
We Are the Body of Christ

1. See chapter 4, by Daniel L. Olson, "The Well-Being of Individuals and the Health of Community." The need for control in retaining identity applies to groups as well as to individuals.

2. See chapter 13, by David A. Ramse, "The Church as Organism: Characteristics of a Young Church."

3. For historical and theological information about the gifts of the various Lutheran traditions, see E. Clifford Nelson, ed., *The Lutherans in North Amer-*

ica (Philadelphia: Fortress Press, 1975); and Kent S. Knutson, "The Community of Faith and the Word: An Inquiry into the Concept of the Church in Contemporary Lutheranism," Ph.D. diss., Columbia University (Ann Arbor: University Microfilms, 1961).

4. The following diagram, like this chapter, is significantly revised from an earlier version published in *Lutheran Partners* 15 (May/June 1999): 26–35.

5. See "Baptism, Eucharist and Ministry," Faith and Order Paper No. 111 (Geneva: World Council of Churches, 1982), in *The Ecumenical Movement: An Anthology of Key Texts and Voices*, ed. Michael Kinnamon and Brian E. Cope (Grand Rapids, Mich.: Eerdmans, 1997), 189–200, on a threefold office of ministry.

6. "Gregory the Great," in *New Catholic Encyclopedia* (New York: McGraw-Hill, 1967), 6:767. This reference, regarding the Bishop of Rome, I apply to all bishops and pastors.

7. See Miroslav Volf, *After Our Likeness: The Church as the Image of the Trinity* (Grand Rapids, Mich.: Eerdmans, 1998), 246–49, on the relationship of charisma and office.

8. Craig L. Nessan, *Beyond Maintenance to Mission: A Theology of the Congregation* (Minneapolis: Fortress Press, 1999).

9. *Together for Ministry: Final Report and Recommendations*, Task Force on the Study of Ministry 1988–1993 (Chicago: ELCA Division for Ministry, 1993). I see the work of the bishop requiring gifts that presuppose those of a pastor but which go beyond them in terms of ministering to the church's oneness, holiness, catholicity, and apostolicity. The ministry of a bishop is itself an office and not just a special function of the ordained office.

Chapter 13
The Church as Organism

1. Julia Coburn and Corry Nap, "The Church in Nepal" (unpublished manuscript, 1992), 3.

2. *MARC Newsletter* 98:1 (March 1998): 6.

3. See chapter 6, by James L. Bailey, "The Pauline Letters as Models for Christian Practice: 1 Thessalonians as a Case Study."

4. See chapter 10, by James R. Nieman, "Practice *Where* You Preach: Conditions for Good Preachers."

5. There is ongoing mission activity in Nepal. These missions are separate from the Nepali church, serving holistically in the name and in the spirit of Jesus Christ to all people, whether Christian or non-Christian.

6. Churches cannot own land or property because they cannot be registered with the government. If a congregation wishes to build its own church structure, this can be accomplished by purchasing it in the name of a trusted parishioner. This practice has often led to dishonesty, conflict, and division.

7. Cindy L. Perry, *Nepali around the World: Emphasizing Nepali Christians of the Himalayas* (Kathmandu, Nepal: Ekta Books, 1997).

8. Donald E. Miller, "The Reinvented Church: Styles and Strategies," *The Christian Century* (December 22–29, 1999): 1250–53, notes that "the fastest growing and largest Churches in the world are cell-based, with all of the Church ministry flowing out of small groupings of people who meet weekly, worshiping together, studying together, praying together and often engaging in highly imaginative service to people in their neighborhoods."

Chapter 14
Mission as an Oriental Fan

1. "Growth of Christianity Declines," *World Vision MARC Newsletter* 99:3 (August 1999): 2.

2. Isaiah 65:17-25.

3. Luke 4:18-19.

4. Revelation 21:1.

5. See chapter 12, by Craig L. Nessan, "We Are the Body of Christ: Ecclesiology for a Church in Mission," on the reign of God as central to contemporary church life.

6. "The medieval approach to missionary effort was 'collective or communal,' unlike modern approaches that are based 'on the principle of individual conversion.'" John Witte Jr., and Richard C. Martin, eds., *Sharing the Book: Religious Perspectives on the Rights and Wrongs of Proselytism* (Maryknoll, N.Y.: Orbis, 1999), 161.

7. "The great obstacles to conversion are social, not theological." "Church planters who enable men to become Christians without crossing such [*race, caste, class, language*] barriers are much more effective than those who place them in men's way" (emphasis added). Donald A. McGavran, *Understanding Church Growth*, 3d ed. (Grand Rapids, Mich.: Eerdmans, 1990), 156, 168. See also Wilbert R. Shenk, ed., *Exploring Church Growth* (Grand Rapids, Mich.: Eerdmans, 1983).

8. Philippians 4:8.

9. Bill Hull, *New Century Disciplemaking: Applying Jesus' Ideas for the Future* (Grand Rapids, Mich.: Fleming H. Revell, 1997), 86.

10. For example, the Taizé community in France.

11. The popularly expressed statement that the X generation is not religious but seeks to be spiritual makes this an urgent task for the churches.

12. *Mission and Evangelism: An Ecumenical Affirmation* (Geneva: World Council of Churches, 1982), 30.

13. Ivy George expresses that phenomenon as follows: "I restate that the 'Great Commission' [Matt. 28:18-20] has been, and continues to be, a text of terror for all those people who do not share the ... ideology of Christian tri-

umphalism." Ivy George, "From Proclamation to Presence: Towards an Asian Hermeneutic of Christian Mission," *Journal of Asian and Asian American Theology* 2:1 (summer 1997): 93.

14. John B. Cobb, *Beyond Dialogue* (Philadelphia: Fortress Press, 1982), and *Transforming Christianity and World* (Maryknoll, N.Y.: Orbis, 1999).

15. David Bosch, *Transforming Mission: Paradigm Shifts in Theology of Mission* (Maryknoll, N.Y.: Orbis, 1994), 5.

16. Even though the gospel and cultures issue was present from the inception of Christianity, it was not until the second half of the twentieth century that this issue was identified as a key missiological concern needing careful and thoughtful attention of both the historical and the younger churches. It has become a theme for several studies, seminars, and conferences, including the World Conference on Mission and Evangelism of the World Council of Churches in Brazil, 1996. Christopher Durisingh, ed., *Called to One Hope: The Gospel in Diverse Cultures* (Geneva: World Council of Churches, 1998).

17. The "towards a global ethic" declaration at the 1993 Parliament of the World's Religions in 1993 in Chicago is an example of one small step in this direction; a further session of the Parliament was held in Cape Town, South Africa, in 1999; and the spiritual leaders millennium summit was called by the United Nations Organization in 2000.

18. All of these barriers and others found in the community would need to be dealt with separately to do full justice to them.

19. See chapter 21, by Peter L. Kjeseth, "After the Jubilee: The Church's Advocacy Role."

20. John Witte Jr. has described the irony of the situation as follows: "We have celebrated the creation of more than thirty new constitutional democracies since 1980 but lamented the eruption of more than thirty new civil wars." Witte and Martin, eds., *Sharing the Book*, xi.

21. *Our Global Neighbourhood: The Report of the Commission on Global Governance* (New York: Oxford University Press, 1995), 125.

22. For example, when France resumed the nuclear testing in the Pacific in 1997, churches and Christians the world over expressed their solidarity with Christians and communities in the Pacific with their renewed understanding of the Christian vocation and the mission call to be stewards of creation.

23. "World Parliament of Religions," *ENI Bulletin* 23 (December 22, 1999): 25, and 17 (September 20, 2000): 5–7. One such recognition is the "spiritual summit" organized by the United Nations, which brought together one thousand of the world's religious and spiritual leaders just before the UN Millennium Heads of State Summit in 2000, the first such gathering to be organized by the UNO in its fifty-four-year history and in which the UN Secretary-General Kofi Annan gave the welcoming address.

24. Frederick R. Wilson, ed., *Your Will Be Done—Mission in Christ's Way: The San Antonio Report* (Geneva: World Council of Churches, 1990), 32.

Chapter 15
Youth and Family Ministry as Congregational and Community Renewal

1. "Preface to the Small Catechism," *The Book of Concord* (Philadelphia: Fortress Press, 1976), 338.

2. "Exploration of 4th Commandment," Luther's Large Catechism (Minneapolis: Augsburg, 1967), 43, par. 70.

3. "The Second Commandment," Luther's Large Catechism, *The Book of Concord* (Philadelphia: Fortress, 1976), 375, par. 77.

4. See chapter 8, by Ralph W. Quere, "The Community of Faith as a Confessional Norm: Universalism and Evangelism."

5. The renewal of commitment to youth can be seen in the great amount of time and attention being given to new ways of teaching confirmation. The fine work of Faith Incubators, Rev. Ken Smith of Janesville, Wisconsin, and the Road Trip Series serve as examples. The increased emphasis in many congregations of adding a mentor ministry to a confirmation program is also a very healthy sign.

6. Peter Benson, keynote speech (presented at the First Annual Healthy Communities Healthy Youth Conference, Bloomington, Minn., October–November, 1997).

7. National Longitudinal Study on Adolescent Health Carolina Population Center, University of North Carolina at Chapel Hill, 1998.

8. James Garbarino in *Lost Boys* (New York: Simon and Schuster, 1999) documents this connection in dramatic ways.

9. Mary Pipher, *The Shelter of Each Other* (New York: Ballantine, 1997).

10. David Anderson, of the Youth and Family Institute of Augsburg College, has made this point abundantly clear and has supported it with an exceptionally effective congregational model called "The Child in Our Hands."

11. John Westerhoff, *Will Our Children Have Faith?* (Minneapolis: Seabury, 1976), and many others make this point about faith transmission.

12. See chapter 16, by L. Shannon Jung, "Discovering Hope: Marks of Vitality and Practices That Form Communities for Mission."

13. Merton Strommen and Richard Hardel, *Passing on the Faith* (Winona, Minn.: Saint Mary's Press, 2000), 98.

14. Paul G. Hill, *Up The Creek with a Paddle: Building Effective Youth and Family Ministry* (Minneapolis: Augsburg Fortress, 1998), ix.

15. See the semiannual sales catalog *Faith Life in the Home Resource Guide*, developed by David Anderson of the Augsburg Youth and Family Institute, Minneapolis, Minn.

Chapter 16
Discovering Hope

1. One of the more systematic efforts to address those questions for town and country congregations was sponsored by the Division for Congregational

Ministries, the Evangelical Lutheran Church in America, and Wartburg Seminary's Center for Theology and Land. Twenty-six vital rural congregations were carefully chosen and invited to be part of a Discovery Event. There, they told amazing stories about their lives. The leadership team has drawn together the results of the event in a book, *Discovering Hope: Building Vitality in Rural Congregations* (Minneapolis: Augsburg Fortress, 2001).

2. See chapter 7, by Duane A. Priebe, "Believing in God through Others; Believing in God for Others."

3. Shannon Jung and Russ May, *Transforming Congregations: Leadership Practices That Form Communities for Mission* (Dubuque, Iowa: Center for Theology and Land, 1999); Alan C. Klass, *In Search of the Unchurched* (Bethesda, Md.: Alban Institute, 1996).

4. Shannon Jung et al., *Rural Ministry: The Shape of the Renewal to Come* (Nashville: Abingdon, 1998). See also Klass, *In Search of the Unchurched.*

5. Jung et al., *Rural Ministry.*

6. See chapter 20, by Elizabeth A. Leeper, "Can This Community Live? A Historical and Contemporary Perspective."

7. Lawrence W. Farris, *Dynamics of Small Town Ministry* (Bethesda, Md.: Alban Institute, 2000).

8. Roland Heifetz, *Leadership without Easy Answers* (Cambridge, Mass.: Belknap, 1994); William Easum, *Sacred Cows Make Gourmet Burgers* (Nashville: Abingdon, 1995); Shannon Jung and Mary Agria, *Rural Congregational Studies: A Guide for Good Shepherds* (Nashville: Abingdon, 1997).

Chapter 17
American Civil Religion

1. Robert N. Bellah, "Civil Religion in America," *Daedalus, Journal of the American Academy of Arts and Sciences* 96 (winter 1967): 1–21.

2. Ibid.

3. Ibid.

4. Ibid.

5. Perry Miller, *Errand into the Wilderness* (Cambridge, Mass.: Belknap, 1956).

6. In early New England, it was the civic order that was adjusted to the will of God; now the flow tends in the other direction, with civic motives being attributed to God.

7. Edmund S. Morgan, *Visible Saints: The History of a Puritan Idea* (New York: New York University Press, 1963).

8. Sidney E. Mead, "The 'Nation with the Soul of a Church,'" in *American Civil Religion,* ed. Russell E. Richey and Donald G. Jones (New York: Harper Forum, 1974), 45. In the immediate aftermath of the terrorist attacks on the World Trade Center in New York City and the Pentagon in Washington, D.C., on September 11, 2001, "God Bless America" became the semiofficial hymn for many national and citywide memorial services.

9. Frances Fitzgerald, *America Revised* (New York: Vintage, 1979).

10. See chapter 5, by Norma Cook Everist, "Re-Membering the Body of Christ: Creating Trustworthy Places to Be Different Together."

11. In January 2001, newly inaugurated president George W. Bush set forth a proposal that would allow for, and even encourage, "faith-based organizations" to apply for government funds for social programs that would "affect people in a positive way" and "change America for the better" (press statement by George W. Bush, January 29, 2001). Immediate questions were raised about the separation of church and state. Beyond those questions, commentators debated whether this would move America to the inclusion of initiatives by a broad range of religious organizations or whether it was singularly intended for support for fundamentalist Christian churches that align themselves closely with the American "good."

12. Paul Johnson, "The Real Message of the Millennium," *Reader's Digest* (December 1999): 62–66.

13. Romans 3:19-20.

14. David W. Noble, *The Eternal Adam and the New World Garden* (New York: Braziller, 1968).

15. Evangelical Lutheran Church in America, *Constitutions, Bylaws, and Continuing Resolutions,* chap. 2:02b (Minneapolis: Augsburg Fortress, 1995).

16. See chapter 8, by Ralph W. Quere, "The Community of Faith as a Confessional Norm: Universalism and Evangelism."

Chapter 18
Imagining the New Community in Christ and the Challenges of Race and Class

1. Second Corinthians 5:17.

2. See Thomas L. Friedman, *The Lexus and the Olive Tree* (New York: Anchor, 2000).

3. See Matt.13:55; Mark 6:4; and Luke 4:22.

4. Mission Statement, Wartburg Theological Seminary, Dubuque, Iowa.

5. There is the erroneous notion in the West that hierarchy and the destructive and abusive use of power are the "sin" of the former European colonies in Africa, Asia, Latin America, and the Caribbean only.

6. Jerome D. Quinn, "Ministry in the New Testament," in *Eucharist and Ministry, Lutherans and Catholics in Dialogue IV*, ed. Paul C. Empie and T. Austin Murphy (New York: USA National Committee of the Lutheran World Federation and Bishops' Committee for Ecumenical and Interreligious Affairs, 1970), 91.

7. See chapter 4, by Daniel L. Olson, "The Well-Being of Individuals and the Health of Community."

8. Ralph F. Smith (Associate Professor of Worship, Wartburg Theological Seminary, 1985–94) characteristically would say, "There is no one way to worship, but some ways are more faithful to the gospel than others."

9. See chapter 1, Thomas H. Schattauer, "Seeking Peace in the Assembly: God's Mission, Our Worship, and the World's Hope."

10. Philippians 2:5ff.

11. Second Corinthians 12:1ff.

12. Galatians 3:28.

13. Brook Larmer, "Latin U.S.A.," *Newsweek* (July 12, 1999): 51.

14. *Harvard Magazine* 1 (September–October 1996): 3.

Chapter 19
The Body of Christ and the Issue of Required Celibacy

1. This does not mean that same-sex behavior was unknown in ancient times. The category "sexual orientation" has a much broader referent than simply behavior. For a discussion of the history of the category, see N. Miller, *Out of the Past: Gay and Lesbian History from 1869 to the Present* (New York: Vintage, 1995). For a discussion of debates surrounding terminology for homosexuality, see David Halperin, *One Hundred Years of Sexuality* (New York: Routledge, 1990).

2. The ELCA rosters three categories of commissioned and consecrated lay leaders: associates in ministry, diaconal ministers, and deaconesses. Since I will be referring to the version of the document *Vision and Expectations* addressed specifically to clergy, I will speak simply of "clergy" throughout the chapter. The same expectations hold true for rostered lay leaders, as detailed in the version of *Vision and Expectations* prepared for them.

3. See chapter 9, by David J. Lull, "Living Together Faithfully with Our Different Readings of the Bible." For an extremely helpful historical analysis and critique of the discussion regarding homosexuality in the ELCA and predecessor bodies, see Christian Scharen, *Married in the Sight of God: Theology, Ethics, and Church Debates over Homosexuality* (Lanham, Md.: University Press of America, 2000).

4. Tim Lull, "Public and Private, Strong and Weak," *Word and World* 10 (1990): 140–46; Christian Batalden Scharen, "Subject to Discipline: Authority, Sexuality, and the Production of Candidates for Ordained Ministry," *Journal of the American Academy of Religion* 66:2 (1998): 313–44.

5. Evangelical Lutheran Church in American (ECLA), *Vision and Expectations* (1990), 3.

6. Ibid., 10–13.

7. Ibid., 13.

8. For an insightful critique of the use of the word "gift" in reference to sexuality, see Martha E. Stortz, "Human Sexuality and the Christian Faith," *Dialog* 32 (1993): 62–76.

9. For examples of contemporary scholarship on 1 Corinthians, see Richard Hays, *First Corinthians* (Louisville: Westminster John Knox, 1997); Dale Martin, *The Corinthian Body* (New Haven, Conn.: Yale University Press, 1995); Margaret M. Mitchell, *Paul and the Rhetoric of Reconciliation: An Exegetical*

Investigation of the Language and Composition of 1 Corinthians (Louisville: Westminster John Knox, 1993); and Antoinette Clark Wire, *The Corinthian Women Prophets* (Minneapolis: Fortress Press, 1990).

10. Martin, *The Corinthian Body*, xv–xviii. I am indebted to Martin's insights throughout my discussion of 1 Corinthians 7.

11. John Poirier and Joseph Frankovic, "Celibacy and Charism in 1 Cor. 7:5-7," *Harvard Theological Review* 89 (1996): 1–18; Geza Vermes, *Jesus the Jew* (Philadelphia: Fortress Press, 1973), 99–102.

12. The experiences of homosexual commissioned and consecrated lay leaders also illustrate this point (see note 2 above).

13. See chapter 11, by Karen L. Bloomquist, "*Communio* as a Basis for Moral Formation, Deliberation, and Action."

14. For examples of theological discussions regarding sexuality and sexual behavior, see Lisa Sowle Cahill, "Sexuality and Christian Ethics: How to Proceed," in *Sexuality and the Sacred: Sources for Theological Reflection,* ed. James Nelson and Sandra Longfellow (Louisville: Westminster John Knox, 1994), 19–27; and Roland Martinson, "Sexuality, Intimacy, and Boundaries," *Word and World* 10 (1990): 114–23.

15. For the analogy of gentile inclusion, I am indebted to the excellent article by Jeffrey Siker, "How to Decide? Homosexual Christians, the Bible, and Gentile Inclusion," *Theology Today* 51 (1994): 219–34.

Chapter 20
Can This Community Live?

1. "Mass suicide involved sedatives, vodka and careful planning," *CNN Interactive*, March 27, 1997 (news on-line); available from www.cnn.com/us/ 9703/27/suicide/index.html; accessed March 27, 1998.

2. This report is denied by the university.

3. Robert W. Balch, "Bo and Peep: A Case Study of the Origins of Messianic Leadership," in *Millennialism and Charisma,* ed. Roy Wallis (Belfast: Queen's University, 1982), 39.

4. "Do's Intro: Purpose-Belief. What Our Purpose Is—The Simple 'Bottom Line,'" in *How and When "Heaven's Gate" (The Door to the Physical Kingdom Level Above Human) May Be Entered* (book on-line); available from http://www.heavensgate.com/book/book.htm.

5. Wknody, "A Matter of Life or Death? YOU Decide," student statement, April 6, 1996, in *How and When "Heaven's Gate."*

6. "Beyond Human—The Last Call, Transcripts of Video Tape Series," session 2, in *How and When "Heaven's Gate."*

7. "Beyond Human—The Last Call," session 1.

8. One of the shocking revelations to come out of the coroner's office was the fact that several victims, including Do himself, had been castrated. See

"Some Members of Suicide Cult Castrated," http://www.cnn.com/US/9703/31/suicide/index.html.

9. "List of Bible Quotes Substantiating Our Position," in *How and When "Heaven's Gate."* All quotations of Christian scripture are from the version used by Do and his movement.

10. "Beyond Human—The Last Call," session 11.

11. "The 17 Steps. Behavioral Guidelines Given in the Early Days of the Classroom," November 1976, in *How and When "Heaven's Gate."*

12. "Additional Guidelines for Learning Control and Restraint—A Self-Examination Exercise," spring 1988, in *How and When "Heaven's Gate."*

13. "Beyond Human—The Last Call," session 8.

14. Thomas Robbins, *Cults, Converts and Charisma: The Sociology of New Religious Movements* (London: Sage, 1988), 105–6.

15. Robert W. Balch and David Taylor, "Seekers and Saucers: The Role of the Cultic Milieu in Joining a UFO Cult," in *Conversion Careers: In and Out of the New Religions*, ed. James T. Richardson (Beverly Hills, Calif.: Sage Publications, 1978), 45, 54. The people who joined Heaven's Gate came from what Balch and Taylor call the "cultic milieu, . . . a loosely integrated network of seekers who drift from one philosophy to another in search of metaphysical truth."

16. See chapter 19, by Gwen B. Sayler, "The Body of Christ and the Issue of Required Celibacy."

17. Justin, *1 Apology* 29.

18. Robert Murray, "The Exhortation to Candidates for Ascetical Vows at Baptism in the Ancient Syriac Church," *New Testament Studies* 21 (1974): 62.

19. Rodney Stark, "How New Religions Succeed: A Theoretical Model," in *The Future of New Religious Movements*, ed. David G. Bromley and Philip E. Hammond (Macon, Ga.: Mercer University Press, 1987), 13.

20. In a *Nightline* interview with Ted Koppel, a former member said that he considered the option of castration in order to control his sexual drive. Later, he left the group, married, and now has a child, very glad that he did not take that ultimate step. Interview by Ted Koppel, "The Heaven's Gate Cult: The Thin Line between Faith and Reason," *ABC Nightline*, 1997.

21. *Apostolic Tradition* XVI.9.

22. Marc Galanter, "New Religious Groups and Large-Group Psychology," in *Scientific Research of New Religions: Divergent Perspectives*, ed. Brock Kilbourne (San Francisco: American Association for the Advancement of Science, 1985), 64–80.

23. Justin, *1 Apology* 46.

24. Justin, *1 Apology* 67.

25. Eusebius, *Ecclesiastical History* VI.43.11.

26. See chapter 17, by Roger W. Fjeld, "American Civil Religion: A De Facto Church."

Chapter 21
After the Jubilee

1. President Clinton, in his state of the union address, January 27, 2000, said, "In a world where over a billion people live on less than a dollar a day, we also have to do our part in the global effort to reduce the debts of the poorest countries." Other statistics suggest that two-thirds of the world's population lives on two dollars or less a day.

2. Bill McKibben in *Mother Jones* (March/April 2000): 37–39.

3. Available at http://www.jubilee2000uk.org/. Jubilee 2000 UK offers consistently the most up-to-date information on the debt cancellation campaign. Its director, Ann Pettifor, has a gift for public encounter. Jubilee 2000 USA (www.j2000usa.org) tracks the U.S. congressional scene.

4. Ann Pettifor of Jubilee 2000 UK denounced the Okinawa meeting as "the squandered summit." Larry Elliot, South African columnist, argued that the failure in Okinawa would galvanize the debt cancellation movement into even greater action. *Daily Mail and Guardian*, July 28, 2000, available at www.mg.co.za.

5. *Newsweek,* February 21, 2000, 40–45. Professor Jeffrey Sachs, director of the Center for International Development at Harvard University, a tireless worker in the debt cancellation campaign, is featured in the article along with Bono and the pope!

6. William Greider's respected study *One World, Ready or Not: The Manic Logic of Global Capitalism* (New York: Simon and Schuster, 1997) warned that the global economic system could easily self-destruct as white-hot global competition, driven by the momentum of unrestricted capital flows, produced far more than the world market could absorb. Samir Amin had for some time documented the failure of neoliberal economics to achieve any kind of just and healthy social balance in *Capitalism in the Age of Globalization: The Management of Contemporary Society* (Cape Town, South Africa: Zed, 1997). The 1998 volume, *Globalization and Progressive Economic Policy,* ed. Dean Baker, Gerald Epstein, Robert Pollin (Cambridge: Cambridge University Press, 1998), documents in balanced detail the essential failures of the Bretton Woods institutions.

7. Available at http://www.house.gov/jec/imf/ifiac.htm.

8. *Can Africa Claim the 21st Century?* Copublication: the African Development Bank; African Economic Research Consortium; Global Coalition for Africa; United Nations Economic Commission for Africa; and the World Bank. English edition, May 2000.

9. When Namibia established its Jubilee 2000 movement with a pre-Okinawa petition campaign, it was the Council of Churches and the Ecumenical Institute in Namibia (EIN) that launched it.

10. As a coalition, Jubilee 2000 represents many streams and rivulets, some going back farther than others. Jubilee 2000 was formally founded in 1990.

11. The reception attracted key people from the administration and from Congress. President Clinton's secretary of the treasury, Larry Summers, and Gene Sperling, the president's adviser on economic policy, addressed the group, as did Representative Jim Leach of Iowa, the original sponsor of H.R. 1095, the main debt cancellation bill before the U.S. Congress. Congresswoman Maxine Waters, feisty black American from California and a leader in the Congressional Black Caucus, thanked the church groups for "making Congress a better place." She later spearheaded the drive July 2000 to authorize funding for Clinton's promises on debt cancellation. Account available at www.j2000usa.org/updates/vote-july.html.

12. A good place to begin is www.loga.org.

13. A group called the Religious Working Group on the World Bank and the IMF initiated a symbolic action called the "Rolling Fast," which called to mind the prophetic public actions of Gandhi and Martin Luther King.

14. Baucus even sent a personal letter to each member of Congress in which he included $1.20 of his own money to illustrate what it would cost each American a year for the next two years to forgive the total debt owed by the HIPC countries to the United States.

15. For example, Hans Ucko, *The Jubilee Challenge: Utopia or Possibility? Jewish and Christian Insights* (Geneva: WCC Publications, 1997), and the entire issue of the *Bulletin for Contextual Theology in Africa* 6:2 (June 1999). See also note 11 above.

16. See chapter 9, by David J. Lull, "Living Together Faithfully with Our Different Readings of the Bible." As people faithfully read Scripture, it can empower them for action.

17. The thirteen countries: Burkina Faso, Cameroon, Lesotho, Malawi, Mozambique, Nigeria, South Africa, Swaziland, Tanzania, Togo, Uganda, Zambia, and Zimbabwe. The Lusaka Declaration was printed in pamphlet form in *Jubilee South*, June 1999, and also is available through http://www.jubilee2000uk.org.

18. Dean F. Murphy, "In Africa, Debt Relief Has Two Sides," *Los Angeles Times,* January 27, 2000. Murphy does a careful report from Uganda, something of a success story. Having endured the stringent Economic Structural Adjustment Programs of the IMF, Uganda has established a poverty elimination fund that is beginning to spell out modest but real success.

19. Typical of the work being done on poverty reduction is the proposal laid out by the Jesuit Center for Theological Reflection in Lusaka, Zambia. Four new "mechanisms" are needed in connection with debt cancellation: (1) a structure to involve civil society in monitoring how savings from debt cancellation are used to help the poor; (2) a structure to analyze each national budget in relation to the poor; (3) a "bilateral counterpart mechanism" that would negotiate with donor agencies and countries to match funds from debt cancellation that are used for special antipoverty projects, such as dealing with the AIDS-HIV pandemic; and (4) a new international debt arbitration

mechanism. Dr. Peter Henriot, coordinator of the Debt Project, has outlined these initiatives in an article in the *Times of Zambia*, August 12, 1999. He denies that these proposals are unrealistic in the present world economic situation. Is it realistic, he asks, to expect that the present arrangement will solve an international debt situation that is "economically untenable, politically destabilizing, socially harmful and ethically unacceptable"?

20. Ulrich Duchrow, "The Jubilee as Seen from Europe," *Bulletin for Contextual Theology in Africa* 6:2 (June 1999): 27–32, esp. 27–29.

21. This charge has been leveled against the United States specifically and against the G8 generally, particularly in connection with economic boycotts. It is an issue to watch carefully.

22. Tahir Sitoto, lecturer in Islamic Studies at the University of Natal, Pietermaritzburg, quotes from an article in *Al-Qalan*, May 1999, by Hussain Vadachia: "The third world during the 80's owed 567 billion dollars to the financial houses of the first world. . . . Twelve years down the road [1992] the same debt had escalated to 1,419 billion dollars, an increase of 250% despite the fact that the debtor countries had repaid their capital debt three times over." Tahir Sitoto, "Jubilee 2000 Campaign for Debt Relief: Towards an Islamic Perspective?" *Bulletin for Contextual Theology in Africa* 6:2: 40.

23. See chapter 6, by James L. Bailey, "The Pauline Letters as Models for Christian Practice: 1 Thessalonians as a Case Study."

24. Luis N. Rivera-Pagan, "Exegetical and Theological Reflections on the Jubilee: From the Context of the Caribbean," *Bulletin for Contextual Theology in Africa* 6:2 (June 1999): 33–38.

25. See chapter 13, by David A. Ramse, "The Church as Organism: Characteristics of a Young Church."

26. Duchrow, "The Jubilee as Seen from Europe," 31.

27. Gerald O. West, "Debt and Jubilee: Systems of Enslavement and Strategies for Liberation," *Bulletin for Contextual Theology in Africa* 6:2 (June 1999): 14–17, quotation, 17. See also the ELCA social statement on economic life, "Sufficient, Sustainable Livelihood for All," esp. p. 4. See also Craig Nessan, "Give Us the Day Our Daily Bread," *Currents* 27:3: 165–91.

28. *Bulletin for Contextual Theology in Africa* 6:2 (June 1999): 18–22, quotation, 20.

29. Paul F. Knitter, *One Earth Many Religions* (New York: Orbis, 1995). Knitter insists that a common ground for multifaith dialogue has been given powerfully in the plight of the poor of the world and in the ecological devastation that has resulted from the present capitalistic global economic system. See Sitoto, "Jubilee 2000 Campaign for Debt Relief."

30. These grassroots organizations are legion. One fascinating example from South Africa is ESSET, Ecumenical Service for Socio-Economic Transformation, an initiative related to the South African Council of Churches (SACC). A "trickle up" axiom from ESSET: rapid growth is not necessarily the path to eradication of poverty; it is the distribution of benefits that matters.

ESSET insists on "economic literacy" for Christian communities and has set up courses and materials to accomplish this goal. In the spirit of the African Renaissance, it advocates with government and business for a twin-track strategy for the eradication of poverty: (1) an employment/intensive growth policy, and (2) policies meeting basic needs, housing, health, and so forth, and providing social safety nets. See *Economic Strategies for Poverty Eradication,* summary pamphlet from a workshop sponsored by ESSET and SACC, August 13, 1998 (printed by Progress Press, ESSET Khotso House, Johannesburg, South Africa).